St. Martin's Press

175 Fifth Avenue, New York, NY 10010
Telephone (212) 674-5151

ADVANCE BOOKS

TITLE:

THE ENGLISH MUSICAL RENAISSANCE

AUTHOR:

PETER J. PIRIE

PRICE:

$16.95

PUBLICATION DATE:

2/29/80

COMMENTS:

ISBN: 0-312-25435-0
79-89437

Peter J. Pirie has been writing and lecturing on music for many years. He has contributed to *Grove's Dictionary of Music and Musicians*.

THE ENGLISH MUSICAL RENAISSANCE

by

PETER J. PIRIE

ST. MARTIN'S PRESS
NEW YORK

For Mildred

CONTENTS

LIST OF ILLUSTRATIONS

following page 96

PREFACE

There have been one or two books in the past on the English music of the twentieth century, and it might be as well to explain in what way this one differs from them. Firstly, it is a strict chronological narrative, a history as well as a critical exegesis. Past books have tended to classify our composers into groups, for instance Late Romantics, and not only are these terms misleading, but the device makes continuity extremely difficult, if not impossible. Secondly, I have taken into account the way social and political factors have influenced our slender musical muse, and in what way they have made our music the rather peculiar thing it is. Thirdly, I have made constant reference to foreign composers, and attempted to place our music in a world context; this may puncture our pride a little, but to isolate our own music is both insular and misleading. Finally, I have noticed two tendencies in considering English music: there are some critics who seem to believe that all our composers are great composers, and that it is all wonderful just because it is English; on the other hand, I have read that all English music is negligible. I wish to create some sort of balance, and take as objective a view as I can; it is doubtful if many, or indeed any, of our composers are of the same stature as the great figures of twentieth-century music, Schoenberg, Berg, Webern, Bartók, Debussy, Stravinsky, Strauss and the rest. But our concert halls would be the poorer if our concerts were confined to major figures only; there are a great many characteristic minor composers who have something unique to say, and a number of English composers can be classed in this group. I have a feeling that there have been some factors in English history and the English character which have prevented us from doing even better than we have; and that also I have explored. But I hope my love of English music may shine through this book; if we do not support our composers, no one else will; although that support must be clear-eyed, and free from self-deception.

P.J.P.

June 1978.

I

THE SOIL

OUR SCATTERED GROUP of islands spreads from within a few miles of the coast of France in the south to the Orkneys and Shetlands in the north, which far islands seem to be an outcrop of Norway. On the map the British Isles do not figure as prominently as their great variety of climate and landscape might seem to imply; they lie poised between the land mass of Europe and the arching neck of Scandinavia like stray pieces of a jigsaw puzzle escaped from the vacant Baltic. The isles are nook-shotten, containing within their small compass a great variety of landscape and light: mountains in Scotland and Wales, chalk hills and sunny sea in the south, farm land in the Midlands, and in the north of England a dark and bronzed landscape at strong variance with the south. The boundaries of the counties are meaningful, and each county suggests its own topography, and in extreme cases a light and atmosphere unique to itself.

In the nineteenth century the industrial revolution spread great conurbations over the north Midlands, Yorkshire and Lancashire, blackened the Welsh valleys with coal, and enlarged London, which had been almost rural in the eighteenth century, until the sprawl of houses reached out towards Brighton in the south. But at the opening of our period, the end of the nineteenth century, much of the English countryside was still unspoiled, and even by the 1950s the north and west of Scotland, and the west of Ireland, remained inviolate, testimony to a great if largely departed beauty that still haunts odd corners over the whole group of islands.

Of all the arts, the English excel in literature. There are a few great painters, notably Turner and Constable, who, appropriately enough, portrayed green farmland, village, and ever-changing light in their sometimes gentle, sometimes visionary pictures, and a few exquisite minor artists like Cotman, or haunted Palmer, whose great master Blake epitomised that aspect of the English character, nurtured on the Jacobean Bible, that gave us Bunyan, Lilburne, Fox and Penn. Hogarth, with his narrative paintings and comment on social life, provides a link between the Nonconformist conscience and politics, which have always been an English concern. Politics have probably tilted our artistic flair in the direction of the arts of persuasion, of which literature is the chief. For it is with the complex-origined, flexible tongue of which the Jacobean Bible is one of the majestic peaks that we have wrought an incomparable literature. Celt, Roman, Saxon, Norman, all gave to that language some aspect of their own until Chaucer consolidated the already unifying disparate elements into a single, expressive tongue. Literature has been the background to all our culture, the only art we have practised without decline or interruption, and no consideration of any of the other arts in Britain can afford to ignore it.

To all intents and purposes the first reference to polyphonic secular music in our literature is the famous passage in the *Descriptio Cambriae* of Giraldus Cambrensis (1147–1220) in which he describes how he heard the Welsh singing in parts. Now Giraldus was writing little more than a century after the Norsemen were finally driven from England, in 1066. We know little of Scandinavian music before this date; indeed, Giraldus's passage is one tiny chink of light in the almost total darkness of the period. Tunstede, writing in 1351, records English singing in parallel thirds, noting that neither Italy nor France knew this device at the time, though it was to become popular later under the name of gymel. This, however, is the mere doubling of the principal part; within a few years of Giraldus's death, and a century before Tunstede, if the most popular dating is correct, we have the so-called "Reading Rota", a canon in six parts. This is quite different, being true counterpoint. Was what Giraldus heard gymel or counterpoint? The sense of the passage seems to indicate the latter.

There are several important points to note here: one is the possible influence of Scandinavian music, an influence that recurs in our history, and suggests a possible deep psychological link; another is that the artistically conservative English actually began by being pioneers, at least as far as the non-Scandinavian mainland of Europe is concerned. It may be no more than a coincidence, but a telling one, that at another turning point in our musical history, at the beginning of the twentieth century, Edward Elgar had an experience similar to that of Giraldus, standing on a hilltop in Wales and listening to the Welsh singing. He used what he heard as the basis for his Introduction and Allegro for strings.

There is an aesthetic unity here that is significant. It is also appropriate that the "Reading Rota" should be a spring song. Many writers have remarked a sense of rebirth in the two or three centuries that followed the Norman conquest; over the whole continent of Europe there was a springtime in the affairs of men. The plague was to continue until the Great Fire, but its worst visitations were over; the belief that the thousand years after the resurrection of Christ would see the end of the world had been proved false. It was the time of the rediscovery of classical scholarship, and first the Goliards, and then the Trouvères, created a tradition of secular song that was gay as no other art is gay, and compared with which the later renaissance has the quality of a full-blown rose compared with the buds of May. This was the great morning of English music, which developed with the rise of English Perpendicular architecture, and the first dawn of English poetry "in summer season when soft was the sun" that was to culminate in Chaucer.

When the English polyphonic style had developed it was one of lucid consonance, full and rich without congestion, and tending to elaborate ornament in the top parts, which sometimes appear to sway on the more static stem of the bass. The first large collection of English music that has come down to us in a decent state is the Old Hall manuscript, formerly in the library of St Edmund's College, Old Hall, Ware, and now acquired by the British Museum. In this MS. we find the names of composers for the first time breaking out of anonymity: Lambe, Typp, Pycard, Byttering. At this time English music began to influence the Continent, and this influence extended until in

John Dunstable (1390–1453) it reached its peak. Even such major figures as Binchois and Dufay acknowledged it. It brought great prestige to England, and there was exchange between the Netherlands and English schools as between equals.*

The life and work of Dunstable represented a high point: during his lifetime England was the centre of the musical world. We have never reached such dizzy eminence since, for after Dunstable English music fell into one of those inexplicable declines which seem usually to coincide with the rise of a strong continental school. The decline after Dunstable is significantly contemporary with the Wars of the Roses, which began in Dunstable's closing years and ended with the reign of Henry VII, the first Tudor. The years between 1460 and 1621 saw the rise of a strong, contrapuntally complex continental school of which the greatest figures were Ockeghem and Josquin des Pres; while the end of the civil war in England ushered in the first of the great Tudor composers, Robert Fayrefax (1464–1521) and John Taverner (1495–1545). They are associated with the Festival Mass, a florid mass on a large scale, jubilant, confident and peculiarly English in its expansive clarity of expression and freedom of technique. These works make a strong contrast with the composers of the earlier Eton Choir Book, which contains works by Browne, Nesbett, Cornysh, Wylkinson and Fawkyner. A setting by Richard Davy in this MS. of the Passion according to St Matthew is one of the earliest of all Passions, and its stark simplicity throws the brilliance of Fayrefax into relief.

In spite of the glory of Fayrefax and Taverner it is with the Elizabethan composers that the average man reaches music that he knows, at any rate by name. The Elizabethans were a late flowering, coming to England as a part of the Renaissance when on the Continent it was already passing. William Byrd

---

* The Coventry Leet Book contains fragments of Dufay's *Missa Caput* (itself founded on a cantus firmus from the Sarum rite) alongside those of an anonymous English mass on "Tu es Petrus", while the Brussels MS. Bibl. Royale 5557 has late masses by Dufay and Busnois with those of Richard Cox and Walter Frye. Manfred Bukofzer, in the *Oxford History of Music*, points out that the Trent, Aosta and Modena manuscripts contain over 200 English compositions, marked as such as a sign of special esteem.

(1543–1623) and Claudio Monteverdi (1567–1633) were near-contemporaries, but the music of the Italian is much more advanced, especially in instrumental technique, than that of the Englishman. Monteverdi carried the madrigal to its fullest possible development, and by accompanying the voices with instruments laid the foundation for his own development of the first historical stage of opera. The English composers followed the example of the Italians, who, with the Netherlanders resident in Italy, invented the madrigal. Yonge published the first version of *Musica Transalpina* in 1588, and Watson *Italian Madrigals Englished* in 1590, but there had been editions of Italian music in England as early as 1568. Many of the lyrics used by English composers were translations of poems which had already been set by the Italians; Gibbons's lovely setting of "The Silver Swan" was almost the last of the madrigals on these words, which in their Italian form had been composed many times. The English madrigal is quite different from the Italian; the deeply expressive, almost symphonic Italian madrigal, in which one may hear, with not too prophetic an ear, the beginning of Verdi in Monteverdi, has only the basic form in common with the spry, lilting English product. The English composers hold their own with the French school, Clement Jannequin and his contemporaries, and it must be said that except for the giants Monteverdi and Gesualdo the general run of English madrigalists is in no wise inferior to their Italian counterparts; the best of Wilbye (1574–1638), Weelkes (1575–1623), Byrd and Gibbons (1583–1625) is surpassed, anywhere in the world at this time, only by the greatest names. In the field of sacred music it is the same story; today we can see that the finest music of Byrd,* Tallis (c. 1505–85) and Gibbons is the equal of most of their European contemporaries, but that those foreign schools produced more composers of this quality than we did.

In instrumental music during the period from the coronation of Henry VIII to the reign of Charles I the English actually pioneered a few things, especially in the field of keyboard

---

* Byrd was a recusant, but this did not prevent his holding official position under Elizabeth; nor did it stop this fervent Catholic from contributing the greatest setting of the reformed service that we possess.

music; but Purcell's opera *Dido and Aeneas* (1685) is a less advanced work than Monteverdi's *L'Incoronazione di Poppea* of 1642. Dowland (b. 1562) died in 1626, a year after Gibbons, and the lute song virtually died with him. On the Continent the predecessors of Bach were composing: Schutz, Buxtehude, and in France Lully, Rameau and François Couperin; in Spain, Bach's exact contemporary Domenico Scarlatti was revolutionising keyboard technique. Purcell's influences, like those of the Elizabethans, were mostly Latin; but after Handel, who was more than half Italian in his musical idiom, the great German hegemony began, and English music entered its darkest hour.

The spread of music printing, the growth of the public concert, the cult of the instrumental virtuoso, all combined to create the image of the composer as a kind of prophet or priest writing for all mankind and all ages; the concept of the musical genius and the immortal masterpiece, these are essentially German concepts. After Bach there was a delicate balance between the predominantly Italian idiom that had come from the seventeenth century and rising German musical nationalism; this balance is seen at its best in Mozart, but in Beethoven the German accent began to predominate, and German nationalism was consciously developed by Weber and perfected by Wagner. If we say that the sheer size of such composers, and their triumphal progress through the world was competition too great for the successors of Purcell to meet, this is only a half-truth. Why didn't the English produce composers of similar stature, who *could* compete?

The historical events of Purcell's time must be taken into account. We have seen that English music has tended to wilt, not unnaturally, in times of civil war, and we must take into account the effect of the Commonwealth. Percy Scholes has written eloquently in defence of the Puritan tradition in music, but the fact remains that music is simply not a Puritan art; literature may be, however, and in fact the great English literary tradition has never been interrupted. The interruption to the development of our music was brief—only eleven years—but this brief break had its effect. The early death of Purcell need not have been so crippling, if only he had had contemporaries of his own stature; Mozart's early death did not stop German music. Neither is there any logical reason why the presence in our midst of Handel need have affected us adversely. The dominant music at the end of the seventeenth century was Italian and sensuous, and largely operatic; even Bach felt its influence. It had been the inspiration of the English madrigalists; and then there followed the operas of Monteverdi, Lully, Alessandro Scarlatti and of Handel himself, in many ways the culmination of this school of opera, and an Italian in training and style. But the Commonwealth had made its contribution towards England's bad conscience as far as sensuous and passionate art was concerned—a contribution which the Restoration only temporarily, and not entirely, alleviated.

William Lawes (1602–45) and his brother Henry (1595–1662) were contemporaries of Purcell, in the last years of Charles I. William, who was killed fighting on the Royalist side, wrote a number of sonatas and consorts of cranky (and very English) individuality. They had no progeny, they were too subjective, too romantic for the increasing formality of music.

It is possible that something in the English genius does not take kindly to classical formalism; the contrast between Racine and Shakespeare is not an isolated instance, although a much-quoted one. We might expect some singularity in the artistic productions of an island divided by sea from the mainland, just as we might expect a certain conservatism; what is less accountable is a tendency to lyrical effusion and dramatic rather than formal construction. It does not amount to rhapsody or formal incoherence. But with the exception of Alexander Pope we have never produced a practitioner of any of the arts in whom the formal interest was paramount.

Eighteenth-century formality was exemplified in the work of William Boyce (1710–79). Boyce's Birthday Odes must not be compared with those of Purcell; yet his symphonies and overtures are individual enough to stand comparison with those of his German contemporary J. C. Bach, and with the early Mozart symphonies. Slight, breezy, wistful, recognisably English, Boyce's symphonies make the London Bach sound every inch a German, and bring out the Teutonic streak even in Mozart. They have a curiously timeless quality—William Walton's *Portsmouth Point* at once claims kinship. Of Boyce's contemporaries, the two Arnes, Thomas the father (1710–76) and Michael the son (1741–86), were concerned with the theatre; the elder Arne was the more distinguished of the two. The next generation—Thomas Attwood (1756–1838), friend of Mozart; John Callcott (1766–1821); William Crotch (1775–1847)—have simply not survived. History records one curious figure, the shy, elusive Cipriani Potter (1792–1871), a contemporary of Beethoven who also wrote nine symphonies; for one brief moment he caught the interest of no less than Richard Wagner, who tried to persuade him that his symphonies really were of value: but in vain. So English a figure! But after the brief moment of glory in which Wagner actually conducted one of his symphonies the darkness closed over Potter, and over English music.

No fact or collection of facts can quite account for it: English music led the world in the fourteenth century, and made a decent show from then on until the appearance of a major composer in Henry Purcell; but from his death until the first works by Elgar almost exactly two hundred years later we were virtually silent. And these years marked the production, by a race that is nearest ethnically to our own—our fellow Saxons— of a succession of major geniuses. We may mark the position of Austria and Germany at the centre of Europe, where all musical roads cross; we may note that German musical education has always been more rational and thorough than ours, and the multiplicity of German musical institutions, which offer a much wider scope for the musical aspirant in all fields. It does not suffice; because of Dunstable, Taverner, Byrd, Tallis and Purcell it does not suffice.

We have noted the effect of external events on our precarious genius. In any country with a stronger artistic environment than ours these events would have had less effect. Napoleon had little deleterious effect on the world of Haydn and Beethoven. But the musical world that grew up after Dunstable in England did not survive into the modern age at all; and it was in England that the birth of the industrial and scientific age took place, in a society in which the musical tradition had been cut short.

Music needs a considerable apparatus for its realisation. Up to the time of Purcell it was reasonably amateur and domestic; but with the onset of the eighteenth century it became increasingly professional and public. It needed printed editions, orchestras, concert halls. These demand a public that values music at least as much as more material things. The French had their republican revolution, but the English were first with the industrial revolution, and it hit harder here than anywhere else. Napoleon was defeated by a nation of shopkeepers, and England was a shop; a brisk, philistine emporium with a stinking factory in the back premises. Haydn came (1791) and went (1795) and the eighteenth century ended, and within a generation the French Revolution passed from the storming of the Bastille by peasants to the loss of Waterloo by Napoleon; from the cry of the eighteenth century for bread to the thunder of the guns of the modern world. England had killed her king in the seventeenth century, but had then turned shudderingly away from republicanism; henceforth she would hold both a superstitious reverence for the old world and a thoroughly practical determination to make hay in the new. This dichotomy made the England of the nineteenth century what it was.

It is this divided aspect of the English character that makes William Blake such a significant figure; almost alone among major artists he thundered against those dark satanic mills. He was right to dread the death of the soul of England, though his England, prophetic, poetic, an England of artists and visionaries, has lived fitfully in the other England alone. His pupil Palmer painted pictures of heart-rending beauty and sadness, full of the knowledge that the brief vision was already passing. For all its material wealth nineteenth-century England was a period of artistic nadir in all but the written word.

The English choral tradition, of bogus reputation, began just before 1850. It had nothing to do with the choral tradition that had come to an end with the death of Henry Purcell, partly naturally, with the rise of instrumental music, and partly as a result of our longest artistic collapse; no attempt should be made to link the Victorians with the Elizabethans, for the tradition had been broken for a hundred and fifty years. The nineteenth-century choral movement started as a social rather than an artistic phenomenon; it was a conscious attempt to improve the morality of the workers of the industrial revolution, whose condition was rapidly sinking into the enormous wretchedness depicted with such sombre power in the drawings of Victorian London by Gustav Doré. The attempt to interest these people in choral singing was of high moral tone and small artistic merit. Curwen had by this time introduced Tonic Sol-fa, and any composer who wanted to succeed had to write music of religious inspiration that was technically easy and aesthetically timid. There was also the influence of the less original works of Mendelssohn, against which George Bernard Shaw inveighed, and what some people fondly imagined to be the music of Handel, but which, heavily edited, confined to the oratorios (they had no idea that their pious idol was a great opera composer) and performed by monster choirs, was unrecognisable as any sort of eighteenth-century music.

The influence of Mendelssohn could be seen at its most potent in the compositions of William Sterndale Bennett (1816–75), limpid and inoffensive stuff, a little more efficient than that of his by now quite forgotten contemporaries, but shallow and without originality nevertheless. The music of Charles Villiers Stanford (1852–1924), Hubert Parry (1848–1918) and Alexander Campbell Mackenzie (1847–1935) was conceived under these social and artistic circumstances, with a very heavy Brahmsian influence also. Though friends of Parry are anxious to point out that he was nearly a socialist and almost a free-thinker, like most of his contemporaries (and like the twentieth-century atheist Ralph Vaughan Williams) he set a lot of the Bible to music. His *Job* has been said in some circles to have started the English Renaissance, but I think Shaw has summed up that claim well enough:

There is not one bar in it that comes within 50,000 miles of the tamest line in the poem. This is the naked, unexaggerated truth. Is anybody surprised by it? Here, on the one hand, is an ancient poem which has lived from civilization to civilization, and has been translated into an English version of haunting beauty and nobility of style, offering to the musician a subject which would have taxed to the uttermost the highest powers of Bach, Handel, Mozart or Wagner. Here on the other hand is not Bach, nor Handel nor Mozart nor Beethoven nor Wagner, not even Mendelssohn or Schumann, but . . .*

Shaw puts his finger on the point. To write a religious choral work at this period of English musical history would have needed burning religious conviction and adherence to some faith other than that of the Established Church, a faith that still had its social inconveniences. When the man arrived, Shaw was one of the first to acknowledge him.

We need to establish the environment and circumstances under which the revival of our music in the twentieth century took place if we are to understand the strengths and weaknesses of that revival. Into this context, late in the century, came some important influences. The most important was that of Wagner. Although his music began to be known in England in the nineteenth century certain events prevented its assimilation until the twentieth, and these were not the obvious barriers of harmonic novelty and difficulty of idiom. The influence of Wagner was of two kinds: the eroticism and harmonic tension of *Tristan*, and the clever primitivism and latent giganticism of *The Ring*. The cult of *Tristan* began among artists, not musicians; we may link the names of Beardsley, Wilde and Whistler with it. Whistler had brought the new developments in painting from France, and Wilde was full of the new French literature; Beardsley was startlingly original, and his present revival is testimony to his strength; his drawings and writings alike are haunted by the erotic side of Wagner—as witness the drawing called "The Wagnerians" and the erotic fantasy in prose *Under the Hill*, which derives directly from *Tannhäuser*. They outraged the establishment.†

* Quoted from *Moving into Aquarius* by Michael Tippett (1959).
† In 1877 John Ruskin published an attack on a Whistler Nocturne in his *Fors Clavigera*; it was libellous, and Whistler sued him. The sure-footed Whistler won this first legal brush of the group with Victorian respectability, but their second encounter they lost disastrously.

The group quite recklessly attacked Victorian society in its weakest spot, that of sexual morals. They were almost exhibitionist about their eroticism, whereas the Victorian keyword was secrecy. Their weakest link was Wilde, and in 1895, following (as so often) in the footsteps of the less vulnerable Whistler, he sued the 8th Marquess of Queensberry for slander. We all know the result; but its effect on the temper of English art during the following decades has not been sufficiently stressed. It delayed the progress of progressive painting and promoted a weak academic school which was still active in the 1940s, when Alfred Munnings, who specialised in painting racehorses, launched his notorious attack on Matisse, by that time established as one of the greatest of twentieth-century painters.

Where we have to take the aesthetic débâcle into account when considering English music is in the cult of *Tristan*, and the support the group gave to the new French composers, and to Debussy especially. I do not know of any English composer of the first fifty years of our century whose music reveals any understanding of, or profound textural influence by, *Tristan*, although several less successful ones copied the more conservative parts of *The Ring*; and as for Debussy, there is little or no trace of his existence in English music until the serial revolution of the 1960s introduced it by way of Boulez. Let us be clear: I am writing about the erotic tug of *Tristan*, the result of chromatic, dissonant suspensions, and its resultant in the harmony of Debussy, notably the exact rather than the tonal transpositions of higher discords. The eroticism, and these harmonic devices, were virtually absent from English music until they had become historical curiosities elsewhere in the world.

The sum total of our musical achievement in the Victorian era was meagre, reactionary and undistinguished. Stanford, who lived until 1924, by which time Schoenberg had introduced serial technique, is shrivelled in the blaze of a composer like Richard Strauss. Some of his songs are worth preserving, and in an ideal world we might hear one or two of his orchestral works occasionally; but most of his choral works are terribly vacuous and devoid of significant invention. Parry's choral music, with the possible exception of *Blest Pair of Sirens*, is dead.

Two other Scots had a spark of imagination denied to Macken-zie: John McEwen (1868–1948) and Hamish MacCunn (1868–1916). McEwen's rhapsody *Grey Galloway* and his Solway Symphony are imaginative beyond the scope of Mackenzie, and we still hear the occasional performance of MacCunn's *Land of the Mountain and the Flood*—it is actually recorded—and *The Ship o' the Fiend*. They are overtures in the style of Gade, and none the worse for that. Arthur Sullivan (1842–1900) stands somewhat apart. Only the collaboration between Brecht and Weill provides a parallel with Sullivan's extraordinary partnership with W. S. Gilbert. Sullivan's "Irish" Symphony of 1866, eleven years before the First Symphony of Brahms, created a sensation, and led some critics to the idea that it was a great symphony; an idea that was immediately shattered when Brahms's First Symphony appeared. Sullivan's serious music weakened as his collaboration with Gilbert, in less serious things, went from strength to strength.

As the end of the nineteenth century approached, Wagner divided his empire with Verdi. Brahms, Tchaikovsky and Dvořák were lately dead or in their last decade; Bruckner and Mahler were heard now and then on the Continent, and Bruckner was already established in Austria as a great composer, but their music was seldom heard outside Austria and Holland, and their names were scarcely known in England. Debussy was a coming force in a France dominated by the pupils of César Franck. England had reached the highest point of her imperial power, and the long life of Queen Victoria was drawing to a close. In 1898 the son of a provincial piano-tuner called Elgar had just written a set of variations for orchestra, and the roving son of a Bradford wool merchant called Delius had settled in France at the age of thirty-six, and was to give a concert of immature compositions, in London, at his own expense, in 1899.

23

2

THE AGE OF ELGAR: I
1890—1911

IT IS IMPORTANT to realise Elgar's sheer isolation, not only from world culture, but also from the musical establishment of Victorian England, itself in the last degree provincial. He was born in the tiny village of Broadheath, Worcester, in 1857, in the very middle of Victoria's reign, the son of a country musician and piano-tuner who was not even classifiable as a professional, but a man 'in trade'; and in class-conscious England this was to have profound consequences for the young Edward Elgar. Feeling the need to compose, he taught himself from the books in his father's shop in Worcester; apart from a few professional violin lessons, he had no other musical instruction.

The Royal Academy of Music had been founded in 1822, and the Royal College opened in 1873. Stanford had studied music at Trinity College, Cambridge, and also in Germany; later in life he taught at his old college and at the Royal College of Music. Parry took his Oxford Mus. Bac. while still at Eton, and also studied with the German Dannreuther, subsequently becoming Director of the Royal College of Music. Mackenzie studied in Germany, and at the Royal Academy of Music, whose Principal he later became. This was the pattern for those few English composers who overcame the prevailing apathy and amateurism of English musical life in the latter half of Victoria's reign, to become tolerably decent professionals. Elgar saw no official institution, never studied in Germany, and left school at fifteen to work in a solicitor's office. He played the violin in local orchestras, wrote quadrilles for a mental home, and picked up his professional skills as he went along. After a year in the solicitor's office he left to assist in his father's music shop, and later to teach music at The

Mount, Great Malvern, a private school for girls. There he met Rosa Burley, who has left an interesting if biased account of these crucial years in Elgar's life.* Miss Burley is highly emotional and perhaps on occasion prejudiced, but her account fits the facts of Elgar's life at this time which have come to light during the last few decades, and what we know of his troubled emotional state.

Elgar was a very sensitive and powerful creative artist who guessed at his own genius; he married a woman who was his social superior and some years older than himself, and for years they suffered social ostracism as a result. He hated teaching; he was to be short of money until he was over fifty; only his friendship with Rosa Burley provided him with an outlet for his pent-up emotions at this time. To her he was devastatingly frank. After setting down, in Elgar's own words, the familiar story of his struggles up to this time (about 1892), Miss Burley records:

Suddenly, without quite knowing how it had begun, I found myself listening to an outpouring of misery that was positively heartrending. Gone were the usual reserve, the hauteur and superiority. In their place was a raw and almost frightening sincerity. . . . Flounderingly, for he was in a pitifully over-wrought state, he told me of his struggle to achieve a musical career. It had always seemed hopeless. . . . Ultimately he began to realise that he was not a potential concert violinist, not even a teacher, but a composer and nothing else. The realisation brought no satisfaction for he knew that, little as he could make by teaching music, he would earn far less by writing it and the drudgery of teaching prevented his being able to compose. Without money and the leisure that money provides, indeed, he believed he would never be able to do so.

"And then," he said as if it were the climax of his misfortunes, "I married."

(pp. 38–9)

* *Edward Elgar: the record of a friendship*, by Rosa C. Burley and Frank C. Carruthers (1972).

25

There is no doubt that by this placing Rosa Burley intends us to assume that Elgar's marriage was a disaster; it is far more likely that Elgar meant it was a financial burden.

Elsewhere in her book Miss Burley correctly diagnoses one source of Elgar's haunting unhappiness as his place in the class structure of Victorian England. Elgar was working class, an unforgivable offence, and to make matters worse he was a Roman Catholic; finally, he had the temerity to believe that composers were valuable artists, who should be given money and honour for their work, and that he was potentially a composer of distinction. During the Victorian period too many composers were clergymen and amateurs. This the Victorians accepted, since most of the music they admired was specifically religious, and to be an amateur removed the stigma of being 'in trade'. The professional composer was a foreigner, was funny, was a clown; it was not a profession for an English gentleman.

Elgar's feelings about his origins are clear from Miss Burley's account:

> The core of the trouble, the festering sore from which there was no escape, was that he was the son of a tradesman and had been brought up in a shop. . . . It is certain that at some time he had suffered a humiliation so cruel and so crushing that he could not bear ever to speak of it, a humiliation that arouses one's indignation at the stupidity that could have afflicted it.
>
> (p. 114)

The humiliations endured behind the counter in a Victorian shop were crushing for anyone with no more pretentions than to be a shop assistant all his life, and with a much thicker skin than Elgar had; what must they have been like for a painfully sensitive man conscious that musical genius was being crushed within him. In his long struggle against the Victorian establishment—a strange struggle of complicity, since Elgar loved and admired and was a part of that which he was forced by his genius to fight—he must have known one humiliation after another, until he was over forty. No wonder he seemed greedy for honours; honours that he never took quite seriously, except inasmuch as they honoured his wife and his profession.

When Miss Burley first met the Elgars, in her own words, "Edward was an unusually youthful thirty-six and she was a rather mature forty-three." Mrs Elgar was, moreover, the daughter of "an Indian Army Officer, General Sir Henry Gee Roberts, K.C.B.". Elgar's *Pomp and Circumstance* mood was pure romantic moonshine; it did not survive his first, very indirect experience of real war in 1914. But an encounter with the daughter of such a man would have been perilous for a dreamer like Elgar. Alice Roberts saw at once that he was a genius, and that perhaps was her prime reason for marrying him. In spite of marrying beneath her she was something of a snob, and a conservative of quaint extremity. Elgar later made friends with Bernard Shaw, who was at that stage in his career a fire-breathing socialist and rebel. Elgar followed his wife's views on religion and politics and rarely contradicted her; but his friendship with Shaw, and with other socialists, bohemians and rebels after her death, seems to indicate that his views were more vague and tolerant than hers.

This sets the stage for the career of Edward Elgar (1857–1934), a career that was vital for the rebirth of music in England.

Elgar's early works were pieces in the drawing-room taste of the time, and choral music in the Victorian style; but instead of reflecting the insipid sentiment of his contemporaries, these pieces were frequently distinguished by vigour and imagination, and a gawky strength that often marks the early works of a genius. Like Frederick Delius (1862–1934), Elgar was isolated, but even more so; Delius did study in Germany for a while (not that it did him much good) and was always more secure financially than Elgar. Elgar wrote his Froissart Overture between 1889 and 1890, when, newly married, he was trying to peddle his music in London; the resemblance to Strauss's *Don Juan* (1888) is striking (but can Elgar have heard the Strauss at this early date?). The opening of the Elgar, with its upward surging figure and brilliant scoring, is as close to Strauss as it is far from Parry and Stanford.

Listening to Froissart today it is possible to wonder why it made so little impact on its first performance in Worcester in 1890;* even today it sounds a vivid and impressive piece. But another factor has to be taken into consideration, and that is the unbridled emotional impact of the music itself. Throughout his early years Elgar had to face criticisms of vulgarity and lack of emotional restraint, and the usual way of dealing with such alleged lapses of taste in Victorian times was to pretend they had not happened.

In 1899, the last year of the old century, Elgar was forty-two; after many years of provincial obscurity he suddenly acquired national fame. Hans Richter, perhaps the most eminent living German conductor, who had been the friend and disciple of Wagner, and had played the horn in the first performance of the Siegfried Idyll, on 19 June 1899 gave the first performance of the Enigma Variations.

With the exception of the finale, which was subjected to revision, this was a clean-cut almost simple work with few problems for an audience of the time. The strong and vivid strokes of the variations are achieved with a minimum of notes, and the melodic and tonal outline is clear throughout. It is an unproblematic work, except in the matter of the "enigma" itself, a theme which, according to Elgar, "goes with" the variation tune. Various solutions, all of them unsatisfactory, have been advanced, but the theme is a subtle one, for all its spare outline, and even an invented counterpoint would be difficult, let alone fitting it to a found theme. It is my suspicion that there is no unstated counter-melody, and the whole thing is a hoax on Elgar's part. A noted practical joker, it would be like him to set the academics a puzzle to which there was no answer. "My friends pictured within" is another matter. It provides an invaluable inventory of the most important people in Elgar's life at this time in his career. One variation has always captured the imagination, and that is the most noble one marked "Nimrod". Nimrod was August Jaeger,

* Rosa Burley, mistakenly remembering that it was performed in the Shire Hall, writes that it was killed by the small dimensions of the place; but in fact nowhere in the Shire Hall can music be performed, so it must have been some other place.

Novello's reader and Elgar's closest musical friend, who saw all his works through the press up to the First Symphony.

Richter also took under his wing a much more complex work than the Enigma Variations, *The Dream of Gerontius*, which was given in Birmingham on 3 October 1900. After the success of Enigma the notable disaster of this first performance* came as all the more of a blow, and Elgar was shattered. He had set enormous store by the work, which he knew to be a masterpiece; he had written on the score: "This is the best of me, for the rest I ate and drank, and slept, loved and hated, like another; my life was as the vapour and is not; but this I saw and knew; this, if anything of mine, is worth your memory." After the performance he wrote to Jaeger:

> I have worked hard for forty years & at the last, Providence denies me a decent hearing of my work; so I submit—I always said God was against art and I still believe it. anything [*sic*] obscene or trivial is blessed in this world and has a reward—I ask for no reward—only to live and hear my work. I still hear it in my heart and in my head so I must be content. Still it is curious to be treated by the old fashioned people as a criminal because my thoughts and ways are beyond them. . . . I have allowed my heart to open once, it is now shut against every religious feeling and every soft, gentle impulse *for ever.*†

This is typical of Elgar's more emotional manner in his letters; it is hardly English, as the English then were, but the letters of Mahler, Berg and Schoenberg, his European contemporaries, reveal a similar lack of emotional restraint. In any case, this

---

* The reasons for the fiasco are now well known: the choirmaster, Dr Swinnerton Heap, died before he had time to train the choir to sing this very difficult and unfamiliar music, and the choir were so put off by it all that they ceased to try for the very elderly Stockley who replaced him; Richter's acquaintance with the score would have served had all the performers known their parts, but was insufficient in the circumstances; the soloists were not suitable, and Miss Burley remarks that Edward Lloyd was more used to singing "I'll Sing Thee Songs of Araby" than complex modern music, while the small, dry voice of Plunket Greene simply could not cope with the dramatic music of the Priest and the Angel of the Agony.

† From Elgar's *Letters to Nimrod*, ed. Percy M. Young (1965).

was a (justified) cry of wild disappointment—the remark about religion need not be taken too seriously, as he was soon at work on *The Apostles*. But the phrase "because my thoughts and ways are beyond them" tells.

If there were practical reasons for the failure of the first performance of *Gerontius*, there is no doubt that the great Elgar —the serious artist of *Gerontius*, *Falstaff* and the Second Symphony—was beyond the majority of his fellow countrymen for years, and personally I feel that he was not appreciated in his full stature until the 1960s. The questions that *Gerontius* posed at the time have largely been resolved, and time has smoothed its unevenness. The first part is now seen to hang together in masterly fashion, while the queasy section in Part Two—the solo of the Angel of the Agony—is falling into place and losing its rebarbative quality. The great things remain great, and the conception as a whole can now be seen in all its white-hot power and originality. Newman's poem is largely doggerel,* but Elgar's music so transcends it that we no longer notice it. At the time of its first performance its sectarian quality gave offence to some for whom the Protestant was the only conceivable faith, and Delius, who was a rationalist, is reported by Eric Fenby to have said, "*Gerontius* is a detestable work, and of course greatly influenced by *Parsifal*." It is hardly likely that the subject matter would appeal to Delius, and no sensitive artist writing at the end of the nineteenth century could fail to take cognisance of Wagner; the influence of so considerable a work as *Parsifal* is not necessarily bad. In any case, it is hard to find it now, except perhaps in the Prelude.

But apart from *Parsifal*, this was the kind of music that was being written by Strauss and Mahler in Europe, as Strauss was quick to see; its kinship with *Tod und Verklärung* has not been commented upon, perhaps because *Gerontius* is the better work. Finally, its historical importance lies in the fact that the

---

* Elgar's literary taste was contradictory and even dubious, in spite of the fact that he was a very well-read man. His library included books by Drayton and Sidney, as well as Holinshed's *Chronicles*. This has the authentic Elgarian ring of naïve romanticism, for if his taste in the words he often set left something to be desired, he had an uncanny knack of knowing what to read for inspiration, and a gift for apt literary allusion.

central figure is not Christ, nor even a saint, but an ordinary man. Technically its sole successor was Walton's *Belshazzar's Feast*, for in spite of *The Apostles* and *The Kingdom* it had no spiritual successors.

It made Elgar as a composer, when at last it was, through Jaeger's agency, performed in Germany. The triumphant performances at the Lower Rhine Festival in 1901 and 1902, the praise of Strauss, and the advocacy of Richter for this and other works by Elgar were signs that not even England could ignore. Elgar was forty-five in 1902, and after 1919, when he was sixty-two, he wrote no more important music until the last, doomed surge of his talent when he was actually dying and could finish nothing. Throughout his life his music, with the exception of the works he wrote for state occasions and as salon music, was taken more on faith than with true comprehension. Elgar sensed this; he never really believed in his success, even after the sensation of the First Symphony, and indeed, during his lifetime his music was truly understood only by a few.

We are told that Elgar received from his father an enthusiasm for Mozart and Berlioz. Berlioz raises some interesting points, since he is clearly one of the strongest influences on Elgar's music; indeed, as with Mahler and Strauss, Elgar's orchestration is unthinkable without Berlioz, and the texture of many passages in his works—from the Abruzzi Serenade of *In the South*, so obviously derived from *Harold in Italy*, to the scherzo of the Second Symphony—suggests that he had Berlioz in his bones. The much-quoted influence of Schumann is as slight as it is obvious. Such passages as the end of the Second Symphony, clearly suggested by that of Brahms's Third, are too isolated and undigested to matter. But to seek a composer without echoes of his contemporaries is to seek a monster; such a composer would be incomprehensible. If we take into account a certain touch of the French composers of the nineteenth century, and just a suspicion of Verdi, we shall see that Elgar was an eclectic whose influences were strongly Latin, while those of Parry and Stanford were largely German, in fact the conservative German music of Brahms. One might also wonder about the highly emotional Roman Catholic church music

Elgar heard in his youth; and to the end of his days he stood in awe of Beethoven.

Elgar is often cited as a typical English composer, and indeed as a typical Englishman. This is rather a naïve view, and it has been progressively eroded since his death. Even during his lifetime those who reacted against what they called his vulgarity were expressing their unconscious realisation that there were many things about him that seemed strange to a more typical Englishman of the period. At its worst Elgar's emotionalism suffused the state and patriotic music he wrote; but this actually pleased the general public, since a nation comes to accept a great deal of emotional vulgarity without recognising it as such, as long as it fits in with the national conventions. Much of Elgar's music did not fit the national conventions, and was a clean break from the rather insipid music of his predecessors. Parry and Stanford, much more reticent and conventional men than Elgar, made many sincere attempts to come to terms with him, but he was too hurt and sensitive, and too suspicious, as a self-taught man, of the academic establishment, for any genial relationship to be established. His relationship with Stanford in particular was a stormy one.

At the turn of the century English musical institutions were stirring into life. The Queen's Hall Promenade Concerts began on 10 August 1895. In Sir Henry Wood's own words (of 1942): "They said there wasn't a public for great music 47 years ago. . . . It was a bold venture, in 1895." During the first years of the century Sir Henry, as permanent conductor of the Queen's Hall Orchestra, cautiously but with iron efficiency improved orchestral standards and nursed the Proms programmes towards an improved and more adventurous repertory. The Hallé Society had been founded in 1857, and from 1899 to 1911 its conductor was the great Hans Richter, Elgar's "true artist and true friend". The London Symphony Orchestra, also to be associated with Elgar, gave its first concert on 9 June 1904. In 1905 Thomas Beecham gave his first London concert, with the Queen's Hall Orchestra; he became the conductor of the New Symphony Orchestra in 1906. The Leeds Festival, founded in 1858, was conducted between 1901 and 1910 by Stanford, who included a number of native works in his programmes, as did Dan Godfrey in such an unlikely place as Bournemouth.

Henry Wood wrote to Delius in 1907:

Please do not suggest an English *Tonkünstler* as, if you heard the local orchestras even in places like Liverpool and Birmingham, you would have a fit. They have improved a good deal in recent years, but are still incapable of playing a modern work by Strauss or yourself; why they cannot even accompany *Elijah* decently!

Which suggests both that standards were improving, and what they must have been like in Victorian times. Elgar helped a lot to improve these standards. He was a commanding conductor, and not only of his own works. His reckless but brilliant direction asked the most of his orchestras, which, after a while, they began to give. He had arrived late, and the first performances of his works in London were accompanied by those of younger men just beginning their careers: Joseph Holbrooke (1878–1958) and Granville Bantock (1868–1946). Holbrooke's symphonic poem, *The Raven*, was given in 1900, William Wallace (1860–1940) having written the first English symphonic poem, *The Passing of Beatrice*, in 1892. Also in 1900 Gustav Holst (1874–1934) wrote his "Cotswold" Symphony. A year later Ralph Vaughan Williams (1872–1958) wrote a song, "Linden Lea", that was to become very popular; he was twenty-nine at that date. Slow beginnings, in an unpropitious time; but not so slow as Elgar's, or that of Delius.

It was perhaps to be expected, given the circumstances of music in England at the time, that the other major figure of the beginning of the renaissance should also be isolated but in many ways Elgar's antithesis. A queasy atheist where Elgar was an uneasy Catholic, a man who flaunted unconventionality with the fanaticism of secret doubt, a rootless bohemian who pretended to despise England, the son of a rich man who remained something of an amateur all his life, Frederick

Delius was a being of iron nerves and cynical toughness who was scornful of all men and secure in his own self-sufficiency. As a composer he was so specialised as to be almost precious, and his technique was so individual that at times it looked amateurish on paper.

Delius's instrument, like Elgar's, was the violin (it is very doubtful whether he played it so well), but he studied in Leipzig (very briefly) with a trio of seeming nonentities: Hans Sitt, a German-oriented musician born in Prague, who composed a small number of works but seems to have devoted most of his life to teaching; Carl Reineke, a very prolific composer, violinist, pianist and pedagogue, whom Busoni, who studied with him for a while, regarded with derision; and Salomon Jadassohn, who wrote more than 130 works, but also many books on musical history. Delius seems to have been indifferent to all three; but possibly they helped give him his abiding distaste for the German classics. According to Sir Thomas Beecham, Delius filled many exercise-books with fugues and contrapuntal exercises. He was probably a better contrapuntist than he is given credit for, and counterpoint was the mainstay of the only lessons he valued, or felt were of use to him—those of that curious character Thomas F. Ward, organist of the Jesuit church of SS. Peter and Paul in Brooklyn, son of a Spanish priest and an Irish kitchen maid.* These lessons were given in Delius's hut in the famous orange grove in Florida, scene of one of the young composer's many attempts to escape from the family wool business. Here too he came under one of the most powerful musical influences of his life, that was to pervade his early music, and inspire an opera and a set of variations: the singing of the American Negroes. Another strong influence on these early years was that of Grieg, who befriended Delius, and supported him against his father.

The crucial dates of these years are those of Ward's teaching, between 1884 and 1885, and the influence of Grieg, which began about 1887 and lasted roughly until Grieg's death in 1907, the year in which Beecham first heard *Appalachia* and

---

* Delius's connections with the Roman Catholic Church were remarkable for so trenchant an atheist; right at the end of his life a young Catholic musician acted as his amanuensis and Boswell.

began his long championing of Delius. Sketches for *A Mass of Life*, and some sections, were about in 1899, and some of the *Mass* was given in the St James's Hall concert on 30 May of that year. In the same concert *Over the Hills and Far Away* was performed. The magical opening of this well-constructed little overture is perhaps the earliest manifestation of that quality which has kept the name of Delius in the forefront of English music from the beginning of the century until today. Heard by the side of the music of his mentor Grieg, any major work of Delius at once makes its superiority felt. Far more original than Grieg once he had matured, and with a unique and commanding musical imagination, Delius none the less does not stand comparison with the German classics (he recognised the fact and railed against "the immortals" in compensation); but his music diminishes far less when compared with that of his contemporaries.

Delius received a number of performances in Europe from 1893 onwards. The rise in Germany of Richard Strauss, with his brash and trenchant power, set a number of conservative musicians against him (the article on Strauss in the first edition of Grove's *Dictionary* is a potent example), and the search for an anti-pope began. There is no doubt that when Richter began to champion Elgar, and a number of German conductors took up the music of Delius, they did so in part out of a reaction against Strauss. Both Elgar and Delius admired Strauss—indeed, his *Don Juan* was one of the few compositions by anyone which Delius admitted he admired—but when Julius Buths, Hans Haym, Fritz Cassirer, Hans Richter and the rest took up the music of these two English composers, for obvious anti-progressive reasons, they not only gave the following generation a further reason for dismissing English music as essentially conservative, but laid the foundations for the subsequent annihilation of the English pair in Germany when the true stature of Strauss was realised. And this coincided with the bitterness of the 1914–18 war, when everything English was hated and derided in Germany—and after which the English turned to French and Russian music in their rejection of all things German.

Wagner's death left a vacuum in German music, a ragged

hole which for a while refused to be filled in. People were astonished to discover to what extent he had become an established classic in Europe during the last decade of the nineteenth century, and the "pain of what is new", in Hans Keller's expressive phrase, passed to Strauss. Wagner's dominating personality and sheer size obscured and distorted the reputations of those who lived under his shadow. Reger and Scriabin attracted more attention in the early twentieth century than Bruckner and Mahler; it was many years before anyone outside Holland and Austria realised that the great German succession had passed to these controversial symphonists, who were to pass it in their turn to Schoenberg and the Second Viennese School. Schoenberg's first atonal music, the Piano Pieces Op. 11, appeared in 1909, and Webern's Op. 1 in 1908. At this stage the world was still trying to come to terms with Richard Strauss, and they attracted little attention outside Vienna.

Linked with Strauss in the English mind as a fellow revolutionary, and actually far more radical, was Claude Debussy. He visited England on a number of occasions between 1902 and 1914, to a mixed response, but when he conducted his own music (indifferently) in London in 1908 he received a welcome that delighted him. He was slowly breaking down that English resistance to the culture of France which had existed since the fall of Oscar Wilde; the obvious French bias of Edward VII, and the dubious German military preparations, assisted him. But the progress of his music among composers in England was slow; Elgar went out of his way to warn young composers against it in his Birmingham lectures of 1905, the only unprogressive passage in those underrated lectures. The English might admire, but did not learn from Debussy. However, his appearances paved the way for Diaghilev, who from 1911 onwards broke down the English reserve against anything that suggested the unrespectable side of European art.

The Wagnerian influence was strong on Bantock, Holbrooke, Ethel Smyth (1858–1944) and Havergal Brian (1877–1972), although it cannot be too strongly stressed that it was the influence of the early operas and parts of *The Ring*, and not of

36

Tristan. Bantock and Holbrooke studied with Frederick Corder (1852–1932) at the Royal Academy of Music. Corder was a Wagnerian (but could not understand Debussy), whereas Stanford at the Royal College would tolerate nothing more modern than Brahms. This dichotomy was to be of great importance in the development of music in England in the first half of the century, and influenced, and divided, a whole generation of English composers; the two Royal Schools reflected the division almost too neatly. Corder's only student of considerable talent was Arnold Bax (1883–1953). The bulk of the really talented pupils went to the College and Stanford: in those years he taught Vaughan Williams, Gustav Holst, John Ireland (1879–1962) and Frank Bridge (1879–1941) among others.

However, examining all the facts, and weighing his pupils' reactions to him, it is hard to resist the conclusion that Stanford's legendary reputation as a teacher has been exaggerated. His methods do not appear to have been subtle; his outlook was anything but liberal and constructive. Harry Plunket Greene, the singer, who admired him, tells us in his book on Stanford: "I have heard him again and again lament the unhealthy mud-ponds from which his ugly ducklings quacked at him"— and we have to remember that these "ugly ducklings" were composers far greater than he. Plunket Greene quotes George Dyson, a very conservative composer, who says that Stanford and his pupils were constantly at war, not over the matter of technique, but over personal development of novel forms of expression. "In a certain sense the very rebellion he fought was the obvious fruit of his methods. And in view of what some of his pupils have since achieved, one is tempted to wonder whether there is anything better a teacher can do for his pupils than drive them into various forms of revolution." But the "revolution" Stanford's pupils were advocating had already taken place in Europe decades before they ever went to Stanford; and the result of his teaching, in the majority of cases, was to reinforce a conservatism that was already present in all his pupils, the only one of whom showed any radical bent in later years was Frank Bridge. Stanford disliked the progressive music of his time, and it is doubtful if he ever really understood Strauss and Debussy. T. F. Dunhill writes in the same book by Plunket Greene: "He was impatient, blunt, and frankly hostile to much of what we are pleased to call modernity. To him music was, as it were, a body of truth, and what was not true was false. To deny truth was heresy. To be lukewarm was to betray one's poverty of soul." Most of the composers Dunhill, Plunket Greene and Stanford regarded as modern have long ago become classics, the over-played routine of our rather conservative concert halls; and by 1935, when Plunket Greene's book was published, most of Schoenberg's and Webern's works, except their last, and all of Alban Berg's had been written. Stanford's reported approach to truth is medieval; that any body of doctrine could be only half true, or that facts are in constant flux, is incompatible with it.

It seems a pity that a teacher who had so little sympathy with the music, not only of his own time, but the more progressive music of the immediately preceding generation, should have been able to exercise so much influence at this juncture in English musical history. It was necessary for this new genera-tion of English composers, who, for the first time since Henry Purcell, revealed creative talent and individuality, to forge a technique and style for themselves that should be contemporary without being a mere imitation of what was going on in Europe; and what was going on in Europe at this time was not Wagner and Liszt, but Strauss, Debussy, Scriabin, and even the young Schoenberg, whose *Gurrelieder* was composed about this time. As it was, it was Brahms who was held up to them by Stanford as a model. And one wonders what Brahms. Take the magnificent and radical recapitulation of the first movement of the Fourth Symphony; suppose any of Stanford's pupils had submitted to him anything as drastic as that? "He who cannot write anything beautiful falls back on the bizarre." Gordon Jacob fell foul of Stanford by improvising in the manner of Debussy; and in answer to Stanford's "Anyone can write that sort of thing, me bhoy" he played in the style of Stanford and replied "And anyone can write that sort of thing too."

What effect Stanford's teaching had on Vaughan Williams

must be a matter for conjecture. Michael Kennedy in *The Works of Ralph Vaughan Williams* (1964) says that Vaughan Williams "attributed Stanford's greatness as a teacher to his intolerance and narrow-mindedness—'if a thing was right it was right; and if it was wrong it was wrong, and there was no question about it.' But RVW was unteachable and fought his teacher."

Their relationship must have been a curious one indeed, complicated by the fact that Stanford was a clever man of talent, while Vaughan Williams was a slow-minded, instinctive genius who never learned to control notes with virtuosity; to the end of his life his manuscripts needed editing and putting in order, they were so chaotic and inaccurate.*

In contrast to Stanford, Corder was mildly progressive, and so permissive a teacher that he also left his mark on his pupils; but a very different mark from that left by Stanford. All his pupils lacked discipline, and even Arnold Bax was slow in finding direction, and in freeing himself from the influence of Strauss which spoils the first of his two piano trios. There was also an early mawkishness, found in such things as *A Celtic Song Cycle* (1906). In the case of Holbrooke, whose works were regularly performed before 1914, we feel that he might have improved his technique, and tightened his form with advantage, and without sacrificing his essential personality. But with Bax it is certain that for better or worse this was his nature, and as time went on he expressed his vision in appropriate technical terms. Corder could do little for him, and Stanford would have provoked open revolt and a notable scandal.

It is possible to exaggerate the importance of a teacher. Elgar and Havergal Brian were self-taught, Delius nearly so, and Bax brought to Corder a technique that was already almost fully formed. But the fact that Vaughan Williams, Holst, Ireland and Bridge went to Stanford, and Holbrooke, Bantock and Bax to Corder is too much of a coincidence to be wholly chance. The odd men out, Bax and Bridge, fit neither the Wagnerian tradition of Corder, which seduced Holbrooke

---

* This was often done during rehearsals, with great waste of time and temper, but towards the end of his career Roy Douglas undertook to put his scores in order; see *Working with RVW*, by Roy Douglas (1972).

and Bantock, nor the English pastoral or Georgian lyricism that were his pupils' retreat from the overwhelming Brahmsian cult of Stanford. Both were eclectic, but their work has a rich and haunted atmosphere that can be compared with the sensuous magic of Keats. In his last years Bridge developed a dark and tragic streak that was his reaction to the 1914–18 war, and Bax had a deep conflict and an epic quality of large-scale organisation that eventually declared itself.

There is no doubt that something big was afoot in English music during these years. All the above composers felt it; the example of Elgar, which in particular inspired Bax, had come at the very moment when a new spirit was abroad in England. Its origins were complex, and its exact nature obscure. The breakdown of the Victorian oratorio tradition, the loosening of the hold of Handel and Mendelssohn, helped. The rediscovery of our heritage of music from the thirteenth to the seventeenth centuries was crucial—and here we must remember the names of Edmund H. Fellowes and Arnold Dolmetsch— and our very belated discovery of folk-song added another, somewhat ambiguous element.

The end of the reign of Queen Victoria brought a sense of relief as much as grief; the era had been womb-like in its suffocating, unquestioned, philistine cosiness (at least if you were rich). The sense of liberation was to some extent illusory, but, because many felt it, not entirely so. There was almost that same sense of *reverdie*, of spring song, that came with the dawn of the high Middle Ages after the long night of darkness that ended in the eleventh century. English music was creating its own spring, and if the optimism was not entirely justified, it created an atmosphere without which the English Renaissance might never have started at all. "O youth! Youth!" wrote Arnold Bax. "The urgency of the triplets running through Walther's trial-song was the habitual rhythm of my mood in those lost years. Absolutely anything was possible of life, nothing too good to be true! Round the corner of the street one might find a Land East of the Sun and West of the Moon . . ."

Over the turn of the century Delius was engaged in a number

of works that are among his greatest and most substantial: *Paris, A Mass of Life, A Village Romeo and Juliet,* and *Sea Drift. Paris* was played for the first time in 1901 at Elberfeld under Hans Haym, and *A Village Romeo and Juliet* was given at the Komische Oper, Berlin, under Fritz Cassirer in 1907. *Paris* is contemporary with some of Grieg's orchestral works, the symphonic poems of Richard Strauss, and the early orchestral works of Debussy. Although it is not in the same class as *Don Juan* and *Till Eulenspiegel,* it is not as inferior to them as might be imagined, and it is certainly superior on all counts to any orchestral work by Grieg.

The symphonic poems of Strauss, derived historically from those of Liszt, are broad in outline and form, and close to the German symphonic tradition; not only can the massively moving orchestral textures of Wagner be heard in them (though tempered by the lucidity of Berlioz) but the massive formal procedures of Brahms also. The nearest things by an Englishman to Strauss's symphonic poems are Elgar's *Falstaff* and his three overtures. *Paris* is less massive in its textures and more fragmented in its formal procedures; at the same time it differs from the music of Debussy in several important respects. In spite of the fact that Delius has been called "the only German impressionist" his music is neither German nor impressionist in sound. The dazzlingly brilliant orchestration of *Paris*—which, considering Delius's musical education (or lack of it) is something of a mystery—is closer to that of Ravel than to Debussy, and its colours are post-impressionist, rather than impressionist. It is sheerly original, but some of its scoring is akin to that of *La Valse* and the Concerto for the Left Hand. Its basis is darkness (it is called "A Nocturne"), a luminous darkness of superb writing for the bass instruments; the use of cellos and basses as colour instruments is quite original. Against this darkness the high strings and percussion glitter with the effect of the lights of a great city, and the wood-wind cry with lonely voices.

"A sense of flow is the main thing," said Delius, and it is that sense of flow which distinguished *Paris* from such things as Holbrooke's *The Raven.* There is little in *Paris* of the Germanic development of Strauss's symphonic poems. It uses several themes, one of them a rhythmic motive that is rather overdone; Delius broods over them, and alternates the brooding with violent orchestral outbursts. In the textures of *Paris* we may note a processional element, a fantastic procession, that is recalled in "Villes" from Britten's *Les Illuminations*. To Rimbaud, Britten and Delius alike, the city of Paris suggests the dancing progress of a motley crowd. Like *La Valse* and the left-hand Concerto *Paris* rises from brooding darkness, but unlike those works it returns to darkness at the end, albeit with one last luminous chord. The flowing lyricism, the sheer weight of the orchestral tutti, the shifting harmony that never clots into moving columns of consecutive dissonances, the strength and variety of the incident: all tend to confirm rather than dissolve the fluctuating tonalities, and all are quite unlike the procedures of Debussy. Debussy moves a discord from step to step of the scale with an exact transposition of its intervals, thus undermining the sense of tonality and producing a curiously static *impression*; Delius does not transpose chords exactly, but allows the intervals of the diatonic scale to dictate their nature; but he often jumps between chromatic chords with a powerful effect of movement. This too is neither impressionist nor Germanic; it is the harmonic idiom of Grieg developed into something more daring and individual. In any case, *Paris* is a sport, a single brilliant essay in virtuoso orchestral writing; there is nothing quite like it in the rest of Delius's output.

A Village Romeo and Juliet was not Delius's first opera; it was almost his last, only the negligible *Margot-le-Rouge* and the controversial *Fennimore and Gerda* following it. *The Magic Fountain, Irmelin* and *Koanga* preceded it. There is a case to be made for the theory that the last three major operas of Delius become not progressively more viable on the stage, but less so. *Koanga* is a perfectly stageworthy opera, equal to those of Lortzing and Marschner which it rather resembles; *A Village Romeo and Juliet* raises serious problems;* *Fennimore and Gerda* is almost unstageable. But *A Village Romeo and Juliet* just comes off if it is treated with tender care and a sense of the

---

* Peter Warlock, in a letter to Delius, suggested that it should be given with all the most advanced techniques of modern stagecraft, and an almost abstract design; and Delius emphatically agreed.

kind of work it is. It includes a Dream Interlude, and I would suggest that the whole opera is a dream interlude, and only effective if treated as such; but it contains some of Delius's finest music.

The opening bars of *A Village Romeo* are breathtaking in their freshness and sense of spring and the open country. When the characters first start to sing it is hard not to be disappointed. After the glorious, sweeping melody, magically scored, the "rude brief recitative" is an awful let-down, as Delius's solo writing often is. When the Dark Fiddler enters the vocal writing improves with him; he takes the stage to music of unearthly enchantment, so strange and full of the air of another world that it constitutes one of music's mysteries of expression. In *A Village Romeo* some of the contradictions of Delius's own character find resolution; the cynicism of the Dark Fiddler and the Vagabonds and the unworldly idealism of the lovers are reconciled in nature music of melting beauty. The scene in which Sali visits Vreli on the last day in her old home is a fine one, and contains vocal writing more sympathetic than is usual with Delius; the Dream Interlude, in which the lovers dream they are being married in the old church in their native village, is not as bad as some writers have suggested. The magnificent passage known as "The Walk to the Paradise Garden"—a later interpolation, designed to cover a scene-change—has become an independent concert piece, the best-known music in the opera. One would think that this great passionate outburst, scored for a large orchestra, and culminating in a mighty surging cry of longing and pain, could hardly be misunderstood; but it has been.*

The culmination of the work, both dramatically and in beauty, is the last scene. Here is Delius's message, but it is not, with apologies to Cecil Gray and others, a death-wish, but the old message he preached to the young whenever he could get hold of them: cherish your youth, grasp every moment of it, take no notice of the old and prudish; you will regret the sins you did not commit more than those you did (an actual saying

* An otherwise excellent opera critic has compared it to Debussy's *Clair de lune*, a study in pianissimo washes for the piano.

of Norman Douglas, with whom Delius had a lot in common).
There is an ambiguity here, for the message is also one of pure
idealism: that nothing whatsoever compensates for the loss of
vision. The ambiguity is resolved by the Dark Fiddler. The
two lovers drown in the sinking boat; a somewhat embarrassing
moment. But down the river the boatmen are singing "Hey ho,
travellers, we a-passing by" and from the veranda of the
Paradise Garden Inn the Dark Fiddler—Delius himself—lifts
his arms in longing towards the lovers, farewell my youth!
It is the farewell of the middle-aged Delius to his youth rather
than any actual death that is pictured in this closing scene; in
that superb gesture by the cynical old vagabond we have a
clue to the psychology of that other cynical old vagabond,
Frederick Delius.

Delius was at work during these years on another large-scale
composition, one often linked with *A Village Romeo*; indeed, the
two are his most famous and most impressive works. Although
passages from *A Mass of Life* were performed in 1899, it was
not given its first full performance until 1909; in 1908 the
second part was sung at the Munich Tonkünstlerfest, but to
give the complete work was one of the first acts of Delian
piety of Thomas Beecham. So Delius, like Elgar, was late in
receiving such recognition as came to him; he was thirty-eight
when *A Village Romeo* was first performed, and forty-six before
the complete performance of *A Mass of Life*.

A Mass of Life is more uneven than *A Village Romeo*, but in a
different way; the opera has its weak passages, but is a stylistic
whole, while the *Mass* is a mixture of styles. The words are
by Nietzsche, from *Also sprach Zarathustra*, and they are better
poetry than philosophy; Delius loved this sort of intemperate,
heady versifying, it confirmed his prejudices, and he did not
look too deeply into the logic of the text. A great performance
of the work, such as Beecham gave so many times, and recorded,
can blind even the most critical to its faults, leaving the
impression that it is a masterpiece. In fact, the whole is greater
than the sum of its parts. The best passages are the orchestral
interludes and the meditative centre of the work. The two
dance choruses have been much criticised; they seem on the
surface to be an odd combination of contrapuntal exercises

with Delius's characteristic lilting dance style, but part of the trouble may lie in the sedate choral style endemic until recently among English choral societies. A young university choir of today, who would take the sensuous and libertarian sentiments to their hearts and sing in the uninhibited way one imagines Delius wanted, might shed unexpected light on these two movements. The massive choral section that opens the work, "Oh Thou my Will", is rather foursquare and unyielding. Delius was evidently aiming at rock-like strength, and to an extent he achieved it, but at the expense of a certain muscle-bound effect. More flexible in rhythm is "Now arise, thou glorious noontide", from the middle of the work. In spite of its mixture of styles the *Mass* is cunningly put together and makes a whole, a unity not broken even by Beecham's constant fiddling with the order of the movements. The final section, which was actually the first to be written, betrays a certain immaturity; but the remarkable thing is that it makes a powerful and thrilling end to the work, with its intoxicating tune, great climax and hushed close. The *"O Mensch! Gib acht!"* of this final section is a link with Mahler, who also set these words of Nietzsche's, in a very different manner, in his Third Symphony.

Appalachia was the work that in 1907 was to convert Beecham to fanatical support of Delius—and Beecham was normally anything but a fanatic and not given to supporting causes. It was written in 1902, and first performed in Elberfeld under Hans Haym. In *Appalachia* we meet for the first time the characteristic Delian loose variations of a special kind. Several of his works are in this form, which is an intriguing echo of the Elizabethan division style. This may be another instance of the pervasive Englishness of Delius's music; it is said that the impressions we receive up to our seventh year have the greatest effect on us, and Delius lived in England until he was eighteen. One must also consider as influences such works as Grieg's Old Norwegian Romance with Variations, Op. 15, which Beecham recorded, and which Delius, with his close acquaintance with both Beecham and Grieg, may have known. The undoubted formidable charm of *Appalachia* is a bit of a mystery, considering the barely digested influences that are in it. Chief of these is the "Negro theme" itself, which is none other than the Quartet from *Rigoletto*. A good deal of plantation music in those days was white man's music transmogrified, and *Appalachia* is an impression of the singing of the Negroes on the orange plantation in Florida. But the piece, in spite of some naïvety, contains a lot of very original music. The opening is an example, with its full, archaic-sounding horns, like those of the opening of Mahler's Third Symphony, yet more Nordic, less earthy. Then there is the sheer originality of the writing for the final chorus, with baritone solo. These little "doxologies" (as Peter Warlock called them) float half-heard through the orchestral texture in a manner that was completely new at the time, though typical of the mature Delius. The entry of the baritone soloist at the end, backed by the chorus, who emerge for the first time into the foreground, is tremendously effective and deeply moving; moving with that odd combination of beauty and sadness which Delius made uniquely his own.

On 4 December 1903, at Ingrave, Vaughan Williams collected his first folk-song. Earlier in the same year Cecil Sharp (1859–1924) heard a Somerset gardener singing "The Seeds of Love", and the folk-song movement had begun. By 1913 it had such a hold that a contemporary music critic reported that a number of new English works all began with a pentatonic theme and had modal harmony. There is no doubt that folk music was a revelation to the academically trained and middle-class composers of the time; Vaughan Williams said that when he first heard "Bushes and Briars" he felt he had known it all his life. It is also possible that he and a number of other English composers so reacted against Wagner and Strauss (not to mention Debussy and the French decadents) that they welcomed a form of music that was diatonic without being major and minor and which, with the words sufficiently bowdlerised, sounded innocent. Although both Vaughan Williams and Holst imagined themselves to be rebels as well as heirs (and indeed, Holst produced a number of Wagner imitations in his student days) and Vaughan Williams later studied with Ravel, the reaction against the "heavy" new music of the

Continent suggests at least subliminal absorption of the attitudes of Stanford; they also instinctively protected themselves against an atonalism that had not yet emerged, but the approach of which could be felt in all the advanced music of the day, not only in Debussy but also in Scriabin (1872–1915).

In these days when folk-song may mean a composed song with jazz influences, sung on television by a young university man with an electric guitar, it is necessary to redefine the thing in the terms of those who first rediscovered it; and to point out the anachronistic nature of its influence. Two points are always made by modern folk-song experts: that there was a folk-song of the town, as well as that of the country, an industrial folk-song; and second that the borders of folk-song have become obscured since the first songs were collected. It must be emphasised that for the composers of the early twentieth century folk-song meant essentially the country song, the spontaneous lyrical effusion of an agricultural community. That song may or may not have had a single composer in the first place (it is difficult to imagine community composition from an initial idea) but it became community property, was modified by the community and handed down through the generations.

The English countryside, the infinitely various but usually gentle landscape of a small island, has always been a part of the vision of the English artist; being confined to an island he regarded that vision as all the more precious, an attitude of mind that had its dangers, for the inward-turning could become narrow and provincial, but that also made for intense individuality. During the first decade of our century the English artist realised that the English countryside as he had known it—the countryside of Constable, Turner, Palmer, Cotman, Wordsworth and Keats—was on the point of vanishing for ever. By the end of the nineteenth century the industrial revolution had taken its toll: factories and mines had proliferated and the numbers and concentration of the working population increased to menacing proportions. The survival of the English countryside became a matter of agonising concern to the English artist; and just at that moment, at the point at which its beauty was about to be obliterated, the English folk-song was discovered. It was, seemingly, a way into the future that avoided the paths Europe was pursuing. It was not, of course, such a path: it was an attempt to put the clock back, but few saw it as such at the time.

The classical and romantic composers of Europe took the folk-song as a matter of course, and absorbed it until it lost most of its significance; folk-songs in the symphonies of Haydn are so well integrated into the context of classical tonal sonata that it is only recently, after much research, that they have been proved to be there. English composers, coming upon their own folk-songs unexpectedly and at a moment of crisis in their musical history, allowed them to shape their musical thinking; instead of the symphony absorbing the folk-song, the folk-song dictated the nature of the musical context. Although Vaughan Williams did not use actual folk-songs in his symphonies after the *London*, folk and modal procedures marked his musical textures at least until the Sixth Symphony. Continental folk music is richer in dance elements than the English; English morris dances and the rest are musically uninteresting, odd tunes like the "Dargason" notwithstanding. The folk-tunes of the British Isles are rich in lyrical elements. Whereas continental composers before Bartók absorbed the modal tunes into the major and minor key system, it became a point of honour among composers like Vaughan Williams, Holst and Butterworth (1885–1916) to write modal music, in which the unaltered folk-song was less uneasy.

The folk-song movement in England, which came later than in any European country except perhaps Hungary, was deeply conservative in its nature, since it strove to preserve a way of life, and a musical idiom, which had already passed. In Hungary two close friends, Béla Bartók (1881–1945) and Zoltán Kodály (1882–1967), demonstrated the two possible reactions to folk music; Kodály pursued the same path as Vaughan Williams, using folk music to reinforce an essentially conservative idiom, while Bartók attempted a daring and largely successful synthesis of folk music and a cautiously revolutionary compositional style. He was assisted in this by the nature of Hungarian folk-song, so different from the English; rhythmically more complex and advanced, and using, in addition to the usual modes, various inflexions and exotic scales from further east.

Though the discovery of folk music was a powerful stimulus to some English composers at the time, it was by no means so for all. Bax, Bridge and Ireland were not affected. Elgar reacted with his famous remark "I am folk music"; Delius went his own sweet way, occasionally using folk melodies to remarkable purpose (*Brigg Fair*, "On hearing the first cuckoo in spring"), but only when they closely resembled his own style of melody. Bantock adopted Hebridean tunes when it suited him; Holbrooke and Brian were too steeped in the Wagnerian idiom to be affected. Hebridean folk-song, more elaborate, rhapsodic and moody than the English variety, became popular as a result of the activities of Marjory Kennedy-Fraser (1857–1930), who began collecting folk-song in 1905.

Holst's early music, in spite (or because!) of his studies with Stanford, is turgidly Wagnerian, according to himself; few have heard these "early horrors". But the first two (tiny) works by Vaughan Williams to have lived seem to anticipate his discovery of folk-song; no wonder the composer of "Linden Lea" (1901) and "Silent Noon" (1903) felt that he had known "Bushes and Briars" all his life. "Linden Lea" wobbles between Victorian ballad and folk-song, but the lovely "Silent Noon", itself but one of a number of settings from Rossetti's *House of Life*, is already quintessential Vaughan Williams, even to the point of being both clumsy and beautiful at the same time. The chords at the opening shout Vaughan Williams to anyone who knows his style; and the tune with which the voice enters is already kin to folk-song.

The two major works of 1903 came from Elgar and Delius, and neither of them were folky. The Elgar was in a form that was already sufficiently moribund for its composer to be uneasy about it: oratorio. He had earlier planned a set of three oratorios concerning the Acts of the Apostles, but only two were actually composed. The first of these, *The Apostles*, belongs to 1903, but we will consider *The Kingdom* of 1906 along with it, since Elgar wrote only *In the South* and the

Introduction and Allegro for strings in the intervening years, and the problems that beset *The Apostles* belong also to *The Kingdom*. Three separate conflicting strands meet in these two oratorios. The first is Elgar's deep religious feeling, at this time unimpaired, which had to find musical expression; the second his progressive nature, which even in these conventional works breaks through from time to time; and the third those conventions themselves, Victorian conventions, to which he was still partly in thrall, and the struggle against which was his life's battle.

In size and singularity Elgar stands alone at the beginning of the English renaissance. He looks both forward and backward, has elements in him of both Stainer and Strauss, is a European figure who is English almost by default. Eclectic to the point at which the manifold elements of a European musical language dissolve in his works, until we are hard put to it to recognise the individual strands, he is English in sudden quiet moments in which the timeless wistful singing of an English spring steals into the music like a waif among warriors; English also in his love of a sheet-anchor from the past to hold his adventures within sight of familiar things. The scores of both *The Apostles* and *The Kingdom* bear the sign "A.M.D.G." and the words are from the Bible, selected with great skill in small detail, but with a seeming lack of direction to which the unwritten score of the third part of the trilogy might have provided a clue. *The Kingdom* ends with a long still chord on the words "Thou O Lord art our Father", in a manner which suggests that the key to the curious mosaic construction of the two completed parts might lie beyond them. If so, it would have to take up a good many threads; for, with a few leading motives to hold the music together, the "plot" of both parts consists of a series of scenes, the connection between which is implicit but not obvious, with a few threads of argument in common. Elgar wished to trace the history of the Church of Christ in the world, with the shofar which links the Jewish and Christian faiths in the two early parts used for the Last Trumpet in the third. He meant the Church in the sense of the ordinary people who were entrusted with the building of Christ's society upon earth, rather than the central figure

Himself: one small revolutionary link with *The Dream of Gerontius*.

When it came to the actual writing of the music Elgar fell back on the old oratorio style, or something like it—possibly out of sheer lack of belief in the form, which unconsciously motivated a retreat from the revolutionary implications of *Gerontius*. This idea is reinforced by the fact that he failed to complete the trilogy. Sir Adrian Boult, interestingly, prefers *The Kingdom* to *Gerontius*; he writes that compared with *The Kingdom*, *Gerontius* is the work of a raw amateur. One sees what he means: *The Kingdom* is more symphonic than *Gerontius*; but in spite of such things as "The Sun Goeth Down" the flame of inspiration burns low in *The Kingdom*; it is less uneven because it never rises to such heights. The sheer audacity of *Gerontius* more than makes up for its unevenness. *The Kingdom* sounds conventional and rather weary.

I feel that of the two later oratorios *The Apostles* contains the best music, and more traces of the progressive Elgar. The massive Prelude to *The Kingdom* sets the tone for its rather pompous nature, but *The Apostles* is more intimate, and in spite of the musically dubious Mary Magdalene episode, has more in it of the tender and subtle Elgar of the Violin Concerto and the slow movement of the First Symphony. I think that the finest section in either of the oratorios is "By the Wayside" in *The Apostles*. The Beatitudes are sung by Christ as He walks, to a movingly typical Elgarian ambling tune. The Apostles comment, each in his own character, and on a number of occasions in this brief section light is thrown on Elgar's own attitude of mind:

THE APOSTLES: He setteth the poor on high from affliction.
JUDAS: He poureth contempt upon princes.

Judas sees just that much further into the implications of Christ's teaching—and, uncannily, into the mind of the seventy-year-old Elgar that was to be. The dialogue continues, until we are brought up sharp by the following:

THE APOSTLES: He that hath mercy on the poor, happy is he.
JUDAS: The poor is hated even of his own neighbour; the rich hath many friends.

Judas's comment is painfully familiar as a sentiment expressed in bitter cynicism in many of Elgar's letters.

The identity of much that is put into the mouth of Judas with some of Elgar's own despairing utterances is disquieting, but psychologically interesting. We find the following terrifying words in Judas's last long monologue after the betrayal;

> Our life is short and tedious, and in the death of a man there is no remedy; neither was there any man known to have returned from the grave. For we are born at all adventure, and we shall be hereafter as though we had never been; for the breath in our nostrils is as smoke, and a little spark in the moving of our heart, which being extinguished, our body shall be turned into ashes, and our spirit shall vanish as the soft air, and our name shall be forgotten in time, and no man have our work in remembrance.

The last phrases about no man having our work in remembrance enshrine Elgar's especial nightmare. These two oratorios sound almost as though they were contemporary with *The Music Makers*, and after the Second Symphony. Compared with the tragic power of that great work they sound tired and negative.

On the Continent two symphonies were being written in 1903 that came to international fame only much later: Sibelius's Second and Mahler's Fifth. The latter was not performed in England until forty years after its completion, and I attended this first performance in England of a work written before I was born. In France in 1903 Debussy's *La Mer* was played for the first time, a work belonging to the new world of music as surely as the Sibelius, and even the Mahler, belonged to the old, and the two Elgar oratorios to an older world still. Also in France, at Grez-sur-Loing, Delius had finished *Sea Drift*, a work which in its individual and inward-turning nature bears the stamp of no particular period. Performed for the first time at Essen in 1906, under George Witte, it has some claim to be considered Delius's most perfect work, and is surely a masterpiece. *La Mer*, in its progressive technique and coldly glittering objectivity, proposes many points that were to be developed by Pierre Boulez; *Sea Drift* is also concerned with the sea, but only as a sympathetic back-cloth to preoccupations as typical of Delius as the pain of a creative artist disappointed in his inmost soul came to be typical of Elgar. The emotional basis of *Sea Drift* is a blend of several subtle and seemingly not very compatible elements fused at white heat into a new synthesis—not a bad description of the creative act itself. In spite of the fact that the pain of loss is an important element in the work, it has a sensuous aspect, derived from the sea and also from first experience. The blend of the magical immanence of sea and sky with actual sexual experience, implicit though never explicit, a marvellous involvement of the emotions of the boy and the pair of birds, develops from the wonder of first discovery to the poignance of first pain.

The score is the usual mature Delius scattering of crotchets, minims and semibreves, anything shorter than a quaver being the exception. Compared with the score of *La Mer*, that of *Sea Drift* looks brutally clumsy, the work of a much coarser sensibility. Great though *La Mer* is, however, it is inhuman; the first total projection of a natural order voided of God and human emotion. The sound of *La Mer* is the notes; in the Debussy score and meaning are more at one than in any previous work. More than in any previous work the score of *Sea Drift* is misleading. It only comes to life in performance, when we realise that this primitive-looking score has been transformed into sound that seems to embody our deepest, most mysterious experience. No two scores, written at the same time and ostensibly on the same subject, have ever so completely represented such different worlds. It is quite impossible to prove the claim I have made for *Sea Drift* (other than by listening to the Beecham record); whereas any claim one may make for *La Mer* can be proved almost casually by reference to the bare notes. There is another, vital technical point; the climax of *Sea Drift*, at the words "O past, O happy life", is marked by a modulation so magical that it is hardly an exaggeration to write that it is the most emotionally profound and technically apt since Schubert. No such emotional use of tonality occurs in *La Mer*; tonality is still there, but it has abdicated, become irrelevant. Any such modulation in *La Mer* would disrupt the sovereign play of pure pattern reft of human caring.

The years 1903 to about 1907 were years of tentative beginnings in England, but mounting achievement in the new music of Europe. In 1904 Mahler completed his Sixth Symphony, a towering masterpiece, and as human as you like, but bitterly despairing. There is nothing in Elgar as nihilistic as this, although harmonically and orchestrally Mahler's Sixth and Elgar's Second have something in common; the harmonic and orchestral colouring used by the two men seem equally and disturbingly prophetic of some catastrophic future. At the same time Sibelius wrote his blandly classical, atavistic Third Symphony, a stage in his development from the romantic first two symphonies to his more personal later works. Béla Bartók emerged in Hungary with his symphonic poem *Kossuth* and two works for piano and orchestra: a Rhapsody and a Scherzo. As yet he was a late-Romantic nationalist. A few works by the younger English composers appeared: Bax's *Celtic Song Cycle*, Bridge's Three Noveletten for string quartet (1906), Holbrooke's tone poems *Ulalume* and *Queen Mab*, and one of Vaughan Williams's earliest essays for orchestra—*In the Fen Country*.

In 1905 a London businessman, William Cobbett, changed the whole face of English chamber music by instituting a prize for chamber works in the Phantasy form. From this date English chamber music appears; before long there were a number of considerable works by English composers, though few of them were in Phantasy form. In its inception in Elizabethan times the Phantasy was a single movement built out of sections of varying tempi; the works that emerged from the competition were single-movement sonatas in which the traditional order of the movements in a full-scale sonata provided the scheme for the sections. The Cobbett Phantasy was meant to encourage composers to discover an English style of chamber music—hence the appeal to a form that had achieved greatness in the Fantazias of Henry Purcell.

The year 1905 was rather a lean one for lasting English music, only Frank Bridge's Phantasy Quartet joining Elgar's magnificent Introduction and Allegro. But Europe provided two massive works: Mahler's Seventh Symphony, with its strange nocturnal scherzos, and Schoenberg's vast and complex symphonic poem *Pelleas und Melisande*. In the choral *Gurrelieder*, Schoenberg had written a work for huge forces that was nevertheless of lucid beauty, but *Pelleas und Melisande* revealed him as reaching an impasse, in which contrapuntal and chromatic complexity battered at tonality for a way out.

The name of Gustav Holst became public in 1906 with two charming folky works that are still in the repertory: A Somerset Rhapsody and Two Songs Without Words. The Somerset Rhapsody is very close in style to the Norfolk Rhapsody No. 1 of Vaughan Williams, the first version of which was written in 1906. A Somerset Rhapsody uses the folk-tunes "The Sheep-shearing Song", "High Germany", and "The Lover's Farewell", and is actually the first orchestral work of the folk-song movement to have lived. In this year Frank Bridge won an international prize at Bologna with his First String Quartet, a beautifully written work revealing Bridge's sensitive, idiomatic writing for the medium. The Bridge personality makes itself felt for the first time in this work, music of delicate colours, redolent of the summer sea, with a strange air of magic always present under the surface. It was the first string quartet by an Englishman to stand beside the great Viennese examples. From round about this time also comes the Piano Quintet, a big work, very professionally written, but rather plain and without much sign of the mature Bridge.

In 1907—the year that Beecham heard *Appalachia* for the first time and experienced what seems to have been for him an almost religious revelation—Delius produced *Songs of Sunset*, *Cynara*, *Brigg Fair* and *On Craig Dhu*. Of these works the most important is *Brigg Fair*, "An English Rhapsody", an orchestral work in Delius's favourite Fitzwilliam Virginal Book free variation form. "Brigg Fair" is a Lincolnshire folk-song which had been collected by Percy Grainger (1882–1961), who passed it on to Delius. The wood-wind writing at the opening of *Brigg Fair* is superb, and the score looks more professional than that of *Sea Drift*. In sound that opening—compared by Cecil Gray to the lifting of the mist from the hills on a summer morning—is utterly English, one of the first moments in this narrative when this elusive quality has been manifest in a work. There are also passages of fresh, jubilant, complex writing for the upper voices, firmly fixed on the dark line of the basses, which are reminiscent of the writing for treble voices in the Festival Masses of the early sixteenth century. Coupled with its very English form these make *Brigg Fair*, as its subtitle suggests, one of Delius's most English works.

How good is *Brigg Fair*? If we compare it with other nationalist works that immediately preceded it, Liszt's Hungarian pieces, Smetana's *Ma Vlast*, Dvorak's Slavonic Rhapsodies, it stands up very well. It lacks the universal quality that makes *Sea Drift* an unmistakable masterpiece, but it is beautiful and fresh, and we should no more decry it for *Sea Drift*'s sake than we should disapprove of *As You Like It* for the sake of *Hamlet*. Rosalind is abroad in *Brigg Fair*, and the Forest of Arden not far off. The other Delius works of this year are not in this class. There is, however, the short unaccompanied choral piece *On Craig Dhu*, which is a perfect small thing, full of atmosphere, conveying as few other things do the magic of English distances. I must confess to a personal dislike of *Songs of Sunset*. I imagine this is what all Delius's music must sound like to those who dislike it, although the work is actually not very typical—a suite of pieces for chorus and orchestra that exactly matches the bogus decadence and mawkish pessimism of Dowson's immature verses: overripe harmony and rather lachrymose melody.

Sea Drift's poet, Walt Whitman, supplied the words for a short piece for chorus and orchestra by Vaughan Williams that was among his first characteristic works—*Towards the Unknown Region*. This composition is usually and appropriately taken as prophetic of the exploring soul of RVW in the years to come, and this product of the first years of his great friendship with Gustav Holst still has the power to move us, although the opening bars on the orchestra will amuse anyone who knows the style of Hubert Parry. It was also a practice run for a much bigger work that was to come in 1909. Frank Bridge wrote a

tone-poem called *Isabella*, which has remained in manuscript.*

In 1907 Gustav Mahler gave the first performance of his
Eighth Symphony, the last work he was to direct himself, or
even hear performed; and also his most massive symphony.
Ravel was going through a Spanish phase, and from this time
date the little opera *L'Heure espagnol* and *Rapsodie espagnol*.
Schoenberg wrote his Second String Quartet, the last movement of which is consciously atonal (although Liszt had
anticipated him many years before with his Bagatelle without
Tonality); Schoenberg's first wholly atonal works were written
in 1909—the piano pieces Op. 11 and the poem for soprano
and orchestra *Erwartung*. Debussy wrote his *Images* for orchestra;
the largest of these is another Spanish piece in three sections
(*Iberia*), there is a belatedly romantic piece in *Rondes des
printemps*, and *Gigues*, a subtle and haunting depiction of the
environs of Soho on a rainy winter evening at the beginning
of the century; it may well have been conceived on the way
to Queen's Hall.

Mahler's glorious reign at the Vienna State Opera came to
an end on the last day of 1907, and he went to New York,
where he was engaged to conduct opera and concerts. It seems
a small point, but it was symptomatic of the end of an era in
European music. Richard Strauss was switching from symphonic poems to opera, and his first opera was the rather
Wagnerian, innocuous *Guntram*. *Feuersnot* was erotic and
mildly shocking; but the epoch-making work was *Salome*, after
Wilde's play, in 1905.

Delius wrote two characteristic orchestral pieces in 1908,
and astonishingly conducted the first performances himself.
These were *In a Summer Garden* (London, December 1909) and
the First Dance Rhapsody (Hereford, Three Choirs, September
1909). He was a helplessly bad conductor, and the performances
were a shambles. *In a Summer Garden* is a rich and lush work,

---

* It is not the only large-scale work from Bridge's early years that has
dropped out of sight; there was an earlier tone-poem still, with the peculiar
title *Comes the mid of night, ends for a while the brooding*, which was finished as
early as 1903.

and was a favourite of Beecham's; inspired by his garden at Grez, and including a reference to the river Loing, it contains Delius's only essay in the style of Debussy. This is in the second half of the piece, after the broad tune on the strings depicting the river (quite unlike Debussy), and Delius uses a fragmented texture and some of the other devices of impressionism; ostensibly, this is a development of the bird-song material of the opening, but its resemblance to Debussy is obvious. It suggests that Delius adapted his technique to his setting. *Paris* is broadly eclectic; his French garden draws him near to Debussy: *Brigg Fair* uses instinctively English procedures, and so does the First Dance Rhapsody. The slow introduction, which ends with a tremendous crash, is wistful and richly coloured with exotic wood-wind, but the main tune is wholly English in flavour; it is rather like a music-hall song that was popular at the beginning of the century. It is wholly enchanting, Delius's vivid orchestration enhancing its beauty as he turns the tune this way and that, letting the changing light catch it. Right at the end the scoring is rather thick, but the Rhapsody remains a unique work.

In 1908 the Cobbett competition had its first substantial effect; the first prize went to Frank Bridge and the second to John Ireland. Their two Phantasy Trios are broadly alike, but in their differences interesting. The Ireland has a lovely tune, full of that elusive emotion that was to make this little master the most English, if one of the most limited, of composers. Bridge, potentially the bigger man, and with a less limited technique, wrote a dark, richly coloured and energetic work which is still full of the Stanford–Brahms influence. It is not unlike a Brahms trio in its dark strength, and the delicate, enchanted Bridge personality is only fitfully in evidence. Both works are still precariously in the repertory. Bridge's powerful Dance Rhapsody received its first performance this year. Quite unlike the Delius works of the same name, and very characteristic of its composer, it is in turns daemonic in its bursting energy and mysterious in its shadowy poetry.

In 1908 also the extraordinary episode of *Apollo and the Seaman* took place. This gigantic work for huge forces was the brain-child of Joseph Holbrooke, was inspired by a poem by Herbert

Trench, and designed to be accompanied by lantern slides of the poem. Holbrooke actually persuaded Thomas Beecham to perform it, and perform it he did.* But the most historically prophetic, and in that sense extraordinary, English work of the year came from Gustav Holst. His chamber opera *Savitri* would not occasion surprise if it were given with the chamber operas of Britten; indeed, *Curlew River* obviously owes a lot to it. It is scored for three soloists, chorus and chamber orchestra, and stands in the greatest contrast to the megalomania of *Apollo and the Seaman*, while the fact that it appeared in the same year as Elgar's First Symphony is simply astonishing, and almost without historical precedent. Here, at one stroke, is the mature Holst, austere and other-worldly, handling the language of cold, thin chords and simple, chant-like vocal lines almost without a slip. It is a very beautiful work, although not 'advanced' in technique in the same way that the works of Schoenberg were advanced, wholly of the twentieth century; perhaps the first English work of which this could be said, since even the music of Elgar looks both forward and backward.

On 3 December 1909, at the Free Trade Hall, Manchester, the Hallé Orchestra under Richter gave the first performance of Elgar's First Symphony. The first London première took place four days later with the London Symphony Orchestra under the same conductor. It was the first great English symphony, and even if Richter's response to it was partly motivated by a dislike of the new music appearing in Europe, that does not detract from its ultimate stature. Richter did not realise it at the time, but one of the reasons for its greatness is precisely that it spoke as an equal the common language of Strauss and Mahler, at least as far as they had developed up to that time. It was Elgar's moment, and he was never again to know a success like this, for the symphony was performed a hundred times in the first year of its life. But even as Elgar wrote it Strauss, in *Elecktra*, was relegating its harmonic language to the past, while Schoenberg, Berg and Webern were inaugur-

* Beecham seems to have regarded the whole affair as a huge joke (surely an expensive one?), to judge by his account of it in his autobiography, *A Mingled Chime* (1944).

ating a new and quite different musical epoch; Stravinsky was writing his student works. Time was moving so fast that it overtook Elgar's lovely work before it had achieved its hundredth performance. Time was also overtaking Gustav Mahler, at work on *Das Lied von der Erde*. The infinite sadness of farewell, the sense of the passing of the old order, had not yet invaded the music of Elgar, as it was to do in later years, and finds no place in the First Symphony. This is one of Elgar's happiest and most extrovert works, and its success was assured by the gay poetry of mood of most of the work, as much as by its sheer size and the mastery of its technique.

The opening theme of the first movement is broad and simple, and is accompanied by a striding bass; it is used as a motto theme, and it mingles with the texture when it appears with increasing freshness and wistful beauty. The Allegro that follows is tense and dramatic, with a first subject of obscure tonality, contrasting strongly with the plain diatonicism of the motto theme. This is, actually, a very radical piece of writing. Hints of the motto theme float through the strident texture like gleams of sunlight, but in spite of the drama of the music the movement ends quietly and simply, with a passage in the coda that has been compared to café music. Its inspiration was probably the similar passage in the coda of Brahms's Second Symphony, but it is wholly English in sound —a definitive statement of that elusive thing, Englishness— and it has the wistful sweetness of Shakespeare at his most gentle.

This symphony was the last music by Elgar to be seen through the press by his friend August Jaeger, who had been ill for many years with tuberculosis, and was now dying. In a poignant letter Nimrod described what the symphony meant to him:

The Scherzo is a real joy & one of the biggest things in all symphonic literature. And that mysterious Lento with its abysmal depths of tone colour and the astounding Finale, an overpowering outburst of optimism & joie de vivre that carries one away in spite of oneself until the superb peroration crowns the whole splendid structure.

It's a great and masterly work & will place you higher among the world's masters than anything you have done. Ill as I am . . . I have bought a ticket & am looking forward to what I fear will be the last great . . .

Perhaps it was the last music Jaeger heard, for he died six months later, and Elgar lost his beloved critic and dearest musical friend. He is more natural in his letters to Jaeger than in any other record we have of him; here is a gay rebel, a boyish, occasionally bitter but invariably pugnacious man, who writes uninhibitedly, without the fears and cautions that so often drove his other correspondence into conventional stiffness. One has the feeling that no one, not even his wife (in some things especially not his wife), understood Elgar's real self—the musical genius—as Nimrod did.

Among significant European musical events of 1909 was the appearance of Bartók's First String Quartet, a large-scale work in which the patent influence of Beethoven's Op. 131, Hungarian nationalism, and radical twentieth-century tendencies achieved an extraordinary balance; no chamber work of such importance had yet been written in England. But in England Vaughan Williams suddenly moved into the foreground with three works, the least important but most popular of which was the music to *The Wasps*. Of more significance was the song cycle *On Wenlock Edge*, settings of poems by A. E. Housman.

One crucial encounter of RVW's early career was that with Ravel, with whom he had studied in 1908. He was supposed to be studying orchestration, but Ravel's influence clearly extended much further than this.* *On Wenlock Edge* almost quotes the Ravel String Quartet in places, while remaining distinctively English. There is a chord of the

---

* It seems certain that the memory of Ravel's teaching stood Vaughan Williams in good stead during the crisis in his art between 1925 and 1930. He had also consulted with Max Bruch in 1897, and it may not be too fanciful to detect something of Max Bruch's woolly textures here and there in his music.

thirteenth, with decorations, in this cycle that has become known as the "Wenlock Edge" chord, and it is redolent of far English horizons. Ravel took a great interest in the cycle, offering to play the piano part when the work was given in Paris. In fact he did not, but what did the good Parisians make of the words? The Shropshire Lad in the Paris of Baudelaire, Verlaine and Rimbaud?

There had been a great revulsion in England against the European influences of the '90s, and for this the fall of Oscar Wilde was responsible. English literature turned in on itself. Distinguished foreigners like Henry James (American) and Joseph Conrad (Polish) apart, the most popular prose was that of Kipling, Rider Haggard and the rising H. G. Wells. Adventure and Empire were in the air, and the brashness and embryo science fiction of Wells were absorbed along with the Poe-inspired writings of Conan Doyle. In poetry the Georgians were in the making. Housman's *A Shropshire Lad* was first published as early as 1896, but his poems were still being set in the 1960s, in spite of a period flavour that was by then almost derisory.

There is not much English poetry that is easy to set, apart from that of the Elizabethans. Far too much of it is too obviously great, and much of it is in unsuitable form and metre; it needed Benjamin Britten to teach composers how to set a sonnet, and even so, the greatest of English sonnets—those of Shakespeare and Milton for instance—are out of the question (one fervently hopes). During the Elizabethan period much poetry was written with a musical setting in mind, but the poetry of Pope and Dryden, for example, offers few opportunities to the composer, and the later poetry of Wordsworth and much of Keats presents in the main insuperable problems which Holst's Choral Symphony only serves to illustrate. The poetry of the German lied, that of Goethe, Mörike, Heine, et al., is lyrical without actually challenging music on its own ground (as so much great English poetry does) and in short verse forms of suitable length, without being superficial; and we know the result. It is profound *in thought*, whereas much English lyrical verse is musically sublime in a way that daunts, and often eclipses, any musical setting.

But not that of A. E. Housman, whose verse has the settability of Heine, without ever approaching Heine's maturity of thought, bitter adult irony, or complexity of interplay between meaning and structure. Housman was a classical scholar, and his poems are an odd amalgam of Greek lyric forms and various English folk influences. They are eminently settable in a mildly sentimental English style, and in that style they have been set by a number of English composers. Vaughan Williams's settings were, to the poet's disgust, the most sophisticated of any—curiously, one of Vaughan Williams's most sophisticated works, technically.

The major Vaughan Williams work of 1909 was *A Sea Symphony*, to words by Whitman. This four-movement symphony was an astonishing challenge for a composer whose works up to this date had been somewhat tentative in scope. It was given its first performance at the Leeds Festival, under the composer, and most appropriately in Leeds Town Hall. In some ways *A Sea Symphony* was the last great gesture of the departing nineteenth century, since contemporary it was not, by continental standards. Elgar's Second Symphony, which was to come in 1911, was an elegy for the whole period, consciously full of grief; but its musical language was slightly more radical, and it was more universal in scope. The gusty optimism of *A Sea Symphony* was that of fifty years before its actual date. It contains a few prophetic elements, but is in the main a vast piece of Victoriana, like Leeds Town Hall, and like Leeds Town Hall has a slightly comical, faintly sentimental grandeur. Some of it sounds like Parry, though Parry never possessed a quarter of the clumsy genius apparent in this work; but its very dimensions, never again attempted by Vaughan Williams in a symphony, reflect the departing age. The opening gesture of the first movement, "A Song for all Seas, all Ships", is a diatonic fanfare for horns and trumpets on the triad of B flat minor, and it is answered, thrillingly, by the chorus with the words "Behold the sea itself". That fanfare sounds rather too feeble to introduce such a truly imposing choral entry, but there is nothing in the symphony to equal that initial inspiration. The first movement mingles the familiar RVW fingerprints with diverse nineteenth-century echoes, as well as those of Parry, but the slow movement, "On the beach at night alone", is pure RVW in its dark meditation; the Scherzo less so. The finale enlarges on "Towards the Unknown Region", and the whole work leaves a feeling of power, and of promise that was in the main fulfilled. It excites affection, even while we smile at some of its naïveties and occasionally suppress a yawn. It was the first wholly choral symphony, and it proclaimed the coming of a major figure in English music.

Arnold Bax, eleven years Vaughan Williams's junior, also began to be known at this time. His list of works for the first decade of the twentieth century is prodigious, but most were withdrawn by him. Some were incorporated into other works. The list includes some ten orchestral pieces, only one of which has been published.* There are a number of tone-poems, two overtures, a set of variations, and a Symphony in F (not to be confused with his Symphony No. 1 in F flat), as well as another large-scale work, really yet another symphony, called *Spring Fire*. This is a beautifully scored composition of fresh and glittering inspiration, in its limpid colours curiously unlike the later, brooding, dramatic Bax, but betraying its composer with one or two fingerprints. This work emphatically calls for revival.

For a long time the only one of these pieces to be published, and occasionally performed, was *In the Faery Hills*. This was the second of three symphonic poems on Irish subjects; the first was called *Into the Twilight* and the third *Rosc-catha*. *In the Faery Hills* is in fact a neat scherzo and trio, for all its original title concerning the Hosting of the Sidhe, and the most obvious thing about it is its economy and technical accomplishment. Like most of the works from this time it is based on a Celtic subject, but it should be realised that Bax's Celtic period was over by the 1920s, and was in any case mixed with strong

---

* Contrary to the usual critical opinion, one of Bax's strong points was self-criticism, and to withdraw so many works at this crucial stage of his career indicates a stoical attitude that was in fact typical of him. There was also a large-scale ballet called *Tamara*, later changed to *King Kojata*, which he kept in a drawer because of scruples of conscience that would not have troubled another man.

Russian influences. *In the Faery Hills* concerns a harper who played a song of human joy to the Sidhe, who cast his harp into the lake so that this demon of sadness should no more trouble them. Restless sadness at the transience of human joy is one of the most consistent aspects of Bax's music, and is also illustrated by one of the most perfect of his early songs, "The White Peace".

The Cobbett prize for 1909 went to John Ireland for his First Sonata for violin and piano, in D minor.* It is curious to realise that the harmonies of this innocent, fragrant work shocked academic opinion at this time—the time of *L'Oiseau de feu* and *Daphnis et Chloë*. It is in three movements, full of that distinctive spring-song feeling that Ireland, of all people, displayed.

L'Oiseau de feu and *Daphnis et Chloë*; these two exquisite and epoch-making pieces, commissioned by Diaghilev and composed by Stravinsky and Ravel respectively, are works remote from English talents, and there is no score by an Englishman which can be compared to them, although Frank Bridge's later *Enter Spring* reveals the influence of the Ravel on a much smaller scale. This kind of sensuous kaleidoscope of sound, projected by virtuoso writing for orchestra, seems to lie outside the scope of English composers. The nearest we have got to it, and that not very far, is Bax's *The Garden of Fand* (1913).

In 1909 Mahler was engaged on his last tragic struggle, and working on his Ninth and Tenth symphonies. The great grim fortress of the Ninth was completed, and is in many ways his greatest symphony. Many years after he left it in pieces Deryck Cooke found that the score of the Tenth could be successfully reconstructed, with only a few bars that are at all conjectural.

Just as in 1908 Holst suddenly produced a prophetic work in *Savitri*, so in 1910 Vaughan Williams wrote a work which reveals most of his personality, and which was a new sound in English music—the Tallis Fantasy. It is in this lovely antiphonal

* Ireland published the Sonata himself in 1911; but after the Second Violin Sonata of 1917 Augener took it over. Augener's catalogue has now been acquired by Stainer & Bell.

work for strings that the modal revival comes of age. It was given for the first time at Gloucester, in the Three Choirs Festival of the year, and in the same year Kreisler and Elgar gave the first performance of Elgar's Violin Concerto in London at a Philharmonic Society concert on 10 November. The two works belong to different ages. For all its archaicism the Vaughan Williams could only have been written in the twentieth century; modal harmony such as this was impossible in the Classical and Romantic periods (except in late Beethoven). But if we think of the Elgar Violin Concerto we think of those of Beethoven and Brahms. It is a little optimistic to compare it with the Beethoven, although not perhaps with the Brahms. The Violin Concerto is one of Elgar's most English-sounding works, in the slow movement, and in the accompanied cadenza to the third; these should be contrasted with the various European influences that are felt in the surging romanticism of the first movement. Such is Elgar's power that the work holds together with the same mastery that Brahms's concerto holds together; but it must be remembered that the Brahms was written in 1878, the Elgar in 1910. For all its seeming modernism in an English context, Elgar's music was beginning to sound old-fashioned in a European one. The Violin Concerto is really a nineteenth-century work. Even the Ninth Symphony of Mahler, its contemporary, uses a language that was beginning to slip into the past. Webern wrote his Five Pieces for Orchestra in 1911, with his atonal and fragmented style fully formed.

To this time belong the first version of Bax's First Piano Sonata, and the first version of the First Violin Sonata, both works being revised years later—the Violin Sonata several times. The former, in its revised form, is a surprisingly accomplished large-scale work for the piano to come from an Englishman at this period. It handles its large design, flamboyant textures and virtuoso piano writing with confidence. The only work written before the First World War that can be compared with it for size and ambition of design is the Sonata in D minor of Benjamin Dale (1885–1943). Dale was a fellow pupil of Corder; remarkably enough, for his sonata is conservative in harmony and Brahmsian in texture. It is in four movements, the last three being parts of a set of variations. Bax's sonata is in one movement, a huge one, obviously modelled on the B minor Sonata of Liszt, but multifarious in its influences: there is a strong Russian flavour (it was conceived in Russia) and its ending, hectically combative whereas Liszt's sonata sinks in defeat, is a riotous evocation of the bells of Moscow. It is one of the first Bax works to reveal his personality in full, although his later works are less luxuriant. The First Violin Sonata is less ambitious, and perhaps it overworks its lovely motto theme. But in contrast to the vivid splashes of purple and scarlet of the Piano Sonata, it is a study in water-colours, full of Bax's wistful early emotional engagement with Ireland.

Beecham conducted his first season at Covent Garden this year, sharing it with Bruno Walter and Percy Pitt. Beecham conducted Strauss's *Elektra* and Delius's *A Village Romeo and Juliet*, and the season also included Ethel Smyth's *The Wreckers*. Ethel Smyth was one of those English composers who studied at Leipzig, and was the first Englishwoman to achieve something of a reputation as a composer. Today *The Wreckers* conveys the rather odd impression of a youthful opera by Brahms; it is full of the sort of thing one finds in the early piano music and the First Piano Concerto (somewhat watered down), and one imagines that Brahms might, in his youth, have had just this combination of conservatism and recklessness when approaching a medium as uncongenial to him as opera. It is not exactly the kind of music that is known to have appealed to Beecham, who was one of those artists who were slowly breaking down England's suspicion of art, Europe and the modern. His work was considerably assisted by the visits of Diaghilev with the Russian Ballet. Under the guise of something very like the pantomime of hallowed British tradition, these gorgeous, sophisticated and exotic entertainments quickly became fashionable, and the whole erotically ambiguous atmosphere of Diaghilev and his troupe was insinuated into the London season.

Edward VII died in 1910, and on 18 May 1911 Gustav Mahler died in Vienna; his death marked off the end of the old order decisively and curtly. It was not until 1914 that the political implications of the period became explicit, but this was a crucial juncture in music as well as politics. Most of the monuments of the twentieth-century revolution in music were composed in these years, in which the distinctive twentieth-century aesthetic was pioneered in all the arts. Tonality had entered its great crisis, and the work of Arnold Schoenberg and his pupils in Vienna began to make its impression on world music. It is customary to refer to the period, which in England corresponded roughly to the reign of Edward VII, as opulent: a time that was looked back upon with nostalgia by all those rich enough to have benefited from its easy-going laxity. But in this time the poor were still poor, and the opulence of the wealthier section of the population threw that terrible poverty into relief. The Labour Party scored its first electoral successes, and one or two Labour members entered Parliament.

An astonishing amount of great music was written between, say, 1908 and 1912, and the period proved fateful, in one way or another, for all the composers working in it. In 1909 Sibelius suffered from a tumour in his throat, which was believed to be malignant. An operation cured it, but for a number of years afterwards it was feared that it might recur. Under this shadow he composed his Fourth Symphony, one of his best works, and one of the greatest symphonies of the century. Sibelius wrote to his publisher that he had put all of himself into it, without compromise; it is economically scored for a sparse orchestra, and its four movements are condensed to their essentials. The work has an extraordinary atmosphere, a brooding, winter nature-mysticism of hypnotic intensity. One of the curiosities of interpretation is that the hedonistic Beecham, who in any case came to it late in life when all his adventurousness had gone, gave an unapproachably great, frightening performance of this darkly daemonic symphony.

In 1911 Richard Strauss completed *Der Rosenkavalier*, thus turning his back on the radical experiments of *Salome* and *Elektra*, and the potential atonality that lurked in these works. Opulent as you like, reflecting the most luxurious aspects of the Vienna in which it is set, *Der Rosenkavalier* is a ravishingly beautiful opera, though at odds with the radical music of the time. But even in this Strauss was taking a formidable step—in this case backwards, for from now on he became a conservative, and for many years lost his touch. Debussy, in collaboration with Gabriele d'Annunzio, wrote *Le Martyre de Saint-Sébastien*, a work of mingled sensuality and tiredness, full of portents for twentieth-century music, and also perhaps the first sign of the weariness due to his incipient cancer, which Arnold Bax suspected in his unhealthy appearance at this time. Debussy heard Stravinsky's *Firebird* in Paris, while Stravinsky was at work on *Petrouchka*; while Bartók produced his first masterpiece outside the field of chamber music, the one-act opera *Duke Bluebeard's Castle*. Schoenberg was at work on *Pierrot Lunaire*, one of the first great achievements of atonality, a setting of poems by the minor Belgian Symbolist Albert Giraud, in a German translation by Otto Hartleben. In this work there are three groups of seven songs, and the accompaniment is for seven instruments; the Second Viennese School was obsessed with number symbolism: hence perhaps twelve-tone music. It also introduces for the first time the device of Sprechstimme, a kind of notated half-sung speech.

England was as yet unacquainted with Sibelius's terse, twisted nature symphony and the long, bitter elegy of Mahler's Ninth. It was to be many years before first Sibelius and then Mahler became a cult with the people of England; neither did England know the serene Third Symphony and Violin Concerto of Nielsen, who was also to become a craze for a few years after the Second World War. We had our own concerns, and in spite of Beecham and Diaghilev, we were still far behind the Continent. The sardonic old exile, Delius, wrote three short works: *Ein Arabeske*, *Life's Dance* and *Summer Night on the River*. The last piece is the companion to *On hearing the first cuckoo in Spring*, which was composed in 1912; *Life's Dance* was absorbed into other things. *Ein Arabeske* is a short work for baritone solo, chorus and orchestra to words by Jans Peter Jacobsen. So short a piece demanding these forces and with Danish words starts with an immediate disadvantage, and this intensely personal and unusual work has not had the popularity its quality deserves. A hymn to Pan, and to the brevity of love and the Nordic summer, it contains some of

Delius's most tense harmonic writing—writing that, in spite of a certain dry nostalgia, is bitter and inhuman in mood; here is the ancient Panic mystery. It has sometimes been compared with Debussy, and with *L'Après-midi d'un faune* in particular. But Debussy was concerned with sensuality, Delius with emotion. Debussy's faun basks in the summer heat; Delius's Pan is a bitter and ambiguous god. If it is to be compared with any work of Debussy, it is with the Villon songs, although even there the resemblance is but slight.

About this time Joseph Holbrooke began a strange venture which has kept his name alive in the mythology of music at a time when not a note of his compositions is heard. This is the trilogy *The Cauldron of Anwyn*, on Welsh mythological subjects, to words by Lord Howard de Walden. The first of these three operas, *The Children of Don*, was performed at the London Opera House in 1912; the second, *Dylan*, at Drury Lane in 1914; and the third, *Bronwen*, by the Carl Rosa Opera Company in Huddersfield in 1929; a few gramophone records of excerpts were issued in the early 1930s. The trilogy earned Holbrooke the title of "The Cockney Wagner"—rather apt if no question of stature is raised. Holbrooke's Second Clarinet Quintet (1910) is a work of beauty and skill, worth playing today, but in spite of vivid colour and some dramatic passages the trilogy suffers from the textural restlessness and bumpy harmony that seems to be a characteristic of pupils of Corder. The cycle is, however, a notable curiosity.

By 1911 both Elgar and Delius had established reputations more substantial than any English composers since Purcell; Vaughan Williams and Holst, whose collaboration was an important factor in their careers, had both made a certain mark, but could not be said to be firmly established; Bax had a few works to his credit that are still played, and so had Ireland. But Frank Bridge was in that position which it was his misfortune to occupy until very recently. A fine string player who had featured in the Joachim Quartet, he was so skilled a score reader that he was in great demand to take on conducting engagements at the last moment, or to perform modern works in which other conductors felt insecure. His music had at this time a fair circulation. From that day to this his piano music has been used for teaching purposes, with the result that many people know his name without guessing his stature. He had by now written a number of orchestral works and chamber compositions of modest scope but complex character. They were always beautifully composed, but like his songs and piano pieces, the earliest of them had a slight flavour of salon music. This wore off in time, with the Brahms–Stanford influence, and a startlingly different personality made itself known. It was recognisably the same man, but it was obvious that Stanford had been stifling an individual, original composer who in the end became very radical indeed. That was later; Bridge's middle-period music was sensuous and joyful, and in things like *Summer* and *The Sea* he wrote music of a sheer beauty of sound unsurpassed by any English composer. There was also a haunted, dark aspect, the counterpart to those attributes of nature in our islands that are evoked by owls, enchanter's nightshade and moths, a loveliness mingled with unease. A decided harmonic stringency began to be felt, and an increasing mastery, while the salon influences slowly vanished. Bridge's technique was so finished that few composers were his equal for easy mastery of his materials; but from the beginning until very recently he has been consistently underestimated.

By 1910 Elgar had behind him the solid success of the First Symphony and the Violin Concerto. Although his complaints of poverty still went on, he was now able to travel, and in Venice and Tintagel between 1910 and 1911 he wrote his Second Symphony, designed, as the dedication has it, to be a loyal tribute to Edward VII. The king died before it was finished, so the symphony is dedicated to his memory. How did the Catholic Elgar, a bit of a prude, and easily shocked, blind himself to the truth about Edward VII, when the monarch's behaviour, the scandals that pursued him all his life, were matters of common knowledge? It is possible that the honours with which Edward showered him, and that monarch's unfailing affability towards him, so blinded the composer's persecuted spirit with gratitude that he saw nothing else. The dedication is still enigmatic, and even slightly shocking; the contrast between this tragic, other-worldly, profoundly intellectual music and the easy-going, licentious monarch is too great. Then there is the superscription: "Rarely, rarely comest thou, Spirit of Delight!" It is hard to find that spirit in the Second Symphony; it is the rarity of its visits that is stressed.

The work was performed on 24 May 1911; a hot day. The Queen's Hall was by no means full, the audience a fashionable one, the coronation only a month away. It is not easy to think back to that occasion, for this world has been swept away in one of the mightiest social revolutions in history, and little of its atmosphere and structure remain in the modern consciousness. Our own privileged society is quite different, less confident, full of a bitter knowledge that these hot-house people were only to acquire, with shattering violence, in 1914, but of which they suspected absolutely nothing on this night. They expected, from what they knew, that Elgar would celebrate the royal and civic pride of the late monarch, mourn his death perhaps, and possibly greet the new king with suitable imperial pomp. They were probably not very musical, and certainly quite innocent of modern music; and Elgar's Second Symphony was his most advanced work, one of the most radical compositions by an Englishman up to that time.

The very opening note must have thrown that audience off balance. Subtly poised in the strings, it projects the music into the heart of the turmoil with a sense of shock, and if the first theme has been called "The Spirit of Delight", note how the brass snarls at its appearance (horns and trumpets, bars 7 and 8). An exulting phrase, perhaps? Elgar never miscalculated in a passage like this, and at this pitch and intensity the effect will be as nasal as if the brass were muted. It is the shock of combat that greets us, as if the Spirit were under siege, and to be taken only by assault. In fact the battle sinks in exhaustion, and is followed by veiled terror. Eight strokes of a spectral bell usher in a theme that resembles one of Gluck's arpeggio representations of evil spirits; once more the battle is joined, and its turmoil does not finally subside until the movement ends with curt power. The familiar Elgarian fingerprints are here, but the structure is at once more complex and more taut than in any previous movement by Elgar; although the first movement is shorter than that of the First Symphony, it seems longer, because of the density of incident. The whole symphony is weightier than the First, more oppressive as well as more impressive.

The opening of the slow movement at least resembles the obsequies of a king, in its solemn processional grief. We know now how like it is to the funeral march without which, it seems, no Mahler symphony is complete. It is doubtful however if anyone in that audience had even heard of Mahler, who at the time had lain in his grave but five days. The audience must have found this movement especially long and trying; no easy mourning for a remote royalty this, but a personal grieving of terrifying intensity.* And the climax of the movement, the Mahlerian climax, with thudding drums and straining strings, must have been completely beyond them; it needed in fact an audience which had become familiar with at least some of Mahler's symphonies—nearly forty years later—for the true stature of the work to be appreciated. Another stumbling-block must have been the strange passage in the Scherzo where the twilight wraith of the first movement becomes a noontide confrontation. Its terror impresses even today.

The last movement, with its familiar opening gambit, Elgar's habitual dotted ambling tune, is deceptive, and the storm soon breaks anew; the great tides of black sound that succeed it indicate that the climactic psychological conflict is upon us. Those off-beat *sforzandos* are a familiar fingerprint, and had been heard at the very beginning of Elgar's career in the quadrilles that he wrote for the mental home; but in this context they strike across the music like the despairing blows of a man fighting for his life. The ending of the symphony brings no consolation, for the Spirit of Delight departs with a sigh like heart-break. When it was over the audience in the

* Some of Elgar's friends may have known that the tragic death of Alfred Rodewald was in Elgar's mind when he wrote it; the sketches for this movement pre-date the rest, and it was designed long before the death of Edward VII.

Queen's Hall applauded half-heartedly, and Elgar was not deceived. He paused on his way from the platform to say to his leader, William Reed: "What's the matter with them, Billy? They sit there like a lot of stuffed pigs."

3

THE AGE OF ELGAR: II
1912—1914

ELGAR'S SECOND SYMPHONY was beyond the comprehension, not only of the rather atypical audience who heard the first performance, but also of the English public as a whole. The first surprise and glory of the English musical renaissance was over, and a new phase had begun. In England the reign of George V brought with it a sense of the dawn of the real twentieth century, after the long Victorian afterglow of Edward VII; and to many it seemed that the dawn was chill. Edward, in spite of his faults as a man, had striven sincerely and successfully for an uneasy peace among European nations who were moving restlessly towards an outcome which none of them really understood, and society in his reign had been genial and expansive like its monarch, but blind and selfish also. Man's technical achievement was about to outstrip his wisdom, and the peace bought by Edward was precarious and personal; moreover he was no longer there to sustain it.

In spite of the ingrained conservatism of English society it was in England that the revolution of the twentieth century began; England gave birth to Darwin and harbour to Marx, who wrote *Das Kapital* in the British Museum; and later Sigmund Freud was to spend his last years here. But this revolution did not begin to affect our art until after the mid-century. The years between 1911 and 1914 were restless, uneasy, without much conviction or emotional colour, charged with a sense of foreboding that was none the less real for being inexplicable and unanalysable by those who experienced it. The writings of H. G. Wells seemed full of blustering optimism and faith in the new religion of science and progress, and were taken as such by his contemporaries; but underneath the surface of his stories was a sense of futility, and his utopias and visions of the

75

future often ended in nightmare and disillusion. The Vorticist movement, started by Wyndham Lewis with Ezra Pound moving in the same direction, carried in it the seeds not of revolution but of the extreme reactionary positions both men were eventually to assume.

Victorian popular music, for all its inanity the forcing-house of twentieth-century mass culture, after a brief spell of real, earthy significance in the music-hall of the Nineties which produced such figures as Marie Lloyd, Albert Chevalier and Gus Elan (and, indirectly, Charlie Chaplin), was suddenly replaced by ragtime and jazz: the powerful product of black New Orleans. Jazz was sardonically acknowledged by Debussy in two exquisite, precious piano pieces, and later put to more substantial use by Stravinsky. Ravel, in the slow movement of his G major Piano Concerto, revealed that he understood the letter and some of the spirit of blues harmony; but, except for Constant Lambert, he was almost alone in this, and the art of Billie Holliday and Bessie Smith never really crossed the gulf between the two cultures, popular and specialised, which had begun to open in the Victorian period and was now unbridgeable.

The composers who began to appear in the second decade of the twentieth century were unlike the older generation of Elgar and Delius, while still lagging far behind the Continent in radical technique. Bax, Bridge and Ireland inhabited a world whose centre was not 1890, but not the Vienna of 1909 either; although Bridge was to approach the latter year in his last works. The self-conscious Englishness of Holst and Vaughan Williams belonged to a definite, limited period of time, a period that came to an end in 1914. Holst was altogether more intellectual in his approach than Vaughan Williams, and he grasped the techniques of early music with less prejudice, as far as the scholarship of his time went; but Bax and Frank Bridge understood the complexities of twentieth-century music far better. England had been so long without a valid music of its own that even the conservative works of these far from radical English composers puzzled scholar and layman alike. Arnold Bax, whose music was not more radical than that of other late Romantics, was considered an incomprehensible modern until 1945; when he suddenly became an outdated survival. Even the music of Elgar, from the Second Symphony onwards, was greeted with coolness and little comprehension.

Between 1912 and 1914 Elgar wrote two major works: *The Music Makers* and *Falstaff*.* Like Strauss's *Ein Heldenleben*, *The Music Makers* is full of self-quotations, and there can be no doubt, from internal evidence, that Elgar included himself among the music-makers. But he had not got the brash self-confidence, or the vainglory, of Richard Strauss, and these autobiographical references are veiled, reticent, abashed, like the man Elgar himself. If the bitterness of disillusion eventually overtakes the unconscionable bragging of *Ein Heldenleben*, the sadness of loss is never far from *The Music Makers*: there is a reference to Nimrod, the Small German, of the Enigma Variations; and at the words "in spite of a dreamer who slumbers, And a singer who sings no more" the music quotes the dying Gerontius "*Novissima hora est . . .*". The work is as singular as it is majestic, and becomes more moving the better you know it.

Falstaff is much more objective and a technically more self-sufficient work than *The Music Makers*, but for all its extroversion it is profoundly revealing.† The term "Symphonic Study" aptly describes a piece more detailed, more intellectual even, than any other work of its kind. The music has a needle-sharp precision, not just in the depiction of incident, but more particularly in its precise construction and finely chiselled themes, the economy of its texture and the crispness of its scoring. Characteristic is the neat way in which the themes

---

* There is a further indication of Elgar's curious literary taste in these works, for the poem by O'Shaughnessy which he set in *The Music Makers* is little more than a pretentious, tasteless jingle, but his preparatory work for the symphonic poem *Falstaff*, and his explanation of its structure afterwards, suggest that he had a formidable knowledge of Shakespeare; certainly he had read all the sources, and the subtitle, "A Symphonic Study", is apt.

† The first recording, made in 1931–2 under the composer, was advertised by HMV at the time as "The Music of Pageantry", and this is typical of the kind of misunderstanding that Elgar has, until recently, provoked. The only section of this complex and profound score which could be said to portray pageantry is Henry V's Coronation procession at the end, and this is deliberately cold and empty.

allocated to Falstaff and Prince Hal form the first and second subjects of a sonata structure. This is typical of Elgar's insight, since the interplay of the two characters in *Henry IV* has much of the character of a sonata. *Falstaff* is pictorial to a degree, and follows the action in minute detail, often with picturesque illustration worthy of Strauss; but comparison with Strauss's symphonic poems reveals the more fastidious nature of Elgar's music. In spite of the two Dream Interludes the work is formally very tight. As Tovey points out, much of the texture is in only two parts, and gives a consummate effect of lightness yet fullness of sound.

Why did Elgar choose Falstaff for his only symphonic poem? He compared himself to the fat knight when he visited Delius at the end of his life, but that was in jest. Elgar had little in common with Falstaff as a man. It seems that he was drawn irresistibly to the psychological conflict explicit in the relationship between Falstaff and Prince Hal, between humanity and authority. The character of the Falstaff of *Henry IV* (as distinguished from the superficial clown of *The Merry Wives*) is itself charged with ambiguity in Shakespeare's text. Created in the first place as an illustration of the frivolous licentiousness of Prince Hal's youth, and the bad company he kept (False staff), the complex and charismatic Falstaff escapes from Shakespeare's hands and captures the reader's sympathy at an early stage in the play. In Elgar's symphonic poem we are with Falstaff right to the end. His repudiation as he halts the Coronation procession to claim the Prince he loved evokes no sympathy for Henry, whose march is hollow and empty; and we realise that at no point in the score has Elgar marked Prince Hal's music "Nobilmente"—his invariable seal of approval. In fact, the Coronation march is marked "Grandioso". Falstaff's repudiation is followed by brazen music for the king and a coda of melting sweetness for the dying Falstaff, in which the theme of the young Prince Hal, now dead to Falstaff and to history, floats like a dream.

In this symphonic study Elgar's own personal psychological crisis finds expression, and it is significant that there was a crescendo of depression, black even for Elgar, in the period before he began it. The immediate impression of a performance of the work is one of skill, lightness, gaiety, even, I might suggest, psychological release—the kind of release which comes when a conflict, long suppressed, becomes explicit to the patient. Though his music was pugnaciously progressive for his country and his time, much of Elgar's personality was repressed in his public life. There were moments when it burst out, and he either raved or wept in public; and in a trusted circle of friends the real man came out in an almost dangerous sense of humour. His letters are either brief outbursts of tense, hysterical emotion, or reveal the art of non-communication carried to extremes; but even the hysteria is couched either in generalised or obviously symbolic terms. His music is another matter. In this one may detect a deep-lying conflict.* The social order of his youth, to which he looked back with nostalgia, and which he reverenced and honoured, had in fact opposed him in his early struggles, and had only reluctantly, and through the agency of foreigners like Richter, Jaeger and Strauss (even Edward VII was half German), acknowledged him as a composer, and then largely on account of his less serious works. This he must have known subconsciously, never daring to admit it to his conscious, official self. He was afraid all his life that this society would in the end betray him, as it had betrayed Falstaff. False staff! That false staff was not the fat knight, with whom Elgar identified, but the Prince; the powers that be. Perhaps we have here a hint as to Elgar's reason for rejecting (on the face of it unjustly) the court of George V, the stiff young Prince, full of duty, who had succeeded the jovial monarch. The cold reception of his Second Symphony confirmed the evaluation that had been forced on him by experience, and which had found instant expression to Billy Reed, the humble working musician who would understand: "Stuffed pigs!"

Falstaff was first played under Elgar at the Leeds Festival on 2 October 1913, and was coldly received. Robin Legge wrote in the *Telegraph* of 4 November 1913 that on its first London performance (3 November) it was played to a "beggarly row

* In some of his letters, to Jaeger in particular (and in his outbursts to Rosa Burley), the conflict becomes suddenly explicit. When off his guard Elgar is the lonely musician fighting against Providence (as he called it) and society.

of half-empty benches". In delicacy and technical mastery *Falstaff* is the peak of Elgar's achievement. It is an adorable masterpiece, and when subjected, with Elgar's own commentary upon it, to analysis, a psychological document of uncanny power. "How ill white hairs become a fool and jester!" Elgar had seen his own hair grow white, and was himself no mean jester; in his youth even artists of the calibre of Clara Schumann had been forced to play between variety turns.* Composers were too often classed with fools and jesters in Elgar's youth, by an establishment whose chief amusement was to go out and kill something.

In 1912 Delius completed *The Song of the High Hills*. This resplendent work has barely come into its own even at the time of writing, and for many years was Delius's least-known concert work. It is in one long movement, and scored for large forces; six horns, bass tuba and two timpani players in the orchestra and a substantial chorus to balance. More than is usual for a work by Delius it is sensitive to interpretation (and his music most certainly does not play itself). There is a long, leisurely, but fresh-sounding orchestral introduction, after which the voices enter very quietly, as if far off, in a wordless chorus not unlike that in *Appalachia*. An important episode is marked "The wide far distance—the great solitude" with four tenors singing as if in solo. The work is climactic, and the climax comes with a passage for eight-part chorus, beginning very quietly, but working up to a majestic crescendo, joined at its peak by the orchestra. There is a coda for orchestra alone, ending in a magical passage in which the timpani play chords. The work demands the most perfect balance of parts, and in Beecham's flawed but still magical performance recorded in the 1940s it gets it.† Although the piece employs most of the late

* So had the great Maggie Teyte, friend of Debussy, as late as the 1930s.
† The Beecham recording has two drawbacks: the great climax is played down by the engineers—even in the LP transfer the texture dulls and becomes distant as the tremendous wave of sound reaches its crest. Then in the coda the tempo is a little too indulgent, with the result that a sense of climax not achieved is followed by anti-climax. It is obvious that this is mainly a technical fault, but it is followed by one of Beecham's extremely rare miscalculations also.

Romantic conventions, it does so in a unique and most original way.

In 1910 Delius had made two important friendships: with Béla Bartók, who remained to the end of his life a champion of Delius's music, of which he had the highest opinion; and with the strange, rather distrait young musician called Philip Heseltine (1894–1930), later known as Peter Warlock, who for a while worked as a music critic, but from 1916 onwards was to appear as a composer. Delius, in his letters to him of this time, scolded him thoroughly, and with some justification, for dissipating his talents and never pushing any project to a conclusion.

The year 1912 saw Frank Bridge's nearest approach to a popular success: the suite called *The Sea*. Bridge was the only English composer to have been born and to die in Sussex—he lived for many years in a house on the downs above Eastbourne, at Friston; from Beachy Head, not far off, there is a tremendous view of coast and sea. Neat and economical, *The Sea* has sparkling orchestration and sensuous harmony; typical middle-period Frank Bridge, and Britten remembered two of its movements, "Moonlight" and "The Storm", in *Peter Grimes*.

Bax's least-played symphonic poem is *Christmas Eve in the Mountains*. First performed in 1912, it is one of a group of orchestral works from before 1914 that has never been printed. Bax describes its first performance in *Farewell My Youth* (1943), and comments: "In it I have tried to suggest the sharp light of the frosty stars and an ecstasy of peace falling for one night of the year upon the troubled Irish hills, haunted by the inhuman Sidhe, and by clinging memories of the tragedy of eight hundred years." That peace was a concept which haunted Bax's music all his life; but how one wishes the Irish would try to forget those eight hundred years.

On 3 September 1912 Sir Henry Wood conducted Schoenberg's Five Orchestral Pieces at a Promenade Concert, and the work was hissed; on 29 May 1913 the ballet *Le Sacre du printemps* was produced in Paris for the first time, and Stravinsky's score provoked the greatest scandal music had known up to that time, a famous riot that exceeded in violence even the notorious performance of *Tannhäuser* in the same city. In

1913 Schoenberg wrote his opera, *Die Glückliche Hand*, aptly translated by Hans Keller as *The Knack*. This was the heroic age of "modern music", the time of the pioneers, and of the birth of the self-conscious avant-garde.

In this period, which saw the beginning of the "modern music" problem, it is worth mentioning Arthur Somervell (1863–1937), composer of many songs, including the inevitable *Shropshire Lad* cycle, and, of more significance, a cycle of songs from Tennyson's *Maud* that manages to be entirely unsentimental, scarifying in places (it captures the note of madness that lurks in that poem), and a small masterpiece generally. In 1913 Somervell wrote his most substantial work, *Thalassa* (The Sea), his one symphony. It has a certain atmosphere and charm, and is a solid, well-constructed work that is not without merit. But he was a conservative of the conservatives in harmonic and tonal idiom, and even Brahms would have thought *Thalassa* old-fashioned. A very English phenomenon. Then there was the first performance of Havergal Brian's overture *Dr Merryheart*. In those days his music was still being performed, and he had not sunk into that long and mysterious neglect which has given his name a spurious glamour, and rendered it even more difficult to make an objective assessment of his work.

Delius's *North Country Sketches*, a suite of pieces from this period, indicates a certain change of style. These reticent, remote impressions are nothing like French impressionism in sound or technique, and are wholly original. There are four movements: "Autumn" (the wind soughs in the trees); "Winter Landscape"; "Dance"; "The March of Spring" (Woodlands, Meadows and Silent Moors). One does not usually associate the music of Delius with autumn and winter, nor with the cold and austere effects that these two seasons call forth in his music; and if "Dance" and "The March of Spring" are full of familiar materials, they are bronzed with the particular colours of the North. It makes one realise how southern the music of this Yorkshire man often is, in atmosphere and colouring, even in *Brigg Fair*; and to speculate that his request to be buried in the south of England may not be so inexplicable after all. By now Delius was suffering from the first symptoms of the illness—imperfectly treated syphilis—which was to paralyse and blind him in the 1920s.

In Europe the sense of political crisis was deepening as 1914 approached; English travellers came back with the news that Europe was daily expecting war, and that at a dozen sensitive points a small incident could set off the explosion. But in England few anticipated such a thing; the summers had been bright and warm for a number of years, and in spite of the restlessness in the air the middle-aged were apt to look back, on the reign of Edward VII at any rate, as a golden age.

On the fringes of the troubled Continent musical life went on much as before: Sibelius, aged fifty, completed his serene Fifth Symphony, unperturbed by the radical developments in other places as it was by the political climate, a work of paradoxical nature, diaphanous in texture, mighty in weight and gravity (but he revised it several times). Stravinsky wrote *Le Rossignol*, in which his high norm of dissonance was maintained, but became thinner and sharper, without the heaviness of *Le Sacre*, as if anticipating a change of style. In England a few composers were working on scores which seem in retrospect to add up to no consistent picture—one year is too short a space to justify the expression "marking time", but there is an odd lack of direction in English music as a whole after *Falstaff* and before 1920. Up to 1912 it might be possible to depict English music as one mighty crescendo from the Enigma Variations to Elgar's Second Symphony and Delius's *Song of the High Hills*; but after 1912 the impetus seemed lost, the major figures to have passed their climactic, the new men to be hardly established.

Holst was working on *The Planets*, a vast and spectacular suite which was to bring him fame and keep his name in the concert programmes in a way that his finer works never achieved. It was to be some time before the suite was finished, and the first performance was actually a private one. Frank Bridge completed two scores that are characteristic of his mature style before he became radical; *Summer* and the *Dance Poem*. He had finished a Dance Rhapsody in 1908, a hammer-and-tongs work of immense vigour, massively scored, and nothing like Delius; *Dance Poem* may be described as a large symphonic waltz with rhapsodic lapses. *Summer,* on the other hand, is Bridge's nearest approach to the style of Delius. A dreamy impression of summer haze for largish orchestra, it can be seen as a moment of that ancient sunlight, cherished by our grandfathers, captured and held in sound that throbs with the hum of insects with a flicker of distant bird-song.

The name of John Ireland came shyly to the fore in this confused time. His first published orchestral work, *The Forgotten Rite,* dates from 1913. He had bought a copy of Arthur Machen's *The House of Souls* from a railway book-stall, and it fired his imagination. Ireland sought out Machen, whose flamboyant appearance rather put him off at first, but it was the beginning of a friendship that brought Ireland much inspiration. Like most of his English contemporaries Ireland was a born nature poet; but, like Frank Bridge but not to the same degree, the dark, mysterious underside of things was always present for him. When Ireland too shook off the Brahms–Stanford influence and developed his own style, that style on the surface might have seemed unduly sunny and sweet—the epitome of the "Georgian" tradition; but under the plangent melodies the harmony was taut and even at times sinister.

Ireland felt the dark tides of the past, and the strange undertones of *The Forgotten Rite* were typical of a shadow that fell on his music from time to time.* The brooding darkness of this work is truly atavistic, and its suggestion daunting; there is nothing of Debussy's sophisticated sensuality here, although there is a touch, quite unconscious I am sure, of "Pagan Night" from *Le Sacre.* Although many of the usual Romantic devices for producing atmosphere are present—horn calls, slowly surging strings, and so on—this is an unusual piece in atmosphere, and so strange in sound that it is not really a conventionally "romantic" piece at all. It is a singularly beautiful work, and the first real indication of what we could expect from John Ireland.

* The piece was written in Le Fauvic in Jersey, another life-long source of inspiration, which had also produced a set of piano pieces, *Decorations* (1913), the first of which is called "The Island Spell". The gentle wash of this piece is one of the few instances of something like impressionism in English music; but its innocence of spirit is far removed from Debussy!

Two professional conductors helped to shape our musical life, and improve our musical standards, in the first quarter of the new century. Beecham's greatest years were 1918–39, but Sir Henry Wood, a less spectacular talent, altered the musical life of England beyond recognition in the years before 1914. He had raised the standards of the Prom programmes from quadrilles and smoking-room ballads to the actual performance mentioned above, of Schoenberg's Five Orchestral Pieces ("Stick it, gentlemen, stick it! This is *nothing* to what you will be expected to play in twenty years' time!"). Apart from the Hallé Orchestra in the north, and the London Symphony Orchestra, English orchestras were somewhat transitory and *ad hoc* affairs attached to one concert hall or another—the New Symphony Orchestra struggled with the impossible acoustics of the Albert Hall, while the Queen's Hall Orchestra —later the New Queen's Hall Orchestra—had been founded to play in the acoustically far superior hall at the top of Regent Street. With this latter band Sir Henry fought his herculean battle over orchestral standards,* until between the wars the Proms were taken over by the fine new BBC Symphony Orchestra, which had been trained by Sir Adrian Boult, who came to the orchestra from Birmingham when it was founded.

It is possible to estimate some rough dates for the English acceptance of some pre-1914 masterpieces: *L'Après-midi* in the 1920s, *Le Sacre* in the 1930s, *Pierrot Lunaire* not until the 1960s. The Sitwells' exhibition of French Impressionist painting at Heals in 1919 rather belatedly introduced to the general public of England the great artistic ferment that had taken place in France in the last part of the nineteenth century and the first decade of the twentieth.

English restlessness was not artistic. George Butterworth, a

---

* One of Sir Henry's greatest achievements was the ending of the "deputy" system. An orchestral player who had attended the rehearsals had no obligation to play at the actual concert if a more lucrative engagement presented itself, but could send a deputy, who had not attended the rehearsals and might well be a less proficient player. This system grew so bad that one foreign conductor complained it was not so much the deputies as the deputies' deputies that he objected to. The system had to be reformed if England was to have permanent orchestras of something like the standard of those in Europe.

young disciple of the folk-song school who was born in 1885 and killed in the First World War, exemplified this restlessness. He was never sure of his vocation, and entered into his musical education with much hesitation. On leaving Trinity College, Oxford, he was for a short time assistant music critic on *The Times* under Fuller-Maitland, and subsequently music master at Radley; he left Radley in 1910, having finally made up his mind to study music seriously, and went to the RCM. He composed two cycles of songs on Housman's *A Shropshire Lad*, and prefaced them with an orchestral Rhapsody of that name; he also wrote "The Banks of Green Willow", and some smaller pieces. It was on his instigation that Vaughan Williams wrote *A London Symphony*, which is dedicated to his memory. "The war, when it came," comments John Rippon drily,* "seemed to provide something to do." This horrific attitude was very common at the time.

"For generations the English had loved Germany", writes R. J. White in *A Short History of England* (1967), "as the land of *Gemütlichkeit*, of Christmas trees, toy soldiers, fairy castles above the Rhine, street-bands, comic professors, and waiters". The French, in spite of the Entente Cordiale, were suspected and disliked far more than the Germans, who were thought of as being less pagan, and more like the English. In spite of the naval race that had been going on for a decade, the obvious vainglory of the new Kaiser, and Germany's mounting competition in the field of industry, right up to 4 August 1914 few really expected war. When it came, fewer still realised its nature.

* In the first part of a two-part article on Butterworth in *The Musical Times* for August 1966.

4

INTERLUDE I
1914–1918

THERE WAS A very general belief that the war would be over by Christmas—just over four months from 4 August 1914. There was great popular enthusiasm for it and general optimism as to its outcome. In fact, England entered the First World War in a state of total unreality, which was shared by the whole country and the majority of politicians; although a few realised, almost intuitively that this was a new experience for mankind, a terror that had never been loosed on the world before.

The effects of the war on English art in general and music in particular were complex and are difficult to analyse; besides, they were gradual, and took effect comparatively slowly. Confusion was the general mode of existence. The one major musical loss was, most curiously—since it was hardly under threat—that most insular and outdated of English musical institutions, the Three Choirs Festival. But the comparatively progressive Proms went on. There was much concern among professional musicians as to how the war would affect their livelihood; there was a meeting in October 1914 in the Small Queen's Hall under Sir Frederick Cowen to discuss their plight. In fact, the number of concerts increased as the war went on; and the number of foreign musicians in the country— thought to be large—was found to have been greatly exaggerated, since many English musicians practised under foreign names.

But German music was under a cloud, a cloud of rather empty patriotism. The tendency of late nineteenth- and early twentieth-century German music to great technical efficiency, massed forces and loud noises, became associated in the English mind with the "*kolossal*" aspects of German militarism, with the result that a very general revulsion was felt against this kind of music. It did not matter that as the war went on English artillery and warships, and the new invention of the tank, excelled the Germans in the colossal and the frightful; it was felt that these things, massive efficiency and power, were essentially un-English and typically German. Ironically, this was true as far as music was concerned; and the fact that German composers could handle vast forces with great skill, create large forms and write with uninhibited expression, while the English could not, was the very reason why German music was superior to English music. That the one English composer who could approach Bruckner, Mahler and Strauss in these things—Edward Elgar—happened to be our greatest, was no accident. Wagner and Strauss were the immediate targets for intolerance. In Strauss's case he was a living composer drawing royalties from his works, as were Max Reger and Hungarians like Bartók and Kodály. It seems likely that anti-German prejudice harmed Bruckner and Mahler most, for Strauss emerged after the war as a classic, and Wagner was being staged at Covent Garden as soon as the war was over. But it was many years before Bruckner and Mahler were accepted by the English public, and it was precisely the *"kolossal"* aspects of their music, and Mahler's lack of emotional restraint, that were picked on by the English critics. There is some irony in this, for Bruckner was essentially a universal Catholic without political understanding, and Mahler, as he himself said, was three times an exile: as a Czech among Germans, as a German among Czechs, and as a Jew in the world.

Among those for whose deaths the First World War was directly responsible was Alberic Magnard who, in spite of his German-sounding name, was a patriotic Frenchman, killed defending his home against the German invaders in their first great thrust into France. Curiously, no composer of even this modest a stature was killed among the forces of the Central Powers, and in spite of general conscription (which reached England last) the Allies lost no major composer. Part of the reason is that, at any rate until the end of the war, the conscripts were so pitifully young; few of them had had time to achieve anything worthy of notice. Composers, especially in England, mature late; and in the England of pre-1914 had little chance of making themselves known until a long struggle had aged them. George Butterworth, the composer, killed on the Somme in 1916, was thirty-one; a comparatively mature age for a war casualty. Ivor Gurney, the other English composer who was a casualty, was born in 1890 and gassed at Passchendaele; after treatment he went back to the front, but was invalided out in 1918. He was certified insane in 1922, but lingered on until 26 December 1937. He is almost better known as a poet than as a composer, but he wrote a number of sensitive and beautiful songs which were published after he died—or after hunger had worsened his insanity. In March 1917 he wrote in the trenches:

> A simpler heart than mine
>   Might have seen beauty clear
> When I could see no sign
>   Of Thee, but only fear.
> Strengthen me, make me see
>   Thy beauty always
> In every happening here

the last lines of which take the breath away.

Of the older composers Vaughan Williams and Holst saw active service although neither of them was wounded. Vaughan Williams was nearer to the fighting than Holst, and conceived the *Pastoral Symphony* in the trenches. Among younger men George Dyson and Arthur Bliss (1891–1975) were in the war, but of these two only Bliss achieved much as a composer. He states in his autobiography that on the outbreak of war he became much concerned with the possibility of life after death, and as a result became a Roman Catholic. Peter Warlock was turned down by a medical board on a mere technicality, but in any case was a conscientious objector, thus establishing a precedent among English musicians which was more thoroughly observed in the Second World War. Frank Bridge was also a pacifist and John Ireland had leanings in that direction. Arnold Bax appears to have had no leanings in any direction, but was not passed by a medical board.

All this had certain effects on music in England. Vaughan Williams was virtually silent for the duration, and Holst made only a couple of appearances.* Elgar and Delius were in their fifties; at one point Delius, by then settled at Grez-sur-Loing, had to flee the advancing Germans, and stayed for a while in England, rather to his disgust. The effect of the war on Elgar was complex and characteristic. On the outbreak of war he joined the Hampstead Special Constabulary, and regretted that he was too old to be a soldier. But he also wrote: "Everything good & nice & clean & fresh & sweet is far away—never to return." The works Elgar wrote during the war were largely occasional; he even consented to set some lines by Kipling, a poet he detested. It was only towards the end of the war, when he settled at Brinkwells, near Fittleworth in Sussex, that he began to compose in earnest again; but the burst was short lived.

What had been accomplished between the first performance of the Enigma Variations in 1899 and the outbreak of war in 1914? As far as the world reputation of English music was concerned, little that was not swept away by the war. In the early years of the century not only Elgar and Delius, but also Ethel Smyth and Joseph Holbrooke were performed in Germany, sometimes in expensive opera mountings; this ceased with the war. After the war Delius had to rely on Beecham to make his name known and perform his music, and he became, by reputation, far more of a narrowly English composer. The insularity that lies always in wait for English art closed in on our music after 1914. Even the achievements of 1900–14 were placed by events in a purely national context after 1918.

The opening years of the English renaissance were without doubt the Age of Elgar, although his reputation declined in his own country as it was snuffed out abroad. That reputation did not revive until after the Second World War, when international conductors of the stature of Solti and Barenboim took up his music once more, and the nature of that music became

* The first of these was a strange occurrence: *The Planets* was completed before he joined the forces, and in 1918 Adrian Boult and some others of his friends gave him the fine present of a private performance of the work in the Queen's Hall.

plain; not imperial pomp but personal exultation and tragedy. By the 1970s Elgar's international stature was higher than it had ever been before, and rested on a surer foundation. The case of Delius is much harder to assess. By 1914 the lives of Elgar and Delius were by no means over, but the list of their works was in each case almost complete; neither added very much to what they had written by that time, and what they did write did not affect their stature appreciably. Both have been attacked as anachronisms in the twentieth century, but as far as their works are concerned they belong to the years 1880–1914; both developed late and were middle-aged before the twentieth century began. They appear less conservative when we get the chronology right.

Since Holst died in the same year as Elgar and Delius we are apt to think of him as belonging to the same generation. In fact, he was two years younger than Vaughan Williams and almost a generation younger than Elgar. His achievement by 1914 was considerable, but his best music lay in the future. Vaughan Williams had done far more, but his two major works, the *Sea Symphony* and the *London Symphony*, were neither of them as accurate pointers to his mature style as the little Tallis Fantasy. The *London Symphony*, written just before the war, was performed for the first time in the Queen's Hall on 27 March 1914. In those days it took just on an hour to play, but it was twice revised, and shortened, to the regret of a number of good judges, to forty-four minutes. It is not quite like any other work of its composer. Dark, mysterious, warm, full of the riotous, colourful atmosphere of a London that has largely departed, this four-movement work, with its richness of scoring, can be placed in a dozen parts of old London that Hitler's bombs and modern speculators have destroyed. The final passing of these loved places seems inherent in its wistfulness; its final march, a last movement of overwhelming dignity and power, is full of foreboding and profoundly moving.

As for Bax and Bridge, Bridge had written the least music by 1914, but the most mature and lasting music. Before 1914 Bax's music had various deleterious characteristics that later vanished from it; turgid imitation of Richard Strauss, and even, in some works, a kind of Pre-Raphaelite insipidity more

English than Baxian.* His very facility and his prodigious technique made things hard for him, until he knew what he wanted to say. But a blazing creative fire, clumsy, smouldering and erratic, informs so much of this gauche early work. The violent First Piano Sonata, the over-long, meandering First Violin Sonata, the neat, vivid *In the Faery Hills*, the long, uneven *Spring Fire*, had established a personality that was as endearing as it was puzzling.

In 1915 Bax produced his first undoubted masterpiece, the vast Piano Quintet. A powerful work in three movements, its form seems to anticipate that of the seven symphonies, especially as the quintet ends with an Epilogue. The piano writing is complex and of virtuoso difficulty, and the mood stormy and wild. The texture strains the medium; is it a symphony manqué?† Bax's Piano Quintet is less queasy in its chromaticism, and has less in it of barn-storming, than that of César Franck, and can be compared in quality, though not in kind, with the more austere, formal Quintets of Brahms and Schumann.

Also to 1915 belongs Bax's Second Violin Sonata, a very different work from the First. The Second is short and decidedly sinister; the title of one of the movements, "The Grey Dancer in the Twilight", has raised much speculation. Is the Grey Dancer Death? Some echo of Flanders seems present. There was also a short, attractive orchestral work called *Nympholept*, which had to wait until the 1950s for its first performance. Akin to *The Happy Forest* and *Summer Music*, this short piece depicts the state of being 'high' on the influence of wild nature in the spring.

"To Catherine aged 9, *Lusitania* 1915" heads the score of Frank Bridge's Lament for Strings; there is a link here with the contemporary Second String Quartet. Both the Lament and

---

* He called an early song, "Golden Guendolen", "A Pre-Raphaelite Song", and his Magnificat of 1906 is inscribed "After a picture by D. G. Rossetti".

† A little later Bax was at work on a piano sonata the first movement of which became the first movement of the official Symphony No. 1 in E flat. There are signs that Bax's path to his first achieved symphony was as strewn with wrecks as that of Brahms.

the final passage of the first movement of the quartet are marked "doloroso". The stark grief of the Lament is hard to bear; here is pain without consolation or compromise. The string quartet is also mature Bridge; its middle movement is a scherzo, with an evanescent quality Britten learned from him. These two works are full of the distress the First World War brought to Bridge. They mark the increasing chromaticism of his style, the beginning of his exploration of European contemporary music which was to culminate in the influence of Alban Berg. But for the practical Bridge the misery could not go unchallenged for long; there is a positive response in his *Two Poems of Richard Jefferies*. The superscription on the second piece is: "How beautiful a delight to make the whole world joyous! The song should never be silent, the dance never still, the laughter should sound like water that runs for ever" ("The Story of my Heart"). Based on prose passages from the great nature mystic, these two pieces for small orchestra mark a change in technique similar to that which was taking place in Bridge's chamber music.

In 1916 Arnold Bax finished the first of three wartime symphonic poems, which had nothing to do with the war, but much to do with his private concerns at the time: *The Garden of Fand*. It is as I have said one of the few completely uninhibited pieces of colour music by an Englishman; but it is rather short-winded, and lacks the size and scope of such things as *Daphnis et Chloë*. Typically, Bax prefaced the score with a long and largely irrelevant piece of prose in English, thus prejudicing the work among foreign conductors—and that means important conductors. Yet the opening words of this introduction are haunting, and not without significance: "The Garden of Fand is the Sea." He goes on to narrate part of the saga of Cuchulain, which has little to do with the music; only at the end does he explain that the symphonic poem is about Irish sailors venturing into the Atlantic and finding Fand's enchanted island. Fand and her women seduce them, so that they do not see the great wave that finally engulfs the island. Nothing is left at the end but the vision out of which the music arose: the hazy distances of the Atlantic in summer. Without ever suggesting the methods of Debussy, the score is of great beauty, and is implicitly if not explicitly sexual in its emotional impact. As such it breaks the unconscious taboo that haunts the greater part of English music.* It seems that this symphonic poem, with the later *November Woods* and *Tintagel*, marks the crisis which occurred in Bax's private life during the war, when his marriage broke down. He had just met Harriet Cohen, the pianist, and his love affair with her dominated the rest of his life. *Tintagel*, together with much piano music, is dedicated to her, and *The Garden of Fand* is surely her portrait. The slight, gentle Elegiac Trio also belongs to 1916.

Delius in these war years finished three large-scale works and started a fourth, all of them controversial. The Violin Concerto and Double Concerto may have been under-rated between the wars, but they were over-rated in the 1950s, while *Eventyr* has never had its due; and the *Requiem* is a very strange case indeed.

The Violin Concerto is the best of Delius's four concertos (the other two are for piano and cello respectively); it is a work of considerable beauty, even though it is based on the composer's overworked formula of air and dance.† The Double Concerto is perhaps the weakest of the three string concertos. In my view *Eventyr* is one of Delius's finest works. The name is Norwegian, and means "adventure". The Nordic theme, a certain darkness in the sound, the orchestration, and above all a kind of pounding gait that is very close to a characteristic rhythm often used later by Bax. An endearing feature is the wild shout that twice punctuates the music and adds considerably to the atmosphere.

The *Requiem* has aroused considerable controversy. Albert Coates gave it its first performance in 1922, after which it was completely ignored for nearly forty years.‡ It was revived in the 1960s, and in the particular atmosphere of the time, a reaction

* Bax himself was to write in *Farewell My Youth* that Parry and Stanford regarded 'sensuous beauty of orchestral tune as something not quite nice'.

† The Cello Concerto of 1921 is similar to that for violin in mood and structure, but less vivid and inspired.

‡ The fact that Beecham never performed it speaks volumes about the opinion of the early Delians, since Beecham even lovingly trotted out the jejune Piano Concerto. Peter Warlock in particular savaged the *Requiem* in his book on Delius.

against the moribund years immediately after 1945, it attracted
a good deal of critical praise. I cannot help feeling that this was
because the work is rather unlike the Delius of *Brigg Fair*, the
First Dance Rhapsody, even *Sea Drift*—the typical English
sound was despised in this decade. Delius was as bigoted an
atheist as some Christians are bigoted, and the worst passages
in the *Requiem* are those sections devoted to didactic denials of
Christianity. When Delius became didactic on this subject in
life he was both rude and a bore, and in his music (*Sea Drift*
apart) he is rarely at his best when writing recitative for baritone. The *Requiem* sounds as though it was composed in a
hurry; it is dedicated to young artists killed in the war—which
may or may not be thought either opportunism or cynicism on
Delius's part, since his attitude to the war was quite cynical
anyway. It has been said that the work was killed, after its
first performance, by "the Christians". In fact its fiercest
critics were pagans who shared Delius's philosophy to a greater
or lesser extent: Beecham, Warlock, Cecil Gray.

It was in 1916 that the up-and-coming critic, Cecil Gray, and
that extraordinary character Peter Warlock joined forces as a
team; and they promptly met Bernard van Dieren (1884–1936).
It is the fate of some musicians to be more memorable as personalities than as composers; this was for a long time the destiny
of Alkan, a composer who greatly interested van Dieren. Bernard van Dieren's strange personality has persisted as a legend
into a time when his music is very seldom heard. In his autobiography *Musical Chairs* (1948) Gray gives an account of his
meeting with van Dieren:

On taking my seat in the gallery [of the Queen's Hall] I
found myself sitting next to a person who attracted my
attention in a way I had never experienced before. Immacu-
lately clad in a suit of unusual cut, with delicately moulded
Latin features, dark hair and eyes, a complexion with the
unearthly pallor of old ivory, and a sardonically twisted
mouth, he seemed the very embodiment and reincarnation
of some figure of the 1830s, of the period in which Berlioz
lived and worked, and wrote the music which I was to hear
that evening for the first time; or you might say that he was

like an apparition from out of the pages of E. T. A. Hoffmann —inhuman almost, giving forth effortlessly, unconsciously, a hypnotic, daemonic power.

On hearing van Dieren play, at a subsequent meeting, some fragments of his music—very badly, according to Gray—Gray became convinced that he was confronted by "one of the most significant musicians of the age".

Van Dieren was born in Holland and educated in Germany, but was resident in England for most of his life. His music was little known in 1916, but Warlock and Gray began a pugnacious crusade on his behalf, and a concert entirely devoted to his music was given in 1917. It was very well attended, and up to a point the publicity on his behalf was successful. But in time it showed diminishing returns as the sheer pugnacity of the approach began to put people off. Both Gray and Warlock studied composition with van Dieren, a course of study that benefited Warlock but not Gray. William Walton (b. 1902) and Constant Lambert (1905–1951) were also greatly influenced by van Dieren; this can be seen in Walton's Viola Concerto and in almost any score of Lambert's, but particularly *Horoscope*. Van Dieren's music, and that of Kaikhosru Sorabji (b. 1892), who was also attached to this group, and who also believed van Dieren to be a great composer, constitutes a mystery. So eccentric and flamboyant are these two personalities, and so aggressive their approach to all things musical, that they have been consigned to a sort of limbo, with their music as good as dead and only the ghosts of their polemics squeaking and gibbering at posterity. This is a pity, since they both wrote much interesting music.

Bax and Ireland both wrote works in 1917 which were among their best. In Bax's case it was *November Woods*, perhaps his most uncompromising score, even less well calculated for easy appeal than the Second Symphony. Bax wrote to Peter Warlock, "Nearly all my longer compositions, the orchestral works at any rate, are based upon aspects and moods of extreme nature and their relation to human emotions. . . ." Like

Sir Edward Elgar

Frederick Delius aged forty

Edward Elgar just after finishing *The Dream of Gerontius* (photographed by a friend).

Going to the Proms: Regent Street, 1897

John Ireland

Peter Warlock

Ralph Vaughan Williams conducting at the Proms,
Royal Albert Hall

Arnold Bax at the White Horse, Storrington

Sir William Walton with George Szell

Frank Bridge and Benjamin Britten: Bridge, front row, left;
Ethel Bridge, front row, right; Britten, back row, right.
The four other men are members of the Brosa String Quartet.

Sir Michael Tippett

Peter Maxwell Davies

Delius, then, an exploitation of the pathetic fallacy. This certainly applies to *November Woods*, which in some ways resembles *Tapiola*, which Sibelius wrote nine years later.* But Sibelius ends his piece in wild fury, while Bax, about two-thirds of the way through, lapses into *pianissimo*, and *November Woods* ends in utter, frozen quiet. There is actually no dynamic climax; the emotional climax is this hushed grieving with which the work ends. Many years later, disappointed and with his loves gone sour, Bax remarked wistfully of *November Woods*, "I was happy *then*"—an extraordinary, though patently sincere, verdict, considering the unrelieved tragedy of what is probably his greatest symphonic poem.

Tintagel, which was sketched in 1917 and finally orchestrated in 1919, completes the cycle of Bax's three best-known symphonic poems. It is also his most popular work, and is quite frequently performed. It bears much the same relationship to Bax's music as a whole as *En Saga* does to the music of Sibelius; it is a better piece than its popularity suggests, and its originality of sound is striking. Its opening suggests the very smell of the sea better than any other music that is known to me. It also prefigures Bax's constructional practice in his symphonies; several elements that are employed even in the purely atmospheric music of its opening—an anacrusis, a hollow fifth, and a triplet among them—form the bricks out of which the main theme, and indeed the whole structure, is built. To confirm the connection with his private life—and of the castle with King Mark—*Tristan* is quoted in the music.

From this period also come three of Bax's least-known works: the two ballets *Between Dusk and Dawn* and *The Frog-Skin*, and the Scherzo for orchestra, the score of which is in the British Museum, and which appears to be unknown. One work of 1917 does radiate happiness: *Moy Mell, The Happy Plain*, Bax's first published essay in a medium in which he was to excel—music for two pianos.

In 1917 Holst began to compose a work for large orchestra and chorus on words he selected from the Apocryphal Acts of

* Bax has been accused of imitating *Tapiola* in *November Woods*, so it is important to establish the priority.

St John, which he called *The Hymn of Jesus*. In spite of the large forces involved it is nearer in spirit to *Savitri* than to *The Planets*; this is the visionary Holst. It is unlike any religious work, or work to religious words, that had been written before. It uses two Gregorian chants, *Pange lingua* and *Vexilla Regis*, and uses them in unconventional ways. The *Pange lingua* is heard at the beginning, given to two trombones, and subsequently to the cor anglais; but the *Vexilla Regis* is sung by the sopranos of the semi-chorus, after which "a few tenors and high baritones" in the distance sing the *Pange lingua*. This is the first of many unconventional devices, including that of giving the *Pange lingua* to the orchestra as a dance tune. The sense of dancing, both as ritual and as a gnostic method of knowing, is strong in the original poem, and is brought out in full in the music. The uniting of two strongly contrasted elements—wild dancing and visionary quiet—is very typical of Holst, as is the ease with which he imposes unity upon them. The spoken words "Glory to Thee, Holy Spirit" have provoked a lot of comment, and the passage is difficult to bring off. Its faults are few and will soon be absorbed by time. It remains a radiant and most original masterpiece.

If both Bax and Bridge achieved maturity in the later war years, so perhaps did John Ireland, whose Second Violin Sonata of 1917, a very beautiful and disturbingly melancholy work, brought him fame in a single night. If this really was the mood of the British people half-way through the First World War, and it seems that it was, then heartbreak is the only word for it. To this year also belongs his Second Piano Trio, and the two works make an impressive pair, with a great deal in common. The Violin Sonata is lyrical, with the effect of a child singing and crying to itself from sheer loss and grief; the Trio was written, according to Ireland himself, with the thought of "the boys going over the top"—it is no less heartbroken, but the heartbreak has a certain doggedness in it, due to the dour, stomping rhythms. Both works are akin to the later Cello Sonata (1923) which is similarly dark and brooding.

The year 1917 was one of bitter endurance, with the armies bogged down in the mud of Flanders, increasingly astringent rationing, shortages, profiteering, conscription, mounting casualty lists. For the shattered and defeated Russian army, and the people of Russia, it was fateful: in October Lenin successfully led the Bolshevik revolution. Scriabin had died in 1915; Rachmaninov, Stravinsky and Prokofiev were exiled and like Diaghilev stranded in France. An odd work by Frank Bridge dates from this year; odd, because it looks backwards. This is the Cello Sonata, a very diatonic, formally perfect, utterly respectable work that is very pleasant but not really like Bridge at all.

In 1918 the Central Powers broke through, and advanced on Paris. As their heavy artillery began to bombard the city of Renoir, Monet, Degas, Verlaine and Rimbaud, Claude Debussy lay dying of cancer. He heard the shells bursting in the streets around him. His last works—the resplendent *Jeux*, the eerily prophetic *Le Martyre de Saint-Sébastien*, the lovely Three Sonatas—were not at that time appreciated at their true worth; he was considered, outside France, to be a played-out mannerist, whose music had become a prey to self-invented clichés. That he was a considerable French composer was dimly realised, but few understood that "Claude de France" was a world figure whose works would influence progressive composers well into the twentieth century. The harmonic density, tonal vagueness, and the erotic undertow in the music of Debussy are what matters; and its, in the best sense, artificiality. Its derivation from the arts of its time rather than from nature or more personal emotions is a significant prophetic factor, one that points to the aesthetic of our own time.

Bax's Symphonic Variations achieved their final form in 1918. This definitive version was dedicated to Harriet Cohen, who used to cut the work when she played it; she had small hands, and the piano part calls for the stretch of a tenth. Each variation is long enough to make a movement in itself, and after the long theme is exposed, each has a title: "Youth", "Nocturne", "Strife", "The Temple", "Play", "Enchantment" and "Triumph"—seven in all. Their connection with Harriet seems obvious, and their respective titles form a compendium of Bax's prevailing musical styles. This work is so rich and powerful (and so difficult) that it is not so well known as it should be. It lasts forty-five minutes, and is taxing to listen to until its complex textures unravel and it becomes familiar. Nevertheless, this was the first large-scale work for piano and orchestra written by an Englishman (astonishingly enough), and it remains unchallenged in its field. There have been few, if any, such works written in England since to compare with it; only Frank Bridge's *Phantasm* for piano and orchestra is a work of comparable mastery. The other large-scale concerto one thinks of is that of Arthur Bliss; but this is not nearly so original, nor so rich in invention. It sounds like an imitation of the Romantic concertos of Tchaikovsky and Rachmaninov; Bax's Symphonic Variations are a new kind of work for piano and orchestra, on the most tremendous scale, so far as length, complexity, brilliance and power of orchestration are concerned. They are kin in spirit and in size to the great Piano Concerto of Ferruccio Busoni. No later comparable work by an Englishman is quite on this scale; only the exquisite, delicate, light-weight concerto of John Ireland, a work of poignant beauty which used to be popular but which is now seldom heard, is as realised and inventive.

After the weak occasional works Elgar wrote from 1914 to 1917, he began to write chamber music: a Violin Sonata, a String Quartet, and a Piano Quintet. Of these three strange, sad pieces the Piano Quintet, though not well written for the medium, is undoubtedly the best. It has a haunted, ghostly atmosphere. It is instructive to compare Elgar's one String Quartet with the first of Bax's three, which was written in 1918, although it did not emerge until the 1920s. It is dedicated to Elgar, but it is typical Bax, and one of the last of his Celtic works. There is an imitation Irish folk-song in the last of its three movements that is dangerously near to the real thing, although Bax disliked the whole folk-song movement. Vivid in colour and overflowing with pungent and indeed popular melody, it has a surging rhythmic urge in the first and last of its three short movements. It is written with a kind of careless ease for the medium. The Elgar is well enough written, and fastidious in tone—indeed, it makes the Bax sound a little vulgar—but it lacks characteristic music, although there is a device in the slow movement that according to Elgar had never been used before.

Extremely characteristic, and a masterpiece, was Elgar's Cello Concerto of 1919; I include it at this point because it seems to belong with the group of chamber works, in spirit and technique, and to achieve where they fall short. Moreover, it was Elgar's last important composition, and was succeeded by a great silence which lasted until he took up composition again, too late, when he was already dying. Like most of his greatest works at this time the Concerto had a poor reception; but a young cellist called Beatrice Harrison took it up and played it repeatedly, finally recording it with the composer. It has been recorded many times since then, but hers is the definitive performance. It is unbearably sad.

The great crunching gesture in multiple stopping with which the soloist opens the Cello Concerto sounds desperate, and the first movement is frenetic under its elegiac tone; it seems to be searching for a purpose. The middle movements of the four alternate lamentation and ghostly whispering, and some of the phrases recall Schumann. The finale attempts an Elgarian muscular Allegro like that of the finale of the First Symphony, but it lacks joy, and the mood of the opening returns with the soloist's great declamatory phrase. Compared with the more expansive Violin Concerto it is an intimate, introverted work, and a singularly comfortless one. When questioned as to its meaning—and it seems to beg that question —Elgar replied that it was "a man's attitude to life". He was at this time increasingly depressed. His early remark about *Gerontius*, "because my thoughts and ways are beyond them", had proved only too prophetic. His acceptance as a national bard did not mean that his major works were understood, and the increasing indifference that greeted them after the Second Symphony began to tell on him. The writing of major works had always cost Elgar dear in terms of financial loss and the draining of nervous energy, and as support for such ventures dwindled his will to write them waned.

Hubert Parry died in 1918. He had made less stir than Stanford, was a more genial figure, and one that the establishment found it easier to adopt. That he had written a memorable tune for Blake's "Jerusalem" seemed entirely characteristic. Certain of his works sustained a vicarious life after his death; *Blest Pair of Sirens*, Lady Radnor's Suite and the Symphonic Variations are still occasionally heard. He lacked Stanford's occasional flicker of imagination, but had instead a solidity that prevented him from writing the occasional bathos into which Stanford fell. Robust, solid and plain, Parry's music was like himself. To say that it lacks originality is almost beside the point; diatonic, marching in regular phrases, contained in neat packages into which the fire of the spirit never enters to cast strange light on familiar processes, it seems entirely conscious, the good-natured manipulation of well-worn phrases. It is pleasant to listen to, if one shuts out of one's mind the far greater works of Brahms and Schumann, who used a similar idiom with poetry and passion. The stuff of great creative ability does not lie in the solid manipulation of familiar rules and patterns, nor in the taste that strives only not to give offence. It walks in strange ways, communicates with unknown forces, is a law unto itself.

By the autumn of 1918 it became obvious that the German initiative was failing. The English blockade of Germany was biting hard, and there was civil riot in Germany. Revolution on the Russian lines was feared. The German soldiers, who had been told that the French were starving, overran prosperous farmlands and the great French wine harvest. Within a few weeks it became clear that the German attack, which had ended three years of futile trench warfare and had brought them within an ace of victory, had defeated itself. There was nothing left for the demoralised remnant of a great army but surrender.

Armistice Day was fixed for 11 November 1918 and when it came England went mad with relief and joy. On the night of the Armistice Londoners filled the streets, and there were scenes that far transcended those following the relief of Mafeking. But England woke to appalling debts, a whole generation of men killed in their youth, a vast new communist state to the east bent on world revolution, and the United States of America effortlessly taking over the world leadership that for a century had been England's. The Treaty of Versailles, which followed the Armistice, resembled the war it was supposed to end; an attempt to deal with a twentieth-century situation in terms of the nineteenth century.

5

BETWEEN THE WARS: I

1919—1930

THE CESSATION OF the war found world music in some confusion. There was a greater premium on the new than at any time since the eighteenth century; but this new art had to be cheerful and even shallow. The world had undergone too much real tragedy and pain for these things to be tolerable in the arts for a long time. The cosy, sentimental light music of the Victorian era gave way to the frenetic gaiety of jazz. There was a greater sophistication and a greater cynicism; this was the Jazz Age.

The gramophone had replaced the music-hall as a medium of popular culture, and the home entertainment which had been popularised by Caruso became the natural medium for jazz. But the first orchestral records were also appearing, even at this early date, before the invention of electrical recording, which became available about 1926. Long before this Edward Elgar seized upon the possibilities of gramophone records and began the systematic recording of a large proportion of his work. His time in the recording studio seemed to take the place of composition, and may have distracted his mind from his private griefs and guilts, which by now almost crippled him.

References to Elgar in many musical books and journals now became positively contemptuous. One of the most typical if intemperate attacks came in a book of otherwise sensitive and independent criticism by Cecil Gray, *A Survey of Contemporary Music* (1924). Gray coined the notorious phrase, "He has rendered unto César the things that are César's, and to Brahms the things that are Brahms's." He described the finale of the Enigma Variations as "undiluted jingoism". Edward J. Dent also expressed his hostility to Elgar's music in print both at home and abroad; Dent's entry on Elgar in Adler's *Handbuch der Musikgeschichte* resulted in a spirited defence of the composer by Peter Warlock, of all people, widely regarded as Gray's other half. Elgar was caught between the adulation of the unmusical for his worst works and the contempt of the fashionable and academic for his best.

With Richard Strauss now regarded as a classic, the place of *enfant terrible* was taken by Igor Stravinsky—for the new music was essentially French and Russian and Stravinsky was adopting French customs. The innocent eccentric Erik Satie became the mentor of the young French composers, including Les Six, of whom perhaps only Milhaud, the Swiss Honegger and Poulenc are remembered today. Ibert and Francaix, outside Les Six, represented the youngest generation. Neither Bruckner nor Mahler had progressed outside Holland, in spite of the propaganda efforts of the very popular Dutch conductor Willem Mengelberg.

The men of the hour in England were a group of young composers who, for the time at least, adopted the Franco-Russian style then fashionable: Arthur Bliss, Eugene Goossens, and William Walton. But there was one isolated and little-known composer who seems to epitomise the sense of blighted, sinister spring that followed the First World War.

William Baines (1899–1922) was only incidentally a victim of the war; conscripted when the conflict was as good as over, he never saw active service, since he was virtually dying of tuberculosis at the time. He contracted influenza in the great outbreak of 1918, and spent his brief national service in hospital. From 1919 until the year of his death a series of short piano pieces was published, and attracted a certain amount of attention; Frederick Dawson the pianist played them a good deal. Then, after he died, his music gradually vanished from sight as it fell out of print, and ceased to be played. He left, however, a Symphony in C minor, a *Poème de Concert* for piano and orchestra, several short orchestral works, a number of chamber compositions and many more piano pieces, including sonatas, which attest to incredible industry on the part of this ailing young cinema pianist during some six years of active compositional life.*

The quality of these works is extraordinarily high; the Symphony is not only viable as a composition but is of a power and originality such as imperatively to demand performance. Freshness, limpidity and a constructive ability of a very high order are combined with an instinctive and original grasp of orchestration. The idiom of advanced composers in Europe was absorbed by Baines without affecting his own basic personality and essential Englishness; the harmony was observed technically and adapted to his own uses, the result being daring but very different in final effect from Scriabin and others, though with a certain kinship with Ravel. The hothouse atmosphere of Debussy is as absent as the hysteria of Scriabin, and in their place is a cool English freshness that is the exact counterpart of the atmospheric effects described in his diary— sunlight on rain, on leaves, on the sea. In the piano pieces these limpid cascades of notes achieve a small formal perfection; but in the Symphony this structural sense becomes a massive architectural grandeur, while the power that is detectable in the climax of some of his piano pieces, notably in *Tides*, is expressed in the Symphony in rugged tutti suggestive of Sibelius, as is his formidable writing for brass. The *Poème de Concert*, a single-movement piano concerto, is similarly of rugged strength and originality.

So short was Baines's life and so compact his output that it is possible to deal with him in this one reference. The music is of such high quality that it is essential that something should be done about it.† This is an example of the English trauma. On the day Baines died a publisher sent him payment for a set of

---

* In 1960 Baines's mother bequeathed his manuscripts to the British Museum, where they repose as Add. MSS 50211–38. These volumes contain a vast quantity of music in forms one would never suspect from the published piano pieces.

† One of his short, exquisite orchestral works, *The Island of the Fay*, recently achieved its first performance at a concert in Smith Square, London. And there exists a record of the piano music issued by Lyrita, but the recording is uncharacteristically dull and the performances unimaginative, although a certain sense of its impact escapes from these disadvantages.

piano pieces; six penny-halfpenny stamps. His mother stuck them in the appropriate page of his pathetic diary.

The most important event of 1920, one not directly musical but full of portent for our music, was the death of Lady Elgar on 7 April. Elgar's collapse was complete, and up to a couple of years before his death he composed very little. It was certainly grief that precipitated the silence, but also guilt; his inner conflicts had proved too much for him.

Bax was at work on the First Symphony, but his most important work of 1920 was the Phantasy for viola and orchestra, first-fruits of his interest in the viola—an interest aroused, as it was with a number of other English composers at this time, by the playing of Lionel Tertis. In addition to the Phantasy Bax wrote only the pleasant *Summer Music* and a strange work called *The Truth about the Russian Dancers*—incidental music to a play by his brother Clifford, in which the heroine is a dancer who dances her part—which Bax later made into short piano pieces.

In 1920 Basil Dean commissioned Delius to write incidental music for James Elroy Flecker's play *Hassan*, which he had acquired in manuscript. (Flecker, a kind of Oriental Georgian, had died of T.B. in 1915.) There were difficulties, and the score was first heard in Darmstadt in 1923, but in September of the same year the play opened in London and ran for 281 performances. *Hassan* is a curious play; as sentimental as a chocolate-box in places, but with occasional lapses into a morbid interest in pain which have brought a charge of latent sadism. Delius's music, apart from the Serenade, which became very popular, includes a chorus of beggars (quite unsentimental and sardonic), a chorus of warriors, full of the usual stuff— "Pale kings of the sunset, beware!"—a number of short pieces, a "Procession of Protracted Death", illustrating one of the cruel episodes in the play, which produces from Delius some grinding, almost repellent music that might be a surprise to some people, and the famous "Journey to Samarkand". In this last piece the middle-aged sweet-maker Hassan, disgusted with the ways of the great, joins as a pilgrim the caravan along the Golden Road to Samarkand. Delius's music for this comes dangerously near to kitsch; but the most haunting, beautiful kitsch it is possible to imagine.

Vaughan Williams had composed in the war years one of his best-known works, the lovely *The Lark Ascending*, for solo violin and small orchestra. This delicate score, vaguely allusive to folk-song, is one of the finest of what one might call the "Back to Nature" school of English music, quite free from the self-consciousness and almost evasive softness of much of Vaughan Williams's music.

In Europe at about this time several major composers produced important works. Ravel wrote *Le Tombeau de Couperin*, typical in its fastidious pastiche, and, like so many Ravel works, arranged for both piano and orchestra. He also wrote *La Valse*, a powerful study of Viennese decadence that is to my mind underrated. The scoring is fascinating in itself, and parallels many effects in the almost contemporary opera *Wozzeck* by Alban Berg. During the 1920s, too, the music of Karol Szymanowski first began to penetrate the musical scene, although he had already composed a number of works which had a certain impact in his native Poland. These included the First Violin Concerto and the Third Symphony, a setting for soprano solo, chorus and orchestra of verses by the Persian poet Rumi, celebrating the splendour of the Eastern night.

Bax's two works for 1921, the short tone-poem *The Happy Forest* and the unaccompanied motet *Mater ora filium*, are works in which his prevailing, and mounting, internal conflict is silent. *The Happy Forest* is slight but enchanting, light in mood and texture, and has been compared with the music of Eric Coates; but the invention is much more fastidious and subtly complex than anything written by that prolific but almost forgotten composer of light music. *Mater ora filium* was the first of a number of choral works which Bax composed during the next few years, and is a considerable landmark. No other modern English composer before this time had written an unaccompanied motet of such complexity and distinction. Bach was not precisely Bax's favourite composer, but it is Bach's motets that this powerful work brings to mind. It is written for double chorus to medieval words, and it exploits the medium with great virtuosity. It is exceedingly difficult, and one has heard some deplorable performances, but when it is well sung its effect is electrifying.

John Ireland's most massive orchestral work, *Mai Dun*, dates from 1921. Typical of his peculiar area of inspiration, it takes its name from a vast prehistoric fortress or earthwork in Dorsetshire, true Arthur Machen country, and the work is essentially a ghostly invocation of the time when it was manned and alive in grim earnest. *Mai Dun* is far from negligible, but it lacks Ireland's usual light touch, and his complaint, expressed in the words "May not be done", is an indication of its infrequent performance. In fact, its orchestration is rather lumpy and gruff, and the gentle Ireland was not convincing when trying to be ferocious. Its greatest strength and beauty lies rather in its quiet passages, its haunting sense of the past.

Vaughan Williams's Third Symphony appeared in 1921, like its two predecessors known not by a number or key but a title—*Pastoral Symphony*. The *Pastoral Symphony* had been conceived by its composer on the Western Front, as he watched the French countryside dissolving under the artillery barrage. It was one more link with the passing beauty of the rural scene, that prime mover of the whole folk-song school. Its inspiration, however, was French; but there is nothing to resemble French harmonic methods in its strikingly original idiom. With Debussy the motive for writing diatonic consecutives—which he rarely did—was a conscious archaicism, decorative and almost condescending; with Vaughan Williams it was the very stuff of his thought. Debussy's natural idiom was chromatic, at the very edge of tonality, and his excursions into the diatonic modal were time-travelling, as Constant Lambert pointed out, where the time to which he travelled was actually exotic to him, and selected for that reason. With Vaughan Williams it was the home he had never left. Debussy was sophisticated even for a twentieth-century Frenchman, while Vaughan Williams belonged far more to the nineteenth century, and was much less sophisticated and subtle than Debussy.

Yet the *Pastoral Symphony* is the first real and characteristic masterpiece of a small group of great works which Vaughan Williams wrote between 1921 and 1934, and which constitute his chief claim to distinction. In spite of its time-recession its musical language is singularly tough and unsentimental; the opening complex of the first movement, with its streams of triads in contrary motion, generates hard, cool dissonance, and the lack of an obvious "tune"—and Vaughan Williams a few years later in the Fifth Symphony did not stay his hand in this respect—strengthens both the music and the sense of remoteness. It is austere, genuinely archaic, and hardly conscious at all; it seems to stem from the primal consciousness of man, by way of the unconscious mind of Vaughan Williams. It manages to be genuinely symphonic while bearing no possible resemblance to any previous symphony; indeed, it sounds more convincingly symphonic than several of Vaughan Williams's later, more conventional symphonies: the Seventh and Eighth, for instance. The one movement that could conceivably be a part of a conventional sonata structure is the Scherzo; the first movement, with its cumulus drift of sound, its sense that it is neither fast nor slow, but essentially motionless, is like nothing else written before or since; one wonders if Vaughan Williams actually knew how original it was. The soprano solo has, alas, become so persistent a feature of pastoral film music that it is by now inclined to drag the music back to earth, and to raise incongruous echoes of a worldly kind in this most unworldly symphony. An air of grave sadness in the last movement, almost like a distant echo of the tragic march in the *London Symphony*, is wholly in keeping.

A genuine interest in ancient music was beginning in England. Edmund Fellowes's *English Madrigal Composers* was published in 1921, and his *Orlando Gibbons* in 1925. Peter Warlock's erudite, beautifully written *The English Ayre* was also published in 1926. Even earlier Arnold Dolmetsch had settled in Haslemere and begun his pioneering work on ancient instruments. The present cult of early music has deeper roots than is sometimes thought.

Abroad, Saint-Saëns died in 1921, an almost incredible link with the past: he had been born in 1835, and had met Berlioz. Perhaps the most significant music of this period was Stravinsky's Symphonies for Wind Instruments in Memory of Debussy. After the barbaric splendour of *Le Sacre du printemps*, and during his neo-classical period, this music is prophetic of his last style.

Austere, dark in texture, the symphonies are different from anything he had written before. There were two works by a composer overshadowed by Stravinsky yet recognisably the same kind of composer, Serge Prokofiev—works that were destined to become among his most popular: the Third Piano Concerto and the opera *The Love for Three Oranges*. The concerto is almost neo-classical in idiom, but not quite; it is typical Prokofiev in its busy, almost steely invention. The opera is not often heard outside Russia, but the suite of orchestral pieces taken from it have carried Prokofiev's name around the world.

There could be no greater contrast with Vaughan Williams's *Pastoral Symphony* than Bax's First, which was completed in 1922. Nicknamed "The Demon" on its first performance, and in a gruff E flat major and minor, its first movement began life as a piano sonata. One can see its origins in the slow harp run-up to the barking motto theme which begins the symphony, and which was to haunt Bax for the rest of his life. The symphony is a brutal landscape, black in colour and violent in mood, with more fast tempo in it than is usual with Bax, and a slow movement of extraordinary power, in which a climactic tonality of C major is undermined and finally shattered by a great pedal on A flat and D flat.

It was the culmination of a series of events that had shattered the easy-going world of Bax's youth: the war, the Easter Rising, in which a number of his friends died, the breakdown of his marriage, and perhaps most of all, his own realisation that his style was too self-indulgent, and that outside England music was becoming more and more radical. It is possible to see the influence of *Le Sacre du printemps* in Bax's First Symphony; certainly the bleak final march suggests Stravinsky, as do also certain aspects of the brass writing in the first movement. The symphony is challenging in its austerity, its harshness, and its forbidding mood; but it is well constructed, closely argued, and immensely imaginative. Only Elgar and Vaughan Williams had attempted works so ambitious at this date, and Bax's symphony was more advanced in idiom than either of the older composers. It is not really a Romantic work. It is too uncompromising in harmonic language, and too honest in its desolate mood.

Temporary musical fame is a strange thing, especially in England. In 1922 the Birmingham Repertory Company produced Rutland Boughton's *The Immortal Hour* at the Regent Theatre in London, where it ran for some time. For a while Boughton became a Great Composer, and certain things from his opera, notably the Faery Song, were considerable favourites, especially among those who did not normally listen to serious music, for years, until they finally faded out. Boughton (1878–1960) studied briefly at the Royal College of Music, afterwards joining Bantock in Birmingham. He composed many operas, and was a fervent Wagnerian; he tried to establish an English Bayreuth for his own works at Glastonbury. The curious thing is how little Wagnerian his music is; if there is such a thing as Pre-Raphaelite music, this is it: weakly melodious in a popular way, harmonically insipid, and wishy-washy in a vaguely Celtic manner. It is more like Floradora than Richard Wagner. Among Boughton's other operas are *The Birth of Arthur*; *The Round Table*; *Alkestis*; *The Queen of Cornwall*, and *The Lily Maid*.

A similar figure was John Foulds (1880–1939), whose *World Requiem* used to be performed at Armistice Day celebrations for a few years after the First World War. This is a curious genre, compound of the over-sweet taste of England in the 1920s, a megalomania that expressed itself in common chords and commonplaces, and a preoccupation with Wardour-Street Orientalism or vaguely Celtic mysticism—Bantock was another victim, and it must be said that Arnold Bax's hard instinct only just saved him from being still another.

William Walton's long association with the Sitwells (which produced the text of *Belshazzar's Feast* among other things) bore its first-fruit in 1922 and 1923 with the first private and public performances of *Façade*. Walton had begun his career with some advanced chamber music, given at ISCM Festivals and the like. *Façade* was something quite different. It was given a private run-through at the Sitwells' house in Chelsea on 24 January 1922, and its first public performance was on 12 June 1923 at the Aeolian Hall. Walton's early chamber music was very serious, but *Façade*, whatever its technical sophistication, conveyed the same determined cheerfulness—so typical of the Twenties—as the work of the French composers of the time. It was an attempt—devastatingly successful—to match Edith Sitwell's virtuoso studies in abstract poetry with appropriate music.

Today *Façade* is a familiar, much played, and beloved piece, both in its original form and in Walton's subsequent arrangement as two suites for full orchestra; but by a series of events, and one must say misunderstandings, it became notorious at the time of the first public performance. I feel that Osbert Sitwell in his autobiographical volume *Laughter in the Next Room* (1949) is either naïve or disingenuous in discounting the notoriety of the Sitwells themselves at this period. Their pronouncements were not far in advance of radical professional opinion, but so provocatively couched as to stir the hostility of those who did not know what it was all about; and they had put on at Heals in 1919 an exhibition of French Impressionist paintings that was the first massive exposure of the English people to a kind of art which is today extremely fashionable, but which then provoked considerable hostility. These paintings were remembered when the critics came to consider *Façade*. So when a work was produced which involved reciting abstract poems through a megaphone, to music by a chamber orchestra which quoted "I do Like to be Beside the Seaside" and sundry other easily recognisable tunes, it is not to be wondered that the less specialised press seized its opportunity: one headline read "Drivel they paid to hear" and another account ended "Surely it is time this sort of thing were stopped".

In the 1970s, when really advanced art is received in the main with bored indifference, the reception given to the gaiety and innocence of *Façade* is drenched with nostalgia. It was a curious, but very typical incident, this early performance of a work by a composer who has by now been adopted by the establishment which he began by scandalising. Ironically, *Façade* gave notice to those who knew what Schoenberg, Berg and Webern were doing at the time that Walton was really a conservative. Osbert Sitwell expresses very mixed feelings about his student, "atonal" works. Could it possibly be that

Sitwellian disapproval changed the whole course of the development of Sir William Walton?

It was becoming obvious at the time, if it had not been before, that Bax and Vaughan Williams were strongly contrasted composers, as Elgar and Delius had been before them. The short, one-movement Piano Quartet of Bax seems to be connected with the First Symphony: drivingly rhythmical and ferocious for the whole of its brief length, its hard percussive nature recalls the orchestral work. On the other hand the Oboe Quintet, in three movements, is a last, rather vapid product of Bax's early obsession with Ireland. It is rather fey. The Viola Sonata, however, is the finest of Bax's works for viola, and a masterpiece. It is difficult to describe the grim First Symphony as Romantic, but this sonata is almost a textbook definition of the term. Its thematic material is exceedingly beautiful, heartbreakingly so, two slow movements flanking a ferocious Scherzo that alone belongs to the world of the First Symphony.

How different from these colourful works is Vaughan Williams's G minor Mass, an *a cappella* work of remote austerity, serene, distantly lovely, in a polyphony that quite innocently permits all kinds of consecutives, yet of unruffled clarity. Yet it puzzled some critics at its first performance. There was also a cantata, after Bunyan, *The Shepherds of the Delectable Mountains*, which Vaughan Williams would use thirty years later in a larger work, with peculiar consequences.

Peculiar also was Holst's first large-scale opera, *The Perfect Fool*, based on the entirely Holstian idea that beauty is boring; it suffered from what his daughter Imogen is apt to call "those tiresome wizards".* Yet the only part of this large parody opera to survive in frequent performance is the Ballet Music, consisting of the Wizard's invocation of the spirits of earth, water and fire. There is a lot of good music locked up in this rather impossible framework. Holst suggested that *A Fugal Overture* should be used to introduce *The Perfect Fool*; it is an excellent piece, as concentrated as the opera is diffuse.

After a misspent youth (*Madame Noy, Rout, Conversations,*

* In her book on the composer (1951).

etc.) Arthur Bliss suddenly returned to the fold of respectability with a massive symphony, called *A Colour Symphony*, an abstract work except that each movement is headed with the name of a colour. It is a fine work, if not quite in the same league as the symphonies of Bax and Vaughan Williams. It was the first symptom of Bliss's essential conservatism.

In 1923 Schoenberg published his first serial music, the Five Piano Pieces, Op. 23. Although serial implications were to be found in a number of free atonal works before this, these piano pieces were the first conscious formulation of the method. They also marked a curious approach on Schoenberg's part to the spirit of neo-classicism, which was to dominate his music for a decade or so after this. Stravinsky's *Les Noces* and Octet, Kodály's *Psalmus Hungaricus* (perhaps his masterpiece), Bloch's exotic and powerful Piano Quintet, Prokofiev's First Violin Concerto, Bartók's Second Violin Sonata, all belong to this year, which also saw the appearance of Sibelius's surprisingly serene, limpid and understated Sixth Symphony.

During 1923-4 Arnold Bax continued his spate of choral works, and produced the massive *St Patrick's Breastplate*, one of his finest works. It is a setting for chorus and orchestra, of the Irish Gaelic hymn *Luireach Naoimh Padraig* (in English translation), with a powerful rhythmic impulse that is part hymn, part march, and with colourful illustrations of the words, which are saturated with nature mysticism. Bax's choral music is infrequently performed; the difficulty of *Mater ora filium*, with its painfully high tessitura for the sopranos, and the large forces required for *St Patrick's Breastplate*, may contribute to this.

Holst produced two major, but problematical, works in 1924. These were the Choral Symphony and the opera *At the Boar's Head*. Apart from the early *Savitri* and the late *The Tale of the Wandering Scholar*, Holst had little luck with opera. Imogen Holst calls *At the Boar's Head* "a brilliant failure". It is a marriage between Shakespeare's text (from *Henry IV*) and folk-song, the various tunes selected to fit the words and the whole counterpointed together with the utmost ingenuity. There are strokes of wit which, Miss Holst remarks, can only be appreciated by those who know the ins and outs of a morris dance. But in the theatre and opera house minute detail is apt to be lost; it is the broad stroke, the powerful dramatic gesture, that is most effective. At home, with a gramophone recording of the work and a score, it might be different; but in any case the score of this opera is out of print.

A study score has recently been issued, for the first time, of the Choral Symphony—presumably to go with the recording. Holst selected the words for this work from Keats, a somewhat unexpected choice. Keats relied on sensuous imagery for his poetry, often of an implicitly sexual nature; he wrote that only the manners of the time prevented him from describing exactly what took place between the lovers at the climax of *The Eve of St Agnes*, and it has recently been stated, convincingly, that his intention in his poetry was to drive a coach and horses through English emotional reticence.* Now, there is no more convincing example of English emotional reticence than Gustav Holst; and can anyone put a finger on a passage in any work of his, other than the last one, *The Tale of the Wandering Scholar*, which is in a special category, in which sex rears its ugly head? Moreover, much of the poetry Holst chose to set, and especially the central movement, the "Ode to a Grecian Urn", comes under that special category of English poetry, mentioned by Bernard Shaw in connection with Parry's setting of the Book of Job, which dwarfs any imaginable musical setting. It is remarkable that Holst succeeded to the extent he did.

His greatest success is the opening movement, the "Hymn to Pan", significantly a purely technical device of great imagination. He asks the chorus to chant, on one note, while the orchestra crawls with chromatics beneath them. There could be no more effective illustration of the words, in which pagan liturgy and nature description are mingled in just the same manner. Similarly, the Scherzo, a setting of "Ever let the fancy roam", comes off magnificently—Holst never failed with a Scherzo. But the Bacchanal that follows the opening invocation to Pan, as Miss Holst remarks, is too full of fourths that are too consistently perfect. The last movement, "Bards of passion

* See Christopher Ricks, *Keats and Embarrassment* (1974).

and of mirth", is majestic and patchy. But the challenge, un-
fortunately too formidable for Holst, is the "Grecian Urn". It
is serene and lovely music, but the coldness of Keats's poem is
that of white heat, and Holst responds with the hygienic neatness of a refrigerator. Like *The Hymn of Jesus*, the Choral Symphony is a work of remarkable individuality, but Keats just
wasn't Holst's poet. We know now that the Choral Symphony
was in no wise prophetic. Music has not gone that way.

In 1924 Charles Villiers Stanford died, in the year after
Schoenberg introduced serial technique, without having come
to terms with Wagner and Listzt, and still describing the music
of Debussy as "all rot". He tried, according to his lights, to
further the careers of those of his pupils he approved of, and
who could endure his brusque methods, and he performed
much conservative English music in Leeds and elsewhere. Yet,
of these pupils, Vaughan Williams remained in essence a conservative, in spite of the Fourth and Sixth Symphonies; Ireland
suffered from excess timidity all his life; Bridge had to struggle
for twenty years to find his true style, and was dropped by the
musical community when he had found it; and we had to wait
until after the Second World War before English composers
caught up with music that was written before the First. The
composers of the early years of the English musical renaissance
wrote a certain amount of fine and valuable music, but if we
eliminate Elgar, Delius and Bax, and remember that Bridge
only became radical about the time of Stanford's death (was
there some psychological connection here?), the verdict must
be that in the struggle of English music to escape from respectability and the insipid, and to achieve both vivid invention and
professional status, and of English creative thought to become
reasonably contemporary, Stanford and Parry were not particularly helpful.

Vaughan Williams's folk-opera, *Hugh the Drover*, was produced in 1924. An English ballad opera, with obvious homage
to Smetana's *The Bartered Bride* (which dates from 1886), was
a peculiar and perilous undertaking at so late a date. The
Smetana was written ten years before Vaughan Williams was
born, and was conservative in its context (that of *Tristan*), yet
if we discount the English composers' habit of consecutives,

and use of modes, Smetana's opera sounds the more modern, and is certainly the more accomplished. Vaughan Williams was not a natural opera composer, and *Hugh the Drover* is perhaps the first indication of his chronic unevenness. He continued to tinker with *Hugh the Drover* for many years, so he must have had doubts about it himself. What did Holst think about it? Vaughan Williams had expressed "cold admiration" for Holst's Choral Symphony. Affection tinged with exasperation might be a modern reaction to the Holst, but it seems that Vaughan Williams saw its coldness, but was puzzled by its boldness. It was beyond him, and Holst's music was to become increasingly beyond his friend's comprehension.

Sibelius finished his last symphony, the Seventh, in 1924, only *Tapiola* coming after, to be followed by the long "silence from Jarvenpaa". The Seventh is one of the works that suffered most in the great reaction against Sibelius after his death, one critic calling it a "rag-bag of a symphony". It is in fact tautly constructed and marvellously logical, a superb summing-up of his life's work. Music from France for 1924 included Poulenc's *Les Biches*, Ibert's *Escales*, Satie's *Relâche*, and Honegger's railway imitation *Pacific 231*. I am fond of them all, but what a tale of arrested development do they collectively tell!

Peter Warlock composed his masterpiece, "The Curlew", in 1924, and it is as different as possible from the French music detailed above. He had a few more years to live, but this "grisly" work (to use his own term) is full of the portent of his fate. One of the few successful settings of the poetry of Yeats, it is for high voice, flute, cor anglais and string quartet, and is a statement of total despair. Yet it is a superb work, richly imaginative, haunting in its wild melancholy, and possessing that curious faculty of all great tragic art, that of the darkness declaring the glory of light. It is quite free of the self-pity that might have vitiated it, and if I have praised it highly, I believe that is no less than its due. It is one of the masterpieces of English music.

Ferruccio Busoni died in 1924, perhaps the greatest pianist between Liszt and the present day, and an original if enigmatic composer. His writings on musical aesthetics were influential at the time, and his two largest works—the vast Piano Concerto and his final, unfinished opera *Doktor Faust*—seem at the time of writing to be coming into their own for the first time since they were written.

Carl Nielsen wrote his Sixth Symphony in 1925. After five amiable and worthy symphonies he produced in his Sixth an uneven, peculiar work showing symptoms of disgust at "modern music". The passing of Busoni, the composition of such a despairing symphony from such a very optimistic composer as Nielsen, were symptoms of the state of music in Europe; contemporary music was gaining ground, and the most radical composers were emerging from obscurity.

The year saw the first performance of Alban Berg's opera *Wozzeck*. This has proved to be the most popular score produced by any of the founding fathers of atonalism, although it did not establish itself west of Berlin until after the Second World War. A BBC concert performance under Sir Adrian Boult in the late 1930s evoked incredulity and mirth in the main.* Listening to *Wozzeck* today, when the work hardly sounds atonal at all, and not all that radical, makes us wonder what all the fuss was about. The libretto was objected to as "squalid", but it is hardly more so than some of Verdi's. The fact is that it is a deeply moving and very human study in compassion, and as a work of music masterly in the extreme. Notice had been given that the atonalists were about to break through.

Here in England two new choral works by Vaughan Williams appeared, *Flos Campi* and *Sancta Civitas*. The former is for small chorus, orchestra, and solo viola, and is one of Vaughan Williams's tributes to the art of Lionel Tertis. In the main Vaughan Williams's music is austere and other-worldly, but *Flos Campi* is sensuous in atmosphere and content; the score is headed by quotations from the Song of Solomon, which is erotic in its very nature; and the music seems erotic by implication. Not very, I might add. It is a very beautiful work, but

---

* The performance was one of several brave gestures by the more enlightened section of the English musical profession at the time; another was a record by Decca of Webern's String Trio which was actually the first recording ever of any music by Webern anywhere in the world.

about as exotic as English curry. It has the same strange mixture of British innocence and Oriental spice.

When *Sancta Civitas* was new it had the reputation of being obscure and advanced. It is a big work, with texts from a miscellany of biblical sources, but it is not very advanced, and the only obscure part of it (for most readers) is the superscription in Greek which heads the score. Since Ursula Vaughan Williams's biography (1964) it is known that the composer was an atheist; but the quotation is from the *Phaedo* of Plato, and is translated thus:

> A man of sense will not insist that things are exactly as I have described them. But I think he will believe that something of the kind is true of the soul and her habitations, seeing that she is shown to be immortal, and that it is worthwhile to stake everything on this belief. The venture is a fair one and he must charm his doubts with spells like these.

The text of *Sancta Civitas* is explicit, indeed, dogmatic, in its assertion of religious belief; and so, actually, is the quotation from Plato. Vaughan Williams was considered in his lifetime to be the epitome of English bluff downrightness, but the more one examines his nature the more evasive and uncertain it appears. He said of his religious works—and there are a great many of them, apart from his editing of hymnals and his composing of hymns—that it was the duty of a composer to supply his community with appropriate music, even if he did not believe in its philosophic basis. But nothing is so sacred as a man's fundamental convictions, and nothing reveals them so completely as the music he writes. To betray those convictions in music is the death of the soul, as a latter-day English composer, Peter Maxwell Davies, was to emphasise in his opera *Taverner*.

The music of *Sancta Civitas* is anything but obscure. It is hard to realise that these innocent sounds were ever considered difficult or baffling. It is formally a bit confused, and there is a section concerning the Rider on a White Horse and his mission of destruction the motivation of which is not clear. Did it refer to Germany and the 1914–18 War? Vaughan Williams really was that naïve on occasion. In that case what is it doing in a work which seems to paint "the soul and her habitations" and to praise God? It is the whole motivation of *Sancta Civitas* that is mysterious, not the, in the main, innocent Anglican-cum-pastoral music, once dubbed by the English dissonant and modern.

There were two chamber works from English composers during 1925; Bax's Second String Quartet and Holst's Terzetto. The latter is one of the earliest examples of thorough-going polytonality—all three parts remain in different keys. The music sounds so euphonious and bland that contemporary listeners were puzzled when they knew how it was constructed, and even Holst himself was taken aback by how normal it sounded. Bax's First and Third String Quartets are fine works, each in its different way, but the Second is oddly experimental. Its movements are badly related and do not fit together too well; the string quartet texture, too, is curiously unconvincing, too loose-knit to belong to that medium.

The year 1926 saw the great Diaghilev rather surprisingly experimenting with young English composers. His ballet company was in its last phase (he was to die three years later) and its great time was past. But he asked Constant Lambert, then only twenty-one, for a ballet, and Lambert responded with *Romeo and Juliet*. It was eventually produced at Monte Carlo on 4 May 1926. During the protracted muddle of the preparations Lambert had actually stood up to Diaghilev—something very few people were capable of doing—but his ballet stood very little chance after the impresario had finished adapting it to his alien tastes. Lambert was writing a lot at this time; when *Romeo and Juliet* was put on in London at His Majesty's on 21 June, his next ballet, *Pomona*, was already on the stocks. Neither have remained in the repertory; the music for both has something of Lambert's lucid melancholy, but they are immature. But what a beginning for so young a man! Another ballet, *The Triumph of Neptune*, was contributed by Lord Berners (1883–1950), a slight but attractive talent, more memorable as a great eccentric.

Bax's contribution to 1926 included the rather tame Third

Piano Sonata—why his piano music fell off so badly late in life when his other music increased in power and mastery remains a mystery—the rich but unremarkable Romantic Overture, and the tremendous Second Symphony, dedicated to Serge Koussevitzky, who gave it its first performance in Boston. What a performance that must have been! One of the peaks of Bax's inspiration, this bitingly original and singular symphony is a throw of genius. It seems to brood over the tragic implications of the First Symphony, and although it is only a couple of minutes longer, sounds like a much bigger work. It is utterly uncompromising and personal, and indeed Bax wrote, "I put a great deal of time and emotion into the writing." Its almost instinctive form succeeds against all the odds. The first movement rises out of the darkness into disruptive ferocity, taking with it a theme that is a near-quotation of the First Symphony's motto theme—in fact it is that theme with a couple of notes by way of extension. As is customary with Bax, the thematic material is exposed in the first few bars. It has been said that the work is "one vast love-song", but the work is too big, too violent, and too destructive to be any such thing. This symphony, surely, is his entirely personal vision, related to the First Symphony, and a working out of the most extreme of the musical problems raised but not solved by that work. Love-song, surely, is the last term that can be applied to the last movement, with its savage destructiveness, in which themes and texture go down in ruin in one last murderous outburst, to be followed by a slow, broken, sinking back into the pit out of which the grim vision arose. Various beautiful melodies do occur in this symphony, which may have some reference to Harriet Cohen; but the violent nihilism of the whole is what will strike most listeners.

Neither Holst nor Vaughan Williams finished anything of importance this year; Vaughan Williams produced *On Christmas Night*, and Holst two rather abortive choral ballets, *The Golden Goose* and *The Morning of the Year*. But this was the year of Walton's overture *Portsmouth Point*, a very brilliant work in which his rhythmic sense is seen at its best. Its inspiration was Rowlandson, and it is full of the spirit of old Boyce.

In Europe several important events occurred. Sibelius bowed

off the musical scene with a supreme masterpiece, the symphonic poem *Tapiola*, one of the greatest works of twentieth-century music. But a new name appeared; that of Dmitri Shostakovich whose First Symphony, written in 1924 at the age of eighteen, emerged from Russia for the first time. A work of great originality and power, it exhibited the influence of a composer who was an object of neglect and even ridicule in western Europe at that time, but who was to make a spectacular recovery thirty years on: Gustav Mahler. It was obvious that in Shostakovich a new talent had emerged,* but politics saw to it that his next three symphonies were unknown in the West until after the Second World War. Hindemith, then in his *Gebrauchsmusik* stage, wrote his opera *Cardillac*, the story of a maniacal jeweller who cannot bear to part with his masterpieces.

Frank Bridge was now entering into his richest period. 1927 saw the emergence of two orchestral works, *Enter Spring* and *There is a willow grows aslant a brook*. The young Benjamin Britten had been "knocked sideways" by *The Sea* at the Norwich Triennial Festival in 1924, when he was ten, and again by *Enter Spring* at the same Festival in 1927. He became Bridge's pupil on the strength of this overwhelming impression. *Enter Spring* is a big, vivid overture, of virtuoso orchestration; like Bax's *The Garden of Fand* it is close to Ravel in brilliance of harmony and glowing scoring. It was in some ways a curious throw-back; the Piano Sonata of 1924 had laid down the elements of Bridge's new, bitter, dissonant style, and *There is a willow* accords to an extent with that style; but although the harmony of *Enter Spring* is more advanced and complex than that of *The Sea*, its spirit is closer to that work than that of the Piano Sonata, or any subsequent work by Bridge. *There is a willow grows aslant a brook*— the title is taken from the description of the death of Ophelia in *Hamlet*—is a quieter work, but closer in spirit to Bridge's new style. Scored for chamber orchestra, it is full of the strange and remote late-Bridge atmosphere; it is made up of a remarkable

* This the West duly acknowledged when Leopold Stokowski's spectacular recording of the First Symphony was released in the 1930s—as with Sibelius, Shostakovich was one of the first composers to achieve recognition outside his own country through the medium of the gramophone record.

number of moods and textures, drawn together with subtle power into an integrated whole.

Frank Bridge's Third String Quartet reveals his new style fully formed. In this remarkable work the fruits of his admiration for Alban Berg can be seen; the very appearance of the score recalls the Lyric Suite. But although the music is radical, it is a very English personality that persists in it. After the usual short slow opening—too short to be called an introduction, a mere nine bars—the Allegro moderato establishes a positively frenetic mood, in spite of that "moderato". Its tone is dark and striving, the very contemporary melodic intervals, introduced in the first slow nine bars, twisting the music here and there. But the second group, which enters after 4 in the score, has a typical English wistful lyricism. It is a long first movement, twenty-five pages, and is succeeded by an Andante con moto that is rather less radical: a wistful, remote movement. The finale is energetic and savage in tone, but ends in a Bax-like Epilogue, serene and slow, with all the instruments muted. It is a very masculine quartet, like Beethoven's "Serioso", and indeed, for all its Bergian appearance and technique it is Beethoven, and especially the Beethoven of the Grosse Fuge, who shares the influence with Berg. The quartet was written in 1926 and first performed in 1927, and it is not surprising that it was head and shoulders above the musical climate of England at this time.

Egdon Heath may well be Holst's masterpiece (but we should remember also *Hammersmith*) and it too was finished in 1927. It shares with *Savitri* as well as *Hammersmith* the quality of being entirely personal, written without reference to any other critic but himself. The score bears an inscription from Thomas Hardy's *The Return of the Native*:

A place perfectly accordant with man's nature—neither ghastly, hateful nor ugly; neither commonplace, unmeaning nor tame; but, like man, slighted and enduring; and withal singularly colossal and mysterious in its swarthy monotony.

The opening, on a few muted double basses, immediately declares the nature of the work; it is predominately quiet, except for dull processional sounds and a brief, frantic trumpet figure. One agrees with Imogen Holst when she writes that some of the string writing is extraordinarily like the sound of the wind in grass. The ending is as quiet and unobtrusive as the opening. I suppose that the work is actually conservative in harmony and idiom, yet such is its individuality that it is contemporary in sound.

There was one significant event in 1928 in the life of Delius. For some years he had been blind and paralysed, and unable to commit his music to paper. A young Yorkshire organist and pianist called Eric Fenby (shades of William Baines!) had fallen in love with Delius's music, and he wrote to the composer asking if he could help. He went to Grez, and after an awkward and stormy beginning Fenby managed to evolve a means of taking down the music dictated by the pitch-deaf, proud and irascible old man, and succeeded in completing a number of scores. In this way were such things as *Cynara* and *A Late Lark* completed, and *A Song of Summer*, *Songs of Farewell* and the Third Violin Sonata composed. It was Fenby's brief hour of glory, and after his book was published (*Delius as I Knew Him*, 1936) and Delius's life-work completed, his subsequent career was muted.

Elsewhere in Europe Ravel composed his *Bolero*, destined to hang round his neck like the albatross, and Stravinsky wrote the slight but lovely *Apollon Musagete*, for strings. Honegger was at work at a series of symphonic movements, and in this year it was *Rugby*, suggested by the game, and less successful than *Pacific 231*.

Vaughan Williams, undeterred by the comparative failure of the surer-footed Holst's Falstaff opera, issued his *Sir John in Love*, on the subject of *The Merry Wives of Windsor*. Loewe had set the *Erlkönig* after Schubert, so there was no reason why Vaughan Williams should not set *The Merry Wives* after Verdi. Unlike the Holst, many of the tunes are original, and the folk-song element is comparatively sparse. There is some lovely music in the work, and it is at no point as sentimental as *Hugh the Drover*, but it has not held the stage, although it has been recorded. None of Vaughan Williams's operas have achieved the validity in the theatre of Holst's *Savitri*, and in this respect they fall far short of the operas of Britten, which are all more or less in the international repertory. The last act of *Sir John in Love* gives the game away by almost quoting Verdi in the pinching chorus; but of course there can be no comparison; *Sir John in Love* is for England only.

Bax and Constant Lambert also produced works in 1928, and Covent Garden staged the first of Eugene Goossens's two operas, *Judith*.* Lambert's was his most popular work, *The Rio Grande*. Most of Lambert is in this small masterpiece for piano solo, alto, chorus and orchestra to words by Sacheverell Sitwell.† For many years it was played at the Proms, and there has usually been a recording of it. It brings together several aspects of Lambert's style: a very sophisticated genuflexion in the direction of jazz, a Mediterranean melancholy with a touch of Virgil about it, a fascination with instrumental timbre, and in particular contemporary piano writing, and his love for the exotic, which manifested itself during these years in a cult of Anna May Wong, the Chinese actress (he even drank Chinese wine in her honour). *The Rio Grande* is a singularly perfect and delectable short work, and if Lambert came to feel that it was celebrated at the expense of his more serious works—for instance the Music for Orchestra of 1927—he had no reason to be ashamed of it, to put it mildly. Music for Orchestra is, however, another matter; it is quite short, twelve minutes compared with the fifteen minutes for *The Rio Grande*, but concentrated and strong. Different too is the Piano Sonata (1928–9). Cecil Gray said that it had a "dark, black, Célinesque quality" inspired by "long, cat-like, nocturnal prowlings through the suburbs of Paris". This hits it off splendidly—it is quite unlike any other piano sonata.

Bax poured out his usual stream of music, an unpublished Violin Sonata in F, a Sonata for Flute and Harp, and three

* The second, *Don Juan de Mañara*, was staged in 1937, with as little success as *Judith*. In the year of writing Goossens's music seems to be enjoying a revival, but it seems unlikely that this will include either of his operas.

† Lambert suggested Edyth Baker for the piano part, and wanted a coloured singer with a good jazz style for the alto, and a coloured chorus; but when it was performed on 17 January 1928 the pianist was Angus Morrison, with the Wireless Chorus and Orchestra under the composer.

pieces for orchestra, as well as the Third Symphony. There are links, both thematic and dramatic, between Bax's first three symphonies, and they can be said to form a series, a single progression, which the Fourth Symphony interrupts before the series is resumed in Nos. 5, 6 and 7. The Third brings the argument of the first two to a comparatively tranquil, but not a final conclusion. Unlike the Seventh, it leaves the door open. The mood is less hectic, the music less strident, than in the first two symphonies. It seems as if some very real and terrible conflict is being resolved by absorption into a legendary past. Dedicated to Sir Henry Wood, and often played at the Proms in the years before Sir Henry's retirement, this used to be Bax's most popular symphony—if the term popular can be applied to any work of his. It is extremely tuneful—and a Bax tune is usually a formidable affair, memorable and individual.

Formally it is less than successful; the main trouble is that the development section of the first movement is at a much slower tempo than the rest—an incorporated slow movement in fact. Perfectly logical, but it brings to a halt a very vigorous movement, which opens with the nearest thing to a twelve-note theme that Bax ever wrote—"adumbrated", according to Bax, by a solo bassoon unaccompanied; and it is indeed a suggestive word. This is joined by other wood-wind voices, and an idea familiar from the first two symphonies begins to heave in the bass. In the Allegro various suggestions from this initial complex are developed, and after the slow central section the first subject appears as a bare rhythm, which is used as a driving force. The slow movement opens with a lovely melody that is exposed—and this is the right word!—perilously for horn and then trumpet. More romantic and easy-going than the slow movements of the first two symphonies, this movement suggests that the conflict has, for a time, lost its bite. The finale begins with one of those galumphing themes Bax often used in such places, and then becomes a kind of dance, the first suggestion of the barbaric war-dance of the finale to the Fifth Symphony. There is some mysterious rustling, and then the Epilogue begins. This Epilogue is one of the loveliest passages in modern music. The theme, descending in long loops in the violins, is haunted, and suggests some early spring evening, chill and sweet; after more rustlings and transformations it finds its inevitable colouring in a solo horn, which begins on a long, high note that falls from the sky as night descends, leaving a final dusky chord. This symphony succeeds in spite of its formal weaknesses, because of the great beauty of its incidents and thematic material.

Until 1929 Walton's music, like that of several other composers of his generation, had been light and amusing, but little more; he was considered an appendage of the Sitwells, and their ambiguous reputation attached itself to him. The first of what was to be a series of major works appeared in 1929: the Viola Concerto. It was first performed at a Promenade concert with Walton conducting and no less a figure than Paul Hindemith as the soloist. In this work, for the first time, the mature Walton personality is manifest; the jazzy rhythmic bounce has found its place in the texture, and is no longer there for itself alone, but as a foil for a formidable melodic gift; a masterly sense of form emerges, in an original and very dramatic organisation of the three movements as the perfect frame for his characteristic themes. Beginning with a poignant melody for the soloist, and proceeding to a first movement full of drama, and a second that is a kind of scherzo full of the snapping rhythms and capricious changes of tempo that were to be a mark of Walton's music at its best, it culminates in a finale which draws these threads together, not in resolution, but in a dramatic and powerful climax that makes the wistful main theme with which the soloist opened the work the only possible conclusion. It is a masterpiece, as Donald Francis Tovey recognised in a famous passage in his *Essays in Musical Analysis* (1936).

Holst's short choral works are beautiful, but without much significance, and in the main his songs with piano are negligible; like a great many twentieth-century composers he neither played the piano well nor thought in its terms. On the other hand, his writing for voice has a typically English "white" facility. But in 1929 there appeared a magnificent set of songs for high voice and piano, to poems by Humbert Wolfe. The piano parts are highly peculiar, yet in their own individual way these scattered groups of notes achieve an extraordinary effect. The vocal line has a cold and laconic mastery that immediately grips the listener, and an imagination that holds him. Here and there among the songs is an attempt at what looks like the conventional romantic approach, as in "A Little Music", "The Dream City" and "The Floral Bandit"; "A Little Music" comes nearest to being a romantic song, but "The Floral Bandit" is too cool to be any such thing, while "The Dream City" has an extraordinary atmosphere: it links itself with Holst's *Hammersmith* of 1930 in its oblique celebration of London, just as that city is, but with an inner clairvoyance that transfigures. Or rather, one might say, as that city was; for the London of the 1930s, vast yet parochial, still with a rural touch even about the City itself, and with a kind of ruinous, ancient beauty, has largely departed; but Humbert Wolfe's line about the lilac like sudden scented wings in the night has caught the time and place for those of us who were there.

Here and there in these songs an individual version of "conventional" piano writing appears, but lop-sided and gauche. Piano writing of an unconventional but exceedingly powerful kind appears in "Betelgeuse", which is the finest song of the group. The grotesque immensity of the star is celebrated in a piano part that moves like the passage of darkness over the void, and a voice part that hovers over it in frozen indifference. The music has the authentic strangeness of science fiction and the cold and unaccountable beauty of Zen art. Interspersed with these songs, the delicate loveliness of "The Dream City", the wistful and exquisite "Persephone", the vast vision of "Betelgeuse", and the remote love-songs and quiet visions, are some daunting meditations on mortality. One of these, "Journey's End", was also set by Frank Bridge, and his superb version aches with protest; but Holst sets this, and three other death poems, with the same blank indifference with which he contemplated Betelgeuse. Even if we feel that these death-songs are alienated in some way from the rest, the set reflects the full range of which Holst was capable; limited but utterly original. These cool songs are among the best written by an Englishman in the twentieth century.

To this time also belongs Holst's short opera based on Helen Waddell's book on the Wandering Scholars of the Middle Ages—a very Holstian theme. *The Wandering Scholar* is a success, at least in artistic terms, after the failure of *The Perfect Fool* and *At the Boar's Head*. It does not quite achieve the profundity of *Savitri*, and indeed is not meant to, being a sparkling comic opera of marvellous agility and economy. There was also a Concerto for two violins, a gentle and lovely work.

Between 12 October and 1 November 1929 Sir Thomas Beecham staged a Delius Festival in London, the first of two, as it happened, since there was a second one in 1946, some time after Delius's death. With the help of Peter Warlock and Eric Fenby he brought the blind and paralysed Delius and the by now ailing Jelka Delius to London, and gave six concerts of his music, four of which were large-scale choral and orchestral concerts conducted by Beecham, and including excerpts from the operas and *A Mass of Life* complete. Magnificently publicised and stage-managed, and superbly conducted by Beecham, the Festival was a sensational success. A little while previously James Gunn's excellent but misleadingly pathetic portrait of the terrible old man helpless in his chair had provoked public sympathy and excited public interest. Now people flocked to the concerts, and Delius was cheered in the streets as he passed from the Langham Hotel to the Queen's Hall in his Bath chair, propelled by Peter Warlock. He sat in the hall surrounded by flowers, and his tall pale figure with its aloof and aristocratic beauty made an unforgettable impression. But an air of mystery surrounds all this fuss. Why this particular composer should suddenly have caught the public's fancy at this time, when in general the English people ignore English composers and dislike English music, is astonishing; five years later these same people were probably asking, Who is Delius? Certainly critical opinion of his music was not mollified, for it was about this time that the phrase "the bath-salts of music" was coined. Most of the sensation was created by the consummate showmanship and dazzling conducting of Thomas Beecham; Beecham could make an otherwise sane audience encore the *Faust* Ballet Music. The Delius Festival was a magnificent and misleading irrelevance.

A musical event which had a more permanent effect on our musical life was the founding of the BBC Symphony Orchestra in 1930. Sir Adrian, then Mr, Boult was appointed its conductor. It marked the first serious incursion of broadcasting into the musical life of England.* There was considerable opposition to wireless telegraphy on the part of the profession at first; it was thought it might lessen the number of live concerts. But when Boult took over the BBC Symphony Orchestra—and turned it into a superb body—it became evident that in fact the Corporation was going to enrich and extend the musical life of England as perhaps no other single factor had done before. And the incursion of the BBC Symphony Orchestra into the Proms, with Sir Henry Wood still the conductor, began a new era for that vital institution.

Vaughan Williams's *Job*, "A Masque for Dancing", was played for the first time at the Norwich Festival on 23 October 1930, and although it did not reach the stage until 5 July 1931 (Cambridge Theatre, London), it belongs to 1930. Blake's *Illustrations of the Book of Job* was published in 1825, and is one of his masterpieces; perhaps, with his final print, "The Ancient of Days", his greatest pictorial work. These superb Romantic prints, together with the Book of Job itself, were Vaughan Williams's starting point for what was to be his greatest jump forward since the *Pastoral Symphony*.

The opening of the Masque is not inviting. It is in Vaughan Williams's pastoral vein, but a long way from the *Pastoral*. Vague and smudgy, it represents Job at the beginning of the biblical narrative, surrounded by his wives and children and his flocks. That the Masque is going to be an exceptional work is indicated as soon as Satan's characteristic theme is heard. Satan's Dance of Triumph is excellent music, and very effective on the stage; one remembers Robert Helpmann's tremendous leap. But the tremendous brass gesture when Satan sits on the

---

* The Company—later the Corporation—had been founded in 1922, although sporadic broadcasting had taken place before then. Lauritz Melchior had broadcast as early as 1920. The first outside opera broadcast was of *The Magic Flute*, in January 1923, and in 1925 *Carmen* was broadcast from the studio. Broadcasts from Covent Garden began in 1926, and from the Queen's Hall in 1927.

throne of God, "Gloria in excelsis Deo!" is magnificent even in concert performance, and on the stage overwhelming. The inspired use of the saxophone for Job's comforters owes nothing to anybody.* Perhaps only an Englishman could have written music so simple as Elihu's Dance of Youth and Beauty and got away with it. It is one of those rare cases where our negative musical quality is turned to good advantage. Another great moment comes with the Pavane and Galliard of the Sons of the Morning. Once again, the music is perilously near to morris dancing, but the power of the orchestration and the richness of the harmony, as well as the inherent drama of Satan's fall from Heaven, save it. We have to go back to the insipid pastoral stuff for the end, but the work as a whole remains enormously impressive.

Two large works by Holst, each displaying a facet of his personality, date from 1930, and one of them is a mysterious and significant composition. Of the Choral Fantasia little need be said. It is a fine work, typical of its composer; the words are by Robert Bridges, for a time Poet Laureate, and begin: "Man born of desire/Cometh out of the night,/A wandr'ing spark of fire,/A lonely word of eternal thought/ Echoing in chance and forgot." It has moments of intense imagination, one of which is its opening, in which organ and orchestra are used to splendid effect. The Fantasia had a tough reception; one critic wrote: "When Holst begins his new Choral Fantasia on a six-four chord of G and a C sharp below that, with an air of take it or leave it, one is inclined to leave it." The Choral Fantasia is not modern at all. But it has an air of lonely magnificence that places it high among Holst's best works.

The other work, however, is so typical of the Holst case and that of English music that it illumines both with a peculiar light. It began with a commission from the BBC Military Band for a work. Now, the "symphonic band", as it is called in America, has an honourable tradition, and many serious composers have written for it. Holst responded with a Prelude

* Vaughan Williams's use of the revolting tone quality of the saxophone—its blatant, gibbering insincerity—was a case like Mozart's discovery of the clarinet. The soul of the saxophone, that very miserable thing, is enshrined in several works by Vaughan Williams, impaled by a big man's scorn.

and Scherzo which he called, unexpectedly, *Hammersmith*.* In the 1950s it gradually dawned on the more perceptive English musicians that *Hammersmith* is one of Holst's finest works. Since then it has been recorded several times and a miniature score has been published. Hammersmith and Sheppey are a long way from Samarkand, Venice, the Garden of Fand, or any other probable places where composers have found inspiration. But Holst discovered what many of us found at that time in London —a strange inner enchantment which had nothing to do with prosperity (there was a depression on) but which was a product of the dusty London streets themselves. It was part of Holst's philosophy that the commonplace could be transfigured if one made contact with its spiritual significance, but I feel fairly certain that no one will do a *Hammersmith* for modern New York, Chicago or Tokyo.

Besides, this was, perhaps, the first full dawn of consciousness that the English musical renaissance was on. Elgar and Delius had fallen silent, and had not much longer to live, but their works, although not appreciated at their full worth, formed a part of the background of English musical awareness. Holst, too, was soon to die, but he was at the height of his powers. Bax, Vaughan Williams, Bridge and Ireland were pouring out characteristic music, the picturesque fringe in the shape of War- lock, Lambert, Sorabji, Berners and the rest was active, and the young men were coming up: Walton, Tippett (b. 1905), Moeran (1894–1950) and Britten (1913–1976). The London concert seasons were moving into a period of glory, and inter- national artists and conductors performed at Queen's Hall— this beloved place was entering into its great time. In spite of the depression London was buzzing with excitement, and for some years the terrible shadow of Hitler would not begin to darken Europe. It was a moment of equipoise, and for those who cared about English music triumph was thrilling in the air.

Humbert Wolfe could write of London River "and night acquainted with the long purple reaches of the Thames": a

---

* When the Eastman-Rochester Wind Band applied, twenty years later, to the publishers for material in order to perform it, those publishers replied that it was not issued by them, and the band had to work hard to convince them that it was.

Thames much as Whistler had painted it, and heard as an august and spiritual presence in the great bass figures that underlie Holst's *Hammersmith* with darkness, meditation and mystery. The curious thing is that even after the squalling music of the "Saturday night crowds" begins, the peace continues; the river is felt to be flowing on unheard, and so is the meditation. The sheer stridency of the Scherzo sections is bold in the extreme; to risk such blatant vulgarity against the sublime meditation of the river music is to risk much. The Scherzo is beautifully constructed, not just in technical terms, but in musical and psychological terms also. The coming and going of the riotous noise over the majestic meditation is calculated with the utmost sensitivity, and the final impression is one of peace. *Hammersmith* is important not only for its intrinsic value as music, but for the uncanny way in which it—and perhaps also "The Dream City" and John Ireland's London Overture —captures the atmosphere of London at an important moment in our musical history.

Much of the squalor that made Victorian London one of the pest-houses of the world had been cleared up, but the picturesqueness had not departed. And above all the environs of Queen's Hall buzzed with excitement. The great music-publishing houses had not yet departed for the suburbs, the provinces or oblivion; Augeners in Great Marlborough Street, Novellos in Wardour Street, the Oxford University Press in Soho Square, the now defunct Murdoch's, which published virtually all the music of Arnold Bax, in Oxford Street hard by Marble Arch, the new building of Boosey and Hawkes at the top of Regent Street, just over the road from Queen's Hall, and many small businesses in the side streets off Oxford Street created an atmosphere indescribable to those who did not know it. Hot and dusty summer just before the Proms began, with the new Telefunken records in the shop windows, a sense that Europe was becoming available at last, and yet that English music was taking its place in the great concert of Europe: *Hammersmith* caught and enshrined that unique combination of excitement and peace.

Arnold Bax and Frank Bridge also produced works in 1930, the latter one of his most important. Bax introduced three pieces: one, the *Overture to a Picaresque Comedy*, is one of the few works of his that has remained popular through all the changes in his fortunes; the second was the subtle and poetic *Nonet*; the third the seldom played and superb *Winter Legends*. The last is for piano and orchestra, in three movements, and almost constitutes another symphony. The mood is stormy and powerful, and the writing for both piano and orchestra glitters with virtuosity.

The Frank Bridge piece was the first of his final masterpieces, the large-scale orchestral works which are his most cogent claim to be considered a significant composer. This was the eloquent *Oration* for cello and orchestra, the longest work Bridge had so far written, and the most massive. It is in the tradition of Bartók or even Berg, a sombre work of progressive harmony and immense power. Bridge's harmony, always radical, had become very advanced by now, and the press was turning against him as a consequence. Not only polytonality, but long passages of dense chromatic discord in which tonality became very tenuous, increased in his work, and his melodic lines began to abound in compound intervals. *Oration* contains a great variety of music, with those mercurial changes of mood and texture which characterise late Frank Bridge. The scoring is the vehicle for some strange and uncanny imaginings; the end in particular is haunted, in a manner common to much of Bridge's late work.

John Ireland's Piano Concerto in E flat was played for the first time at a Promenade concert in Queen's Hall on 2 October 1930, with the usual conductor, Sir Henry Wood, and Helen Perkin—with whom Ireland had at that time an equivocal friendship—at the piano. It is unlike any earlier English concerto, while remaining quintessentially English. Its finest predecessor, Bax's Symphonic Variations, is very different in scale, spirit and technique—a vast and stormy Nordic landscape. Ireland's concerto is more on the scale of those of Prokofiev, three of whose piano concertos had been written by this time, but is otherwise unlike them. To the present writer it suggests the Chelsea of the 1920s, and is linked with the London Pieces for piano (1917–20) and the later London Overture (1936). There is a mysterious slow introduction to the first movement, and in the slow central movement some sombre moments, but for the rest it is full of that wistful gaiety which is so much England, Chelsea, John Ireland. The high spirits of the first and third movements dance with sunshine, the third movement being the familiar Ireland toccata, but the heavy brass adds another dimension to the music, foreshadowed by the percussion outburst which leads to it from the slow movement. But the heart of the work is the extraordinary episode in the finale in which solo piano and solo violin seem to be playing a passage from a sonata together; wistful to the point of tears, a heart-searching melody of lad's love in an innocent world before the winter came.* This is a wholly lovely work, which any country but ours would cherish as its authentic voice.

Peter Warlock's death—presumably by suicide—in the last days of 1930 closed an era in English music, and subtly changed the whole musical scene. However beautiful and accomplished his songs may be, it must be admitted that his life was too short, and his output too small, to make him a composer of major significance. Nevertheless, he was a figure of major significance; he featured in no less than six novels, including two masterpieces by major writers, Aldous Huxley's *Antic Hay* and D. H. Lawrence's *Women in Love*. The whole period of his activity— roughly from about 1910 to his death in 1930—is permeated with his personality; he affected not only the small but rowdy group that surrounded him and Cecil Gray, but a wider field which included Epstein, Augustus John, Robert Nicholls, Lawrence, Huxley, Bartók, Delius, Moeran, Lambert and many other figures of the time. As Cecil Gray writes in his biography, no one who knew Warlock could forget him; like him or loathe him, he remained in their memory. "The peculiar glamour and enchantment of those days, and they were many, remain indelibly associated with Philip [i.e. Warlock] in one's mind; it is almost as if he created this halcyon quality of perfect spring and early summer skies—as if it emanated from him, so to speak, and had no independent existence apart from him." There was, actually, something of this feeling about the whole period, in spite of the mounting social and political distress; and even in

* The tune is actually by Helen Perkin.

the Thirties it continued—a sense that music had an infinite meaning and joy, a radiance that in later years was not to be found upon the earth. I doubt if it emanated from Peter Warlock; it was the spirit of the English musical renaissance itself.

Among those who obviously did not like Warlock was Sir Thomas Beecham, who in his biography of Delius portrays Warlock as a callow and opinionated young puppy. In fact Warlock was far ahead of his time in musical sensibility, not only in his recognition and appreciation of major European composers who were at that time considered by the English to be either bogus or insane—Bartók, Berg, Schoenberg and the rest—but in his discovery of ancient music, which is now such a cult. Warlock's realisation that the *Orfeo* of Monteverdi is one of the operatic masterpieces of all time is particularly impressive. It has taken us forty years to catch up with him. His temperament was insecure, and he was in some ways a social menace, but musically Beecham was wrong and Warlock right. Warlock's book on *The English Ayre*, his collaboration with Gray on the first monograph on Gesualdo and his publications of Tudor and Jacobean music are not unworthy of the English musicological tradition that was being founded by Richard Terry and Arnold Dolmetsch. I have written that his output was small and confined to short works. But this is almost true of such a major figure as Hugo Wolf, and some of Warlock's best songs can almost be set beside those of Wolf. Gray exaggerated his importance; but with Henry Purcell and Benjamin Britten he has written some of the greatest English songs.

Of these "The Curlew" must take pride of place; it emphasises the fact that his work shows a steady improvement right up to his tragically premature death, and that his last songs are his best; also that his music becomes steadily more radical. Such things as the Webster dirges for chorus, "Corpus Christi", "The Frostbound Wood" and "The Fox" reveal a radical bent that might have carried Warlock far.

Gray recalls his last tragic outburst at the musical inadequacy of England:

We arranged, however, to meet after the concert at a public-house near by, and I must confess that in spite of what I had told him to expect I was unprepared and even alarmed to observe the state of misery and dejection into which the performance [of some of his part songs] had plunged him. After a short space of devastating silence he suddenly burst out into a furious diatribe against the infamy of compromise—how it were better to have done with everything, once and for all, rather than tolerate the mediocre, the second-rate, the imperfect; how one should make no concessions and resolutely insist on everything or nothing.

The time was just before Christmas, a feast that Warlock had celebrated with the loveliest of modern carols, but which he hated venomously, as many sensitive people do. On the morning of 17 December, shortly after his last meeting with Gray, Peter Warlock put out his cat and turned on the gas.

6

BETWEEN THE WARS: II
1931—1939

ON THE CONTINENT the neo-classical style had become fashionable among a group of influential composers who were in the main conservative, although they numbered Stravinsky among their ranks, and Schoenberg was for a while affected by the idea. The early 1930s marked its peak and its decline. Stravinsky had just completed his neo-classical Violin Concerto, one of the most typical, and best, works of this phase of his career. French neo-classical music was much played, although the popular press made jokes about "back to Bach" and "Mozart with wrong notes". But Webern had recently finished his Symphony Op. 21, a masterpiece of concentrated serialism, two short movements pregnant with meaning, the second of which is a theme and variations; this was also the period of Schoenberg's opera, *Von Heute auf Morgen*, which was something of a portent; the first attempt to write a serial comic opera. Their works hardly touched the musical life of England at all. The Stravinsky was accepted, more or less, but the Webern and Schoenberg might not have existed as far as England was concerned.

In 1931 the National Government was formed under Ramsay MacDonald, the leader of the Labour Party, and the residue of that party (which never forgave him) formed a tiny Opposition and went into the wilderness until 1945. It is true that English music was inspired by a sense of rebirth, and our standards of performance were rising fast; a certain euphoria was in the air in English musical life. On the other hand there was economic and political crisis, mounting unemployment, and a great contrast between the lives of the rich and the poor. It was the age of community singing and hiking, but also of Hunger Marches.

A new Bax symphony was becoming an annual event. The year 1931 saw the birth of No. 4.* Bax continued to worry about the too introspective and rhapsodic nature of his work, and the Fourth Symphony, in consequence of this, was more extrovert, athletic and brilliant than the first three. Like No. 3 it is melodically attractive and formally weak. The first movement escapes the weakness of the Third's first movement, which was an allegro with a central slow movement; by what sounds like an heroic effort Bax keeps the tempo steady throughout. But the music is sectional, the progress jerky and restless. The slow movement repeats the formulae of that of the Third, but lacks the remote and haunting magic of the earlier work. The finale is scrappy and unconvincing. Bax tries to pull the music together in the Epilogue, a *Tempo di marcia trionfale* of considerable power; but the Epilogue is unconvincingly prepared, it just happens at the end, rather inconsequentially. In spite of these strictures the Fourth emerges as a work of immense charm and picaresque incident; but Bax was in trouble, and he knew it.

His last symphonic poem, *The Tale the Pinetrees Knew*, was also written at this time, and, with its arch and cumbersome title, is the weakest of the symphonic poems. Unlike the Fourth Symphony it is a convincing sonata structure, but also unlike the Fourth its material is vague and insipid. It leans heavily on Sibelius's *En Saga*; although the model is said to have been *Tapiola*, it is nothing like *Tapiola*. It in no wise compares with the wartime trilogy of *The Garden of Fand, November Woods* and *Tintagel*.

Sibelius was in the air, and Cecil Gray's book on him, published in 1931, helped to push the English musical public towards the first of those Scandinavian cults to which it has been subject ever since. In 1930 the Finnish government sponsored the issue of gramophone records of the first two symphonies, conducted by Kajanus, issued by Columbia, and with an English orchestra. In 1932 the Sibelius Society was founded, and by

---

* Like No. 2, the Fourth Symphony received its first performance in America, this time by the San Francisco Symphony Orchestra under Basil Cameron. Its first English performance was at a Courtauld–Sargent concert.

the outbreak of war most of Sibelius's major works had been recorded by the Society, including Beecham's magnificent performance of the Fourth Symphony.

Let there be no mistake; Sibelius is a giant. But his cult in England and America was profoundly suspect. He was being used as a smoke-screen to hide more radical developments in Europe, and raised as an anti-Pope to Schoenberg. As yet Walton was untouched by the Sibelius influence, which was to affect his First Symphony; his offering for 1931 paid more homage to Stravinsky. This was *Belshazzar's Feast*, a piece of choral barbarism with text arranged by Osbert Sitwell from Daniel v and Psalms 137 and 81, with passages from Revelations xviii. It has rapidly become one of the most popular works in the repertory. Its forces are large without rivalling those of Mahler's Eighth or Berlioz's *Requiem*, but its power is tremendous, a glittering piece of compositional virtuosity, and strongly original, in spite of the distinct Stravinskyan influence on a few places, notably the praise of the false gods. There are passages of intense lyricism, especially in "By the Waters of Babylon", the use of a single shouted word ("Slain!") that is a stroke of genius in its context, and a final impact that, even after almost 50 years, is stunning.

At this time came two large-scale works for piano and orchestra: Vaughan Williams's Piano Concerto and Frank Bridge's *Phantasm*. The Vaughan Williams was written for Harriet Cohen, with her small hands; but, as in the similar case of Bax's Symphonic Variations, this concerto demands a pianist of such phenomenal stretch and stamina that Vaughan Williams subsequently arranged it for two pianos and orchestra. Harriet Cohen was unlucky in her dedications: the concerto is one of Vaughan Williams's weakest works, at any rate from this fruitful period. It makes a lot of fuss in a vaguely neo-classical manner, but the trouble is that neither the material nor its treatment is memorable. It is the work's dullness, not its difficulty, that accounts for the fact that it is seldom performed.

Quite different is Bridge's *Phantasm*; this compares in every way with Bax's Symphonic Variations in richness of material and power of development, and is just about the only English work for the medium that does.* The sombre and powerful work is framed within a piano cadenza, and is based on several themes. The development is long and fantastic, with the "Phantasm" theme undergoing sinister metamorphoses, and when the climax comes, led by a persistent drum passage, it is on this same theme, transformed into a towering spectre which gibbers across the orchestra like a vast shadow. This theme has an eerie and unaccountable atmosphere, and its final appearance leads into the piano cadenza, which vanishes quietly into the bass of the instrument. This was another major work by Bridge, and unlike *Oration* it was actually published, in two-piano score, and remained in print for a while.

The year 1932 saw the appearance of another Bax symphony, and this one revealed that he was out of his bad patch. The form of the Fifth Symphony is virtually flawless, taut and dramatic; it is nearer to conventional sonata style than any previous Bax symphony. The first movement is a brooding, threatening, legendary affair which grows out of the opening drum beat and a menacing theme in the Chalumeau region of the clarinets. The slow movement opens with a remarkable and thrilling effect; under an arch of ice, etched by the violins high on their E strings and a glittering harp figure, the trumpets blaze out in ringing fanfares; "The cataract blows its trumpet from the height." The finale starts, ominously and significantly, with what Bax calls a "liturgical" theme. The conflict of the first three symphonies has been resumed. It quickly gives way to a wild dance, on a subject that emphasises the unity of the symphony. After a while the liturgical theme can be heard growing in the texture, and it grows in strength until it is thundered out by the whole orchestra in the Epilogue; another astonishing orchestral effect, a modern symphony orchestra playing medieval-sounding chant. The Fifth ushers in the last sequence of Bax's symphonies, in storm and stress. The Cello Concerto of the same year is slighter, gently romantic, a not very striking work.

* I heard the first performance of *Phantasm*, with the composer conducting and Kathleen Long at the piano, on 10 January 1934, the fifth of a series of six concerts of English music organised by the BBC.

On 30 January 1933 Adolf Hitler became German Chancellor, and the "Long Week-End" began to move towards its appalling end. The economic crisis was still with us, with dole queues longer than ever; in this situation the Government was more concerned with avoiding socialism than containing the dictators. The music of the year was not very important: Bax's almost unknown Scherzo for orchestra, remarkable only inasmuch as it used to be said that Bax couldn't write a scherzo (he wrote a number), and Holst's Brook Green Suite and Lyric Movement for viola and orchestra, the latter a gentle piece that John Ireland might have written, although Ireland would have given it a more memorable tune. Then there was a new work by John Ireland himself which was an exception to the otherwise unexciting output of the year: the Legend for Piano and Orchestra, one of his best works. It was based on two experiences; the first was in a Downland church that had a leper's squint, the other a vision he had of dancing children while he was sitting on the Downs.* He wrote to his friend the occultist Arthur Machen about this vision, and Machen replied with a laconic postcard: "Oh, you've seen them too." The resultant piece is a single movement for piano and orchestra, beginning with horn calls and mysterious passages for piano, the leper's squint music, and proceeding to an equally mysterious dance-like middle section for the ghostly children. It is a complex score, covering a variety of moods, with virtuoso piano writing. This is one of Ireland's best large-scale works; indeed, it is one of his few completely successful extended scores. Its serious and indeed uncanny atmosphere recalls at moments the Bridge of *Phantasm*.

In 1934, within a few months of each other, all the founding fathers of the English musical renaissance died: Elgar, Delius and Holst. There was an especial poignancy about the death of Elgar, because it had become known, a couple of years

---

* Ireland was in the habit of frequenting the South Downs between Storrington and Angmering—he eventually bought the windmill at West Chiltington and lived there during the last years of his life. The South Downs like the Channel Islands inspired a number of his works; the Downland Suite, the Concertino Pastorale, the piano pieces *Equinox* and *Amberley Wild Brooks*, and also this Legend.

previously, that he had broken his long self-imposed silence and was at work at no less than three major compositions.*

It was Edward Elgar who raised music in England from the dead, and the renaissance was his. He was the greatest of the three composers who began the twentieth-century revival in England, and although he contributed a surprisingly small number of major works, a high proportion of these works became in time accepted masterpieces. He was the first English composer since Purcell to establish a respectable status, and his greatness rests not only in his works, and in what he did for English music generally, but in what he overcame to achieve this. In breaking the strangle-hold of the respectable amateur on English music he made the renaissance possible, and started the slow growth of a viable musical environment in England, which had lacked such a thing for two hundred years.

His reputation in the future is likely to rest on the two Symphonies, the two Concertos, the three Overtures, the Enigma Variations and the Introduction and Allegro; and of the choral works, *Gerontius*. As far as *The Apostles* and *The Kingdom* are concerned, Elgar himself had already reached the conclusion, half-way through *The Kingdom*, that this kind of music was dead; and he was right. *Gerontius* was a revolutionary work in the England of the 1900s; the other two were regressive, belonging more in spirit to the Victorian age. Elgar knew it; and did not finish the trilogy. The conflict in his nature was between the radical and the conservative, and we owe all that is best of him, including *Gerontius*, to the radical side of his nature.

The conflict extended into his social and married life, and right into his innermost spirit. The image of him as a deeply conservative, soldierly man whose natural environment was state occasions in the presence of royalty has been steadily eroded since his death. His dangerous sense of humour emerged first, and then his emotional crisis over the Birmingham lec-

* These were the Third Symphony, a Piano Concerto, and an opera, *The Spanish Lady*, based on Ben Jonson's *The Devil is an Ass*. The BBC were sufficiently confident of performing the symphony they had commissioned that they announced its first performance; in the event, Adrian Boult, a great Elgarian and friend of the composer, conducted the First Symphony in its place.

tures; it became known that he was so emotional that he was not incapable of making a public scene. The fact that he was of plebeian origins, and that society crucified him for it in his youth and remembered it until late in his life, is a recent discovery. He was proud that he had achieved so much, in spite of his humble background. He once wrote "Beware of the Dog" under a list of his honours, and when the procession conferring on him the freedom of Worcester passed the little music shop at the window of which his father stood watching, Elgar paused to stand bareheaded before that humble man.

One should not expect Elgar to be too consistent in his attitudes, and he seems to have been politically entirely naïve, not realising, except perhaps unconsciously (hence some of his conflicts), how his emotional intuitions conflicted with the views ostensibly held by his public self. But Alice Elgar was single-minded and quite consistent in her attitudes. He was radical, emotional, and unconventional in his essential nature, and her idea of good behaviour was the opposite of these things; but without them he would not have been a genius. It must be evident by now that to expect Edward Elgar to have behaved like the product of an English public school is a joke as black as it is pitiful. He was the greatest composer England has produced because he was as he was. All this would be an intrusion in bad taste if it were not for the fact that so many people have called him an enigma, and questioned his behaviour. It was precisely what we would expect under the circumstances, and enigmas arise from not facing the truth.

It is an extraordinary coincidence that Delius, Elgar's opposite, yet the one composer of the older generation nearest to him in stature, should have died in the same year. Since 1928 he had composed, with Eric Fenby's help, *Songs of Farewell*, and a number of works based on old materials, including the *Idyll*, rehashed from *Margot-le-Rouge*. Elgar took on the establishment on its own ground, with a curious combination of complicity and defiance, fighting half himself; Delius scorned the establishment, going his own way with a sarcastic attitude towards the whole of English convention and respectability. Beecham's curious funeral oration, made at the graveside at Limpsfield, rings hollow and false. What would the cynical old atheist have said to the thought that his spirit was benignly watching the whole absurd proceedings? Perhaps Beecham was overcome with doubt as to whether Delius should have been buried in England in any case. Fenby, who knew him better than anyone else, thought it quite wrong. If Delius warmed at all towards England at the end it was due to Beecham's propaganda for his music, culminating in the Delius Festival. As he departed from that Festival, he asked that his blind eyes should be directed towards our receding coast, and that at any rate has an authentic ring. In the end he cared only for his own music, and honoured only those who honoured it.

But if his resting place should have been Grez, no matter what his contempt for English hypocrisy, his music has a persistent Englishness. Technically, in its use of a certain variation technique, its warm, full harmony, its decorative treatment of the wood-wind, and in its combination of the sensuous, the simple and the passionate, the music of Delius claims kinship with all the most typical English music of four hundred years. Besides, he owed everything to English conductors, Beecham, Barbirolli and Wood especially.

Holst died just as his music had reached its best. His last work was a scherzo, designed for an abstract, purely instrumental, symphony that was never finished. This characteristic movement, like so many Holst pieces in scherzo form, is effective and crisp, but with a symphonic sense that was new. His achievement was more fragmentary and tentative than that of Elgar and Delius, but it has been said that it was more in the spirit of the contemporary aesthetic than that of the other two, being austere and objective. As the twentieth century closes, that is seen to be untrue. Mahler is not only the most significant composer of the century but also the most popular composer of today, and in his wake a great Romantic revival is in progress. Holst's austerity and objectivity, once fashionable, are beginning to date as badly as Cubist furniture. Moreover, the progress of music from Mahler through Schoenberg to Webern, Stockhausen and Boulez has left Holst without any pretensions to modernity at all. Like Vaughan Williams he was a reactionary. But his achievement outweighs his historical position. Apart from one great instance, his influence was largely on amateurs;

to an extent his teaching helped to create the enormous audience for classical music today. His style died with him, and the one composer who showed his influence and was badly affected by his death was Vaughan Williams. If Holst had been granted his friend's iron constitution and great life-span it might have been seen in the end that Holst was the greater composer of the two. He was certainly the more learned and consistent.

The same period that saw the death of the founders of the renaissance saw the production, by the next generation of composers, Vaughan Williams, Bax and Walton, of symphonies that may be their respective composers' masterpieces. Vaughan Williams's Symphony No. 4 in F minor was performed for the first time on 10 April 1935, by the BBC Symphony Orchestra under Adrian Boult, who wrote to the composer afterwards, "I got the bit between my teeth." I was there, and in common with everyone else I was taken aback by the stark violence of the work. The opening harmony, *fortissimo* on the whole orchestra, is in minor seconds, bare and exposed, the sheer sound of it is overwhelming. The references to *Job* are also significant, particularly as they are derived from the Satan music. The Symphony in F minor is mildly radical in a context of Vaughan Williams's other music; but in a world context we have to place it beside such established masterpieces as Stravinsky's *Le Sacre du printemps*, Bartók's *The Amazing Mandarin*, Schoenberg's *Pierrot Lunaire* and *Erwartung*, and Berg's *Wozzeck* and *Lulu*, most of which predate the F minor Symphony by a number of years. Webern's Symphony was written in 1928. In this context the F minor Symphony, magnificent though it is, suddenly looks extremely old-fashioned; which indeed, at that date, it was. It is really remarkable to note the fuss that was made about it, and one must say that it reveals how deeply conservative England still was.

There are a number of ways in which the F minor is kin to the *Pastoral*; both are basically hard, and free from a certain softness of texture and sentimentality which occasionally occur in the music of Vaughan Williams—the Max Bruch touch. It is dedicated to Arnold Bax, but more than in any other work by Vaughan Williams it reveals the direct influence of Holst. The

Scherzo might have been written by Holst, so like it is to his usual style. From now on Vaughan Williams seems progressively to have lost direction, even, after the Sixth Symphony, to have gone into decline. The death of Holst is all the more to be deplored; it is just such advice as Holst had to give that makes the progression from the *London Symphony*, through *Job* to the F minor Symphony that of Vaughan Williams's most convincing work.

As for the rest of the F minor Symphony, after that shattering opening in seconds, the slow movement sounds as though a self-conscious effort was being made to write something different from Vaughan Williams's usual slow movements, with results that at times suggest pre-atonal Schoenberg; but the movement is perfectly fitting in its context. The transition from Scherzo to finale was copied from Beethoven's Fifth, as Vaughan Williams admitted, and the finale manages to sound tremendous in spite of its exceedingly silly main theme; the Epilogue is perhaps the most superb music Vaughan Williams ever wrote. The critics of the time dubbed as "atonal" a symphony that insists throughout on F minor and its related keys.

The second of these three symphonies was William Walton's First. Walton is a slow worker, and this is a big work; moreover, the first movement operates at such a pitch of intensity that a finale problem is automatically posed.* Like Vaughan Williams's Fourth it is a symphony of tension and violence, but it is also a longer work, more complex, more heavily scored; and if the Vaughan Williams is conceded to be a statement of something very like anger, Walton's symphony is dominated by tension, and builds slowly to a violence so extreme that at the time of its first performance the long-delayed finale was thought to have overreached itself. It is an odd fact that whereas Vaughan Williams's F minor symphony, with its regulation first and second subjects, its insistence on F minor and its daylight scoring, was called atonal, the far more tonally ambiguous Walton attracted no such sobriquet. The organising principle of Walton's symphony is not block chords in keys as in the

* Walton was so long in completing the symphony that it was performed without its finale by Sir Hamilton Harty and the London Symphony Orchestra in November 1934. The complete symphony was played for the first time in October 1935.

Vaughan Williams, but restless discords held within tonality by incessant pedal points and bass ostinati. The general norm of dissonance is higher than in the Vaughan Williams, in spite of the minor seconds at the opening of the F minor Symphony, and the construction of a subtlety such as to render the Vaughan Williams simplistic by comparison. The tension of the first movement is well-nigh unbearable, and when it ends in explosive chords, its question unanswered and its tension unresolved, it is followed by a lighter-footed but equally explosive scherzo marked *"con malizia"*. As an early critic remarked, against whom directed? Motiveless, undirected malice is a daunting thought. The dumbfounding answer would appear to be that the malice was directed against Walton's late girl-friend, whom he had just changed for someone else; the delay in completing the finale was also partly due to this circumstance.

The symphony was written against an historical back-cloth of mounting terror; here in England, where the improvement in our artistic environment was beginning to be felt, we lived vicariously, more and more conscious that we but usurped our lives. The fate of Guernica seemed to say to us: you are next. London, Vienna, Paris, you are next. With most of my intelligence and temperament I resist the idea that music expresses anything but itself, but I have to admit that Walton's First Symphony conveys for me that unique and powerful atmosphere as nothing else does. Do we employ so great an orchestra, such terrible rhythms and discords, such volleying storms of sound, to announce that we have changed our girl-friend? No more than that the furious anger of Vaughan Williams's F minor Symphony was just Uncle Ralph in a paddy. Is Walton joking, or hiding something? When we take the last of the three, Bax's Sixth, equally violent and filled with foreboding, but in Bax's personal way, and reflect that they all appeared together, then we must feel that all three symphonies must have owed something to the tragic tension of the times.

Bax's Sixth Symphony was also given its first performance by Sir Hamilton Harty, at a Royal Philharmonic Society concert on 21 November 1935. It was written in 1934, mainly in Morar, Inverness-shire, one of the most remote and wild parts of the Western Highlands, Bax's principal workshop at this time. Like the preceding, and the following, symphonies, the Sixth opens at a higher degree of dissonance than he had used before—a harsh and grinding sound. The first movement begins *moderato*, but with immoderate music. Bax uses an ostinato, played by most of the basses, including the third trombone. Over this a shrill figure outlined in seconds is heard in wood-wind and horns; this music continues for eight pages, and culminates in a mighty series of modulatory chords, a vertiginous wrench in eight bars from C sharp minor to C minor. True to Bax's usual practice, the ensuing Allegro is the opening material speeded up in the new key; doubly speeded up, since the ostinato resumes, not only in *allegro* but also with halved note-values. Bax by no means always writes a clear-cut second subject, and even here this wistful, tentative tune for flutes in the quietest part of their compass is derived from earlier material. Bax had always been affected by the fate of frail beauty in a violent world, and in the most obvious of musical terms this movement seems to comment on this aspect of reality. The slow movement suggests a development of the process; it opens in a mood that seems to recall Dante's happiness remembered in sorrow. The melody that haunts it is of great beauty, and it alternates with a lamenting Scotch snap. In the course of the movement the first tune takes on a ghostly aspect, and passes away at the end in a procession of ghosts over a pulsing drum.

The finale is a scherzo of sinister aspect, introduced by two subjects, one aspiring, the other liturgical, and it culminates in a climax that suggests some psychic force of explosive power at last released. At the climax of its destructive violence the liturgical theme is heard. As the fragments sink broken into silence the Epilogue enters a world of beauty and peace, but hardly this world. The long horn solo unites the two themes, and all the horns intone a last benediction, and with their final chords the music turns to the major. The great conflict that had raged in Bax's symphonies from the first was finally resolved, and his last and seventh symphony was to be untouched by it.

Alban Berg died in 1935. He left as his last testament a Violin Concerto written "In Memory of an Angel", the angel being the daughter of Alma Gropius, Gustav Mahler's widow, and a second opera, *Lulu*. He was to become, for the ordinary music-lover, the most approachable of the Second Viennese School, although at this time in England he was little known and less understood.

In 1935 Ernest Moeran published two small pieces for orchestra, *Lonely Waters* and *Whythorne's Shadow*. Moeran's father came from Norfolk, but his mother from Ireland, and the two geographical influences joined innumerable musical ones to contend within him. The Norfolk influence can be seen in *Lonely Waters*, which is based on a fragment of Norfolk folk-song; it is a lovely piece, and the scrap of melody floats wraith-like in a texture which evokes the mystery and the strange light of the Broads. *Whythorne's Shadow* is an arrangement of a part-song by that composer, the words of which compare the flatterer with a shadow that bends and sways with the flattered person; so Moeran's piece is itself a pretty piece of flattery. Moeran's most substantial lessons were from John Ireland, but his studies were interrupted by the 1914–18 War, in which he was wounded.

In this same year Arthur Bliss wrote one of his most impressive works: Music for Strings, a large-scale composition in three movements, which was given at the Salzburg Festival of 1935 by the Vienna Philharmonic Orchestra under Adrian Boult. Behind this work lies the Introduction and Allegro of Elgar; Bliss's music was becoming more and more Elgarian as the years went by. It is a work of restrained romanticism and rich, if English, colouring, recalling, in some of its aspects, the harmonic flavour and melodic shape of the Clarinet Quintet of 1931. In this year also Bliss collaborated with H. G. Wells in the spectacular film *The Shape of Things to Come*. The music Bliss wrote for it has good claims to being the finest film music ever composed. (The March is a popular concert item even today.) Both film and music were filled with the terror and tension of the 1930s.

A new symphonist appeared this year in Edmund Rubbra (b. 1901), another late developer, pupil of Cyril Scott (1879–1970), Holst and Vaughan Williams. From 1935 to 1941 he was to write four symphonies, his best-known, the Fifth, appearing in 1949. A pupil of Cyril Scott is a rarity,* one of Holst or Vaughan Williams much less so. It is hard to find any element of Scott's elegance and lightness of touch in Rubbra, and not much of Holst's clarity and economy; the prevailing influence is of Vaughan Williams, although there is a certain madrigalian strain. But Rubbra's First Symphony is unlike any of his subsequent ones: gawky, with angular scoring, spiky but brimming with life and rhythmic impetus, it seems to owe a lot to Holst. The Scherzo, with the title "Périgordine", exhibits a light touch and a sense of humour which he was to lose. Rubbra's later symphonies appeal to many, but seem to me stereotyped, thick in texture and orchestration, and increasingly reactionary in technique.

Constant Lambert had pursued an erratic career from the first, dogged by ill-health and bohemianism, and later crippled as a composer by his strenuous, and largely unthanked, efforts on behalf of English ballet. But from 1932 he had been working on a large-scale composition for chorus and orchestra, *Summer's Last Will and Testament.* Summer's last will and testament was the plague, and the work is a setting in suite-like form of various Tudor plague poems, mostly familiar. Will Summer was also Henry VIII's jester, so the very title has a sardonic humour. The piece was not a success on its first performance on 29 January 1936; the public expected something lighter and more frivolous from Lambert—forgetting, if they had ever known, his elegiac side, as exemplified by his Piano Concerto written in memory of Peter Warlock. Even after the war ill-luck pursued it, and a performance by the BBC led one critic to describe it as "not even competent". This is quite untrue; whatever else one can say about it, it is technically brilliant, as well as—in the present writer's opinion—haunting, vivid, sardonic, and beautifully constructed. It is old-fashioned in the context of the music that was being written at the time in Europe; but Lambert was never a member of the avant-garde.

* Scott composed a number of large-scale works which are never heard these days (although a group of them has been recorded by Lyrita), and many short piano pieces, once very popular. The two piano concertos, also recorded by Lyrita, are worth remembering, especially the late Second. He seems to have darkened and intensified his style after 1945, although none of the works he wrote were performed.

He championed Sibelius and van Dieren, and this was not forgiven him when the progressive critics came to power in the 1960s. But if you do not look for what is not there, *Summer's Last Will and Testament* remains a powerful work.

Bernard van Dieren had been mortally ill for some time, and on 24 April 1936 he died. His music is little known in the 1970s, but his influence was widespread and his actual achievement far from negligible. Van Dieren exploited a curious kind of dissonant counterpoint, tonal in basis, but so chromatic and with so loose a grip of its tonal centre that during his lifetime his name was often coupled with that of Schoenberg. His music is very different from Schoenberg's, however; it has a Latin lyricism and a sense of almost sixteenth-century flow that contrasts strongly with Schoenberg's Germanic thematicism and rhythmic complexity. Van Dieren went on composing in spite of his ill-health, writing, among other things, an opera, *The Tailor*, a Chinese Symphony, several string quartets, some of them for unusual combinations, and a number of songs, including the exquisite "Spenser Sonnet" for high voice and eleven instruments. At its best his music has a luminous serenity and even ecstasy that is distinctly rare in twentieth-century music. He deserves revival.*

The self-critical John Ireland was always slow to produce large-scale works, but in 1936 came *A London Overture*, one of his most endearing pieces. It was written as a pendant to his *London Pieces* for piano, in much the same way as Butterworth's *Shropshire Lad* Rhapsody was designed as an epilogue to his two sets of Housman songs. London had always fascinated Ireland since his days as a Chelsea organist, and it was the lighter side of the city that touched his imagination. His *London Pieces* are full of sunlight, and his "Ballad of London Nights" of brilliance. *A London Overture* begins with a typical Ireland brooding introduction, but proceeds to a cheeky Allegro based on the bus conductor's cry of "Piccadilly!"; the Lavender Seller's song also appears. The orchestration is both sensuously beautiful and brilliant. This is a splendid overture, one of the greatest of orchestral works inspired by London.

* To the usual disadvantage for English music that van Dieren's music is out of print must be added the extra one that little of it was ever printed.

Between 1935 and 1936 Vaughan Williams composed *Five Tudor Portraits*, and in 1936 was published *The Poisoned Kiss*, an operetta he had been at work on, on and off, since 1926, and which was to be revised again between 1956 and 1957. The *Tudor Portraits* continued some of the tendencies discernible in his music during the previous two decades, with the addition of earthy humour. That humour declines into amateur charades in the opera, which continues the tale of his lack of operatic success; but the *Tudor Portraits* is a considerable work. For alto and baritone soloists, chorus and orchestra, it is a setting of five poems by the sixteenth-century poet John Skelton, sometime Rector of Diss. The two most remarkable numbers are the first and the third: "The Tunning of Elinor Rumming" is an excursion into fairly elementary humour, but "Epitaph on John Jayberd of Diss" is something more. "Elinor Rumming" is enlivened by its pawky orchestration and brilliantly characterful writing for the alto soloist; "John Jayberd" is a perfectly poisonous essay in black humour, a diatribe against a fellow clergyman who provoked Skelton's wrath, in dog-Latin and vile English verse. Pungent, raucous and savage, these two of the portraits indicate how powerful and imaginative he could be when he let himself go.

Short overtures with picaresque titles were something of an addiction with Arnold Bax, and in 1936 he produced two more: *Rogue's Comedy* and *Overture to Adventure*. They are much what might be expected of Bax in this vein: distinguished if not outstanding music, technically accomplished and greatly entertaining. In some respects *Overture to Adventure* points the way to the style of the Seventh Symphony, in spite of its greater brilliance of sound. This year also saw the first performance of one of Bax's best chamber works. The Third String Quartet received its first performance at the Aeolian Hall* in Bond Street; the artists were the Griller Quartet and Harriet Cohen, and the concert also included the Piano Quartet and Piano Quintet. The Third is Bax's finest string quartet; a long work lasting some forty minutes, it is less dramatic, and better written for the medium than the Second. It is neatly constructed, and in a rather spare style which also looks forward to his final works, including the Seventh Symphony.

* Now used by the BBC and no longer the scene of public concerts.

In 1937 King George V died; he was succeeded by the heir apparent, Edward VIII, who was never crowned. William Walton's march, *Crown Imperial*, was written for the coronation of Edward's brother who after the abdication came to the throne as George VI.

It was the year of Vaughan Williams's most impressive excursion into opera, a one-act work based on J. M. Synge's *Riders to the Sea*. This was an unexpected subject for Vaughan Williams. *The Sea Symphony* is not really about the sea, and hardly reflects its sound and smell; it is about spiritual exploration. *The Pastoral Symphony* might, for all its power, be called the "Agricultural Symphony", for Vaughan Williams's interests did not extend to actual wild nature. Synge's play concerns a thoroughly wild and merciless sea, compassion, and fatalistic suffering; in this story of an old Irishwoman's loss of her sons to the sea it is the sea itself that is the chief protagonist. Unlike Vaughan Williams's practice in his other operas, there is no division into arias or tunes here; the vocal style is recitative in the main. But the sea, heard in the orchestra, comments and menaces throughout. It is hard to say, if one came on it new, without knowing who it was by, whether one would identify it as by Vaughan Williams at all. Yet the piece manages to be extremely impressive in spite of the perfunctory and unmemorable vocal parts.

Utterly different is the little piece Vaughan Williams wrote to celebrate the jubilee of Sir Henry Wood. *Serenade to Music* is based on the loveliest tribute ever paid by words to music, the famous passage in *The Merchant of Venice* beginning; "How sweet the moonlight sleeps upon this bank!/Here will we sit, and let the sound of music/Creep in our ears." The sweet words are matched with some of the most melodically inspired music Vaughan Williams was ever to write, set for sixteen solo voices, matched, for the first performance, to sixteen famous English singers of the time who had sung under Sir Henry Wood.

Arthur Bliss developed an interest in the ballet in 1937 which resulted that year in his first and finest essay in the medium, the very dramatic and colourful ballet *Checkmate*. A famous double bill at Sadler's Wells was *Checkmate* and *Job*— and indeed, one needed the radiant optimism of the Vaughan

Williams in the same programme as Bliss's blackly pessimistic mime of the triumph of death over love at a game of chess. Robert Helpmann, tremendous in the athletic part of Satan in *Job*, was also outstanding in *Checkmate*, in the almost static role of the Red King (Love), as various Black Queens (Death) writhed and twisted and raced around him. The music is among the most varied and imaginative Bliss ever wrote.

Sadler's Wells had reached a peak of great richness and achievement, largely through the efforts as conductor, artistic director, and composer of Constant Lambert, whose ballet *Horoscope* was staged in 1937. It is a sign of the best ballet scores that they enter the concert repertory whatever their fate in the theatre, and this is true of *Horoscope*. It marks a great leap forward from the early ballets; the music is splendidly realised, the personality comes through pungently and unmistakably. Although concerned with the dubious theories of astrology (as was also, of course, Holst's *The Planets*), Lambert's music can only be described as Virgilian, and the personal relationships of the story are emotional and real, and only marginally concerned with the stars. He had by now evolved a mature style, one composed of poignant melody, piquant harmony, and a great variety of rhythmic effects, scored in the French manner, lucid and sensuous. An individual mood of gaiety overlaying sadness is the predominant expression.

There was little of importance from Bax, but Frank Bridge signalled another development of his style with the Fourth String Quartet. There is in this work a lightening of the textures after the harsh strength of the Third Quartet, but no compromise in the harmony. It is as if Bridge were seeking a synthesis of his earlier style, that of the *Novelleten* and *Three Idylls* for string quartet with that of the Third Quartet. The mastery of string quartet writing is even more in evidence. He was re-integrating diatonic harmony into a style now completely chromatic, although still tonal.

The name of Benjamin Britten emerged in 1937 with his Variations on a Theme of Frank Bridge. Boyd Neel had been asked to take his string orchestra to the Salzburg Festival, to perform a new English work; he asked Britten, then little known, to write such a piece, and Britten completed the short score in ten days, and produced the finished work in four more weeks. The theme on which the Variations is based is taken from Bridge's Idyll No. 2 for string quartet. In 1937 few Englishmen knew the string writing of Mahler, who influenced Britten strongly; many of Britten's effects are anticipated by Ravel and Debussy. The string writing of today's avant-garde leaves Britten far behind; nevertheless the Variations is a great work, full of Britten's individuality and technical skill. It was appreciated in England at the time, but the English public still regarded Britten with suspicion, a suspicion that was not allayed by his Piano Concerto of the following year.

Karol Szymanowski and Maurice Ravel—radical-conservatives whose music is sensuous, decorative and deeply civilised—both died in 1937. Ravel's is the stronger reputation, even today, but the music of Szymanowski, highly original and inventive, is still performed, and seems to be having a revival in the 1970s. At the time even Ravel's reputation was ambiguous; the Left Hand Concerto, a masterpiece, received a bad press in this country. Things have changed since then.

From an unexpected source there came a large-scale English work: Moeran's Symphony in G minor. It was a sudden excursion into the largest forms by a composer whose music up to that time had been in the main slight and tentative. It attracted a certain amount of hostile criticism at the time—Compton Mackenzie said it "slapped against the mind like a jellyfish". Its faults are formal looseness and a domestic emotional atmosphere, qualities that would appear to appeal to the English public, to judge by the popularity of those minor works of Vaughan Williams that exhibit these qualities. But its endearing nature and a certain inventiveness have outlived its faults, and it is still alive today. The prevalent influences on Moeran are there, raw and undigested: Sibelius, Bax, Ireland, perhaps a touch of Delius; his friendships with Warlock and van Dieren are also in evidence. The strongest source is Sibelius, who is almost quoted once or twice.

By 1938 the availability of wireless music, the development of the gramophone, and the beneficent influence of the BBC on our musical life—especially that of the by now superb BBC Symphony Orchestra under Sir Adrian Boult—had begun to educate the English public into a wider acceptance of music than ever before. This acceptance was to be interrupted, and indeed badly jolted by the war, but by the time Arnold Bax's Violin Concerto was written this increase in sensibility was having some paradoxical results. Ironically, Bax was so upset by what he thought, undoubtedly correctly, to be the exaggerated praise of his Violin Concerto at the expense of his symphonies, that he thought of withdrawing the Concerto altogether.* Conscience may also have had something to do with it. The first movement of the concerto is simply peculiar. It begins in orthodox manner, with an orchestral ritornello followed by the entry of the soloist. But after eleven pages of piano score this first movement abruptly begins again with a Ballad, which lasts for only six pages before a Scherzo intervenes and in eight more pages ends the movement in mid-air, having never started and never arrived. The slow movement is normal enough, but not untouched by that turgidity and congestion which afflicts Bax in his weaker works. The finale is full of the arch stage-Irish atmosphere that spoiled the Oboe Quintet. If Bax writes "Celtic" music after 1920, which he seldom does, then the work is a disaster. Some of Bax's worst faults are on display in this rather cheap piece, and no wonder he suffered a guilty conscience about it.

Vaughan Williams was a very prolific composer—much more prolific than the account of his more important works would suggest. As an example of his normal activity the year 1938, in which he composed no work of significance, is revealing; in this year he wrote: *England's Pleasant Land* (for a pageant); Liturgical Settings of the Holy Communion; "All Hail the Power" (hymn); Double Trio for string sextet; Partita for Double String Orchestra (arranged from the above); *The Bridal Day* (masque); and *Epithalamion*, arranged from the above. To see his work whole, it is important to realise that his work-list consists of many such ephemera, with his important music scattered among a mass of occasional music

---

* It is curious to remember that this concerto was actually popular at the time, for today a salutary readjustment of our values has meant that the symphonies have all been recorded, while that unfortunate concerto has been forgotten.

which is rarely, if ever, performed today; indeed, it belongs to special occasions, and provincial ones at that.

The self-critical John Ireland looked out a trio he had written in 1913, and refurbished it for publication in 1938. What did he do to this 25-year-old work to make it sound as if he had written it in 1938? If one takes the three piano trios in turn, of 1908, 1917, and 1913–1938, each is stylistically in accord with its period in Ireland's life, the Third not excepted. The Third is as expansive and genial as any other work of this, a happy period for him. It is the big, bright sound, the sweeping melodies, and the large scale of the work that seem to place it so firmly in the 1930s rather than 1913.

Alan Rawsthorne (1905–71) made a name for himself in 1938 with his Symphonic Studies. It is possible that he never surpassed this vivid and characterful work. As time went on his music became more diatonic—it was said that his favourite key was C major—and less gruff. It became more introverted and elusive while becoming simpler in material. But this severe and magnificently constructed work, with its complex counterpoint and its rough and dramatic gestures, with a grey orchestration perfectly in accord with its material, created an impression that has lasted.

The years 1938–9 were full of terrified diplomacy. Hitler was busy revising the Versailles Treaty all over the map of Europe, and before each revision there was a flurried attempt by Western statesmen to tell him not to do it, and when he did, not to do it again. Chamberlain's return from Munich on 30 September 1938 with the prospect of "peace for our time", was greeted with hysterical relief; but no one really believed it. The people of England drifted into Armageddon like sleepwalkers.

Britten's Piano Concerto was performed for the first time in 1938, at a Promenade concert with the composer as soloist. His music was attracting attention; but it was felt to be clever (that is, technically competent) and there is no harsher word in English music criticism. Certainly his music at this time suggested emotional immaturity; it was brilliant, beautifully constructed, with a high, clear colouring and a kind of brittle gaiety. Now and then a touch of magic floated over the surface, a beauty wistful and elusive. His music for the documentary film, *Night Mail*, and the film itself, are full of a magic that was soon to depart from the earth, a last clinging to the numinous quality of ordinary things. It was, perhaps, a late development of the pastoral vision of the folk-song composers (rabbits scuttling from the wheels of the express in early dawn); the country dream—had it been anything but the vague pleasure of a townee week-ending, all unaware of the ghost of Captain Swing?—had passed to the suburbs, as the suburbs engulfed the countryside.

Michael Tippett (b. 1905) made less stir than Britten. He came to professional music late, having been a teacher; his First Piano Sonata puzzled England in 1938. It was lucid and diatonic, its slow movement quoted "Searching for Lambs" in the most respectable manner; but its style was elusive, and it was, for all its tonal simplicity, in some strange way modern music. Tippett's First String Quartet had been performed in 1935 (it was revised in 1943); it was tough and intellectual, and made no great impact. Then came his Concerto for Double String Orchestra in the last days of peace, and made a far greater impression. Here was the Tippett style, not fully formed, but recognisable for the first time. Through the elusive complexity of the string writing came several haunting, wistful, very individual tunes. Tunes were not to be a feature of his mature style, and that style developed from now on.

The year 1939 was a full one musically. One would never guess what the prevailing atmosphere was like from John Ireland's Concertino Pastorale for strings. This serenely beautiful work is full of the peace Ireland attained in his later years, after he went to live in Sussex as a near neighbour of his friend Arnold Bax. The three movements of Concertino Pastorale are headed Eclogue, Threnody and Toccata; the music is full of Ireland's characteristic melody, and its rhythms, easy flow and delicate writing for strings give it a poignant beauty unique in English music. It bears a certain superficial resemblance to Frank Bridge's Suite for Strings (1908); but even at that early date the Bridge was more radical in technique, more equivocal in spirit.

Frank Bridge completed in 1938 a short work on which he had been working since 1934, Divertimenti; a curious title for four tiny movements for flute, oboe, clarinet and bassoon. Why the plural? Together they make a Divertimento, but each is too short for a separate work, even if a Divertimento were possible in one movement. This is Bridge's closest approach to the sheer condensation and radical textures of Webern. The concentration of the musical thought is extreme, and, with the String Trio published posthumously, it suggests that Bridge may have been acquainted with Webern's music. The second piece, Nocturne, has a melodic line composed almost entirely of compound intervals, although scored for flute and oboe alone; it looks like some piece by a post-1945 composer. The Scherzetto third movement for clarinet and bassoon is also jagged in outline. The Bagatelle finale has figuration suggesting that of the first movement of Beethoven's Quartet Op. 135, in which a theme is constructed out of crushed grace-notes. The whole work takes only twenty-seven pages of score. An enigmatic and intriguing little masterpiece.

In 1939 there was a World's Fair in New York, and several commissions were made, including works from Arthur Bliss and Arnold Bax. The occasion fitted Bliss perfectly, and he responded with a big, showy Piano Concerto; but the visionary Bax, retiring more and more into himself as old loves faded and the world changed into a place that no longer held a refuge for visions, was a strange recipient for a commission to write something dedicated to "The People of America". Bliss's Piano Concerto was performed for the first time in Carnegie Hall on 10 June 1939; the orchestra was the New York Philharmonic conducted by Sir Adrian Boult, and the soloist was Solomon. It is in three movements, and the composer tried, appropriately enough, to recapture something of the spirit of the late-Romantic display concertos of Tchaikovsky and Rachmaninov. Bliss's Piano Concerto makes a great splash, but does not come up with a single memorable tune. The theme that follows the spectacular opening flourish tries hard to emulate Tchaikovsky, but is an artificial construction of several fussy figures which are repeated too often and refuse to coalesce. The slow movement has a rich, almost Baxian texture, but the material must reluctantly be described as undistinguished. All the material has a contrived air, and in such a work the themes should sound spontaneous to the point of vulgarity; the concerto fancier is deprived of his tune, while the more serious musician is likely to be repelled by the brashness of the work.

Bax responded to his commission, as usual, by making no concessions whatsoever. His Seventh Symphony, duly dedicated to "The People of America", is the last of the visionary seven, a work oddly unlike the others in several respects but in its unusual reticence perhaps the most visionary, if not the most vivid, of them all. The conflict has departed, the work has its very being in some remote country of the spirit, but the vision is held at arm's length, contemplated over an abyss of time. Put more technically, this is recognisably a Bax symphony, but few if any of the obsessive Bax fingerprints are there. The circus animals have deserted; and it is astonishing, and revealing, to discover that in the end he did not need them.

The opening is deceptive. After the usual pedal-point in the bass has been established a theme enters in the clarinets that looks like a twin to that which opens the Fifth Symphony. But there is no slow introduction; the tempo is plain *allegro* from the first bar. The effect is entirely different. No compound theme in the bass urges on a tempo that is already fast; there is no trace of the ubiquitous motto theme of the First Symphony; no liturgical theme menaces the shadows that are not there. It is as clear as sunshine. The first big climax is marked *Poco largamente*, but it is over quickly, and most unusually succeeded by *Molto vivace*; the thematic material is good, but plain, the orchestration lean. But the first movement, as usual, is a vast structure, and it ends with a long, quiet coda.

The slow movement, too, is different; it has been called Bax's only unsuccessful slow movement, but that is not necessarily so. The cor anglais solo is different, and once more there are less notes than usual. But at 10 in the score comes a more typical "In Legendary Mood", and the lower winds sing out a typical Bax melody—and that is always a term of praise. Throughout the symphony there are a number of passages in which the brass choir plays alone, almost in the manner of Bruckner, and it happens even here, in the slow movement.

The climax, when it comes, is less noisy and passionate than in any previous Bax symphony. The die-out of this movement is long, quiet, and beautiful.

The finale is once more exceptional; it is a theme and variations. There is a slow introduction, with the ghost of the slow movement of the Fifth in evidence in an opening fanfare for horns under string tremolos. The theme is plain, and the variations which follow take the course of the usual Bax finale; but the plainness of the theme, which is simple but far from weak, colours the music with the same poise and understatement that marks the whole symphony. The scoring is still sparse, but exceptionally beautiful, with some colouring that is quite original; the last variation is marked *Vivace*, but ends in a massive tutti marked, typically, *Molto moderato e maestoso*. The climax is majestic and noble, but not threatening, violent or passionate, and it leads straight into the Epilogue. This is Bax's longest and quietest Epilogue; it begins with the variation subject in its original form and unadorned except for light accompaniment, *poco cantabile*, in the cellos. The strings have the main material throughout, the rest of the instruments accompanying very lightly; gradually the strings lose momentum and become still, in long chords high in their compass; silence steals upon the scene in utter consummation and luminous peace. It is the end.

On 23 August the Nazis signed a non-aggression pact with the Soviet Union, an act which ripped the last veils of illusion from the eyes of those who understood politics at all. They now regarded war as inevitable. Yet the hope remained that at this peak of culture, one of the great moments in human history, with Picasso, Matisse, Yeats, Eliot, Schoenberg, Stravinsky, Bartók, Strauss and many others in their glory, and the great cities so vast and so vulnerable to air attack, man would not be so foolish; the governments would turn away, at the last moment, from the abyss. On 2 September Hitler invaded Poland, his bombers striking at Warsaw. Chamberlain once more told him to stop it, but it is doubtful if Hitler took him very seriously. At 11 a.m. on 3 September 1939 Chamberlain broadcast to the people of England, in a voice weak with defeat, that England was at war with Germany.

7

INTERLUDE II
1939–1945

3 SEPTEMBER 1939 marked the end of the English musical renaissance as a historical phenomenon. The music that was written after this was no longer the breaking of almost virgin soil, and the founding fathers had done their work and were dead. Elgar's A flat Symphony was the first symphony by an Englishman to live; but by 1939 nearly twenty English symphonies of stature had been composed. After the war the great emotional impetus of the renaissance was over, leaving English music exposed with its backlog of conservatism—an exposure all the more naked because the rest of the world had by now accepted the twentieth-century revolution.

That the folk-music cult was dead, or almost dead, was a blessing. It achieved a certain dubious liberation for Holst and Vaughan Williams, it is true, but it was not an advance, it was a retreat, and if a few lovely but minor works were written under its influence, that influence became more and more destructive as the years passed, until after 1945 those composers, and there were a few, who persisted in this pastoral nationalism destroyed themselves by doing so. Elgar, Delius, Bax, Ireland, Bridge and Walton were unaffected by the cult.

A more elusive thing was the unconscious Englishness of the composers who were untouched by the folk-music influence. The English got folk music more severely than any other nation, but the composers I have listed above as immune from it are usually classed as Romantics, neo-Romantics, or belated Romantics. I do not think these labels are useful or even accurate. English 'romanticism' was quite different from the European sort, and not attached to the mainstream. The romanticism of these composers, if it can be called that, is not a thing that began in the nineteenth century; it has always been there.

It can be found in Dunstable and Taverner, Byrd and Bull, and above all in the Fitzwilliam Virginal Book. This romantic spirit permeated all our arts, and can be found in Keats, Shelley and Wordsworth. The nature music of the Elizabethans ("Will you walk the woods so wild"), the mysticism of Blake and Palmer, the landscapes of Turner and Constable, owe nothing to Europe. In fact, Blake was a universal figure, while Turner was seminal for the Impressionist movement in France, inspiring rather than following a great European school. England's romanticism was its own, born of the isolation I have described in my opening chapter.

If this romanticism was another aspect of our insularity, it was more fruitful and valuable than the folk-song cult; the best works of Vaughan Williams and Holst are not their folk-song compositions. But our music was more insular than the rest of our culture. It can hardly have escaped the informed reader that the socially conscious, essentially socialist poets and writers who came to the fore in the 1930s, Auden, Spender, MacNeice, Isherwood, have not been mentioned by me at all until now. I had no reason to do so, since apart from Britten, in a few immature works, our composers ignored them completely. (Auden, indeed, wrote libretti for Stravinsky and Henze, but for no English composer, apart from those early works of Britten.) The poetry most English composers set was Georgian; even the poetic revolution associated with the names of Eliot and Pound did not affect them.

This was the state of English musical culture when war broke out. It was already evident that the first impetus of the renaissance had waned: the reputations of Elgar and Delius fluctuated, Vaughan Williams was becoming a familiar figure in our musical life, the reputation of Holst was rather remote, Bax and Bridge were ageing but not really accepted, Ireland enjoyed the small reputation he had always had, Walton was still considered to be a coming man, although all his greatest works were in fact written, Tippett was hardly known, Britten was still dismissed as a smart alec, and a host of smaller reputations bobbed along in the flow. English music was in the process of uneasy transition, and what the war would do to it no one knew. Cecil Gray predicted that it would do nothing but good, and wake us from our immemorial illusions; there was profound irony in this opinion.

In 1939 the war itself had never happened. After the initial siren there was no air raid, and after the declaration there was no attack. There was a growing feeling that the whole thing might fizzle out, and the phrase "the phoney war" was born. The Proms, and certain other concerts, continued, and Myra Hess, a pianist of distinction, organised a series of Lunch-time Concerts at the National Gallery, at which a number of English chamber works were given their first performances. Boosey and Hawkes gave a series of more orthodox concerts at which the *Michelangelo Sonnets* were performed for the first time, by Britten and Pears. These masterly and very popular songs increased Britten's reputation among the more musical of the English public, and from now on the "smart alec" label began, very slowly, to fade.

If the left-wing movement of the inter-war years had little effect on English music, by contrast with its significant transformation of literature, pacifism, another potent force in the 1930s but with little effect on literature, began to influence the lives of English composers now that conscription was in force. Frank Bridge had been a conscious pacifist, Ireland a half-hearted one, in the Great War; now both Britten and Tippett joined the 56,000 who registered as conscientious objectors. The war caught Britten in America, with Auden and Isherwood; Auden and Isherwood stayed, Britten returned to face a tribunal. He was given unconditional exemption. Tippett, a rather more articulate man of ideas than Britten, and much less of the public school boy in speech and appearance, was not given exemption and went to prison. Personal tragedy at this time, and his prison experiences, caused Tippett to consult a Jungian analyst, with results which were personally felicitous and musically most fruitful.

It was a strange, fragmented culture which gradually evolved during the war; there was a curious pub-and-air-raid-shelter artistic society, through which the figures of Dylan Thomas, Constant Lambert and Elizabeth Lutyens (b. 1906) drifted inconsequentially. Elizabeth Lutyens was an important phenomenon, although her exact stature as a composer has even now not been decided. From the beginning of her slowly adopted, and initially tentatively held, career as a composer she has been an atonalist and serialist; she was England's first. Others were to follow; but although 3 September 1939 was a real watershed, older composers were still writing. Among the most significant English compositions of the early war years were Bridge's *Rebus*, Ireland's *Sarnia* and Walton's Violin Concerto.

Rebus was Bridge's last completed work; it was finished on 2 August 1940, at his home in Friston, and he died on 10 January 1941. A nine-minute work of fifty pages, its links are with the Fourth String Quartet; like that work *Rebus* belongs to a new phase in Bridge's development, a synthesis of his most advanced late style and a renewed diatonicism. It is a brilliant work, suggesting a more radical *Enter Spring*; in the midst of the brilliance there is quiet music of ghostly import kin to the late String Trio, and a new-found lyricism exemplified by the second subject, which is given initially to that most typical instrument of the English musical renaissance, the viola. In masterly sonata form, this overture raises the question of what a symphony by Bridge would have been like.*

Walton's Violin Concerto was commissioned by Heifetz, and received its first performance on 7 December 1939 in Cleveland, Ohio, conducted by Rodzinsky. England heard it for the first time on 1 November 1941. After this work something inexplicable happened to Walton's style (although the same thing seemed to be happening to Richard Strauss); he abandoned many of his fingerprints, and his music became much less vivid and exciting. *Scapino*, the first version of which came in 1940 (it was revised in 1950), is kin in many ways to the Violin Concerto. Walton's familiar may be thought of as Harlequin, the elusive, mocking, yet romantic figure of the *commedia dell'arte*. He presides over both the Violin Concerto and *Scapino*, although the latter is named for that other, less familiar figure of the same tradition, whose name is derived from the root "to escape". In both works the Harlequin element, capricious, elemental, with kaleidoscopic changes of rhythm, colour and texture, reaches its highest point of development.

* The question is partly answered by the first movement of an unfinished Symphony for Strings in MS. in the Parry Room.

The Concerto combines these elements with the most pungent Latin melody Walton had so far used, a melodic idiom which looks back to the slight but lovely orchestral work *Siesta* of 1926. The first movement is slowish, and its lyrical element is a 16-bar theme of classical beauty and proportion. The second is a Scherzo, full of violent outbursts that contrast abruptly with a garlicky Latin tune. These two elements do not conflict in the Baxian sense, rather do they collide and chase each other, in a kind of diabolical flirtation. In this also there is a sense of the classical Italian comedy; Walton eventually went to live on an Italian island. Affinities with the Viola Concerto present themselves in the finale, but the Violin Concerto is altogether more pungent and brilliant. In fact, with *Scapino*, the Violin Concerto marks the apex of brilliance in Walton's music, a brilliance that now left him.

Ireland's *Sarnia*, "An Island Sequence", was the most accomplished piano work he had written since the Sonata. He had preceded it with a charming suite called *Green Ways*, which seemed almost to be a run-up for the more ambitious work; for *Sarnia* is on a scale and depth suggesting the two sets of *Images* of Debussy, although the technique is nothing like his. It was the last work Ireland conceived in his beloved Channel Islands before they were invaded by the Germans, although it was actually written out in London. The score bears the inscription "The Island of Guernsey was known to the Romans, who named it Sarnia", and the first movement has a quotation from Pomponius Mela describing primitive music heard at night. It has three movements, "Le Catioroc", "In a May Morning" and "Song of the Springtides". The last two are examples of characteristic Ireland short forms, the wistful meditation and the toccata; if Ireland tends to over-use these forms, these are his best examples of them. But "Le Catioroc" is something more, for all that it has its roots in *The Forgotten Rite* and *Mai Dun*. Its atmosphere is more uncanny than that of any other Ireland piece, and savage at the same time; it is a thing of night, sinister and threatening, rising to shrill and spectral sounds, and returning to the night. Another affinity might be Ravel's *Gaspard de la nuit*, and an English one Bridge's *Phantasm*.

Britten's first two successful song cycles were to Italian and French poems respectively; both were daring experiments, but the French cycle was the most daring. *Les Illuminations* is a finer cycle than was generally realised in 1940 when it was performed for the first time. It was dedicated to, and first sung by, Sophie Wyss, but only when the songs were taken up by Peter Pears, Britten's life-long companion and interpreter, did the extraordinary beauty and originality of this set of songs for high voice and string orchestra become apparent. To set the lyrics of Arthur Rimbaud was very daring for an Englishman; perhaps only Mallarmé is more idiomatically French and more obscure than this curious, but glorious, juvenile delinquent whose superb life's work was complete before he came of age. *Les Illuminations* and the *Sinfonia da Requiem* of about the same time are among the least often performed of Britten's non-operatic works; they have never quite lived down the fact that they belong to a time when Britten and his music were suspect.*

It is astonishing how aptly Britten has caught Rimbaud's peculiar accent in *Les Illuminations*; the rhythms exactly match the French poet's vicious patter, and the harmony and writing for strings uncannily suggest the atmosphere of this diabolist mystic. There is just a touch of Mahler (Fifth Symphony) in the string writing, but the French influences are vague and insubstantial; perhaps the Ravel of *Rapsodie espagnol*? Or the same score seen through the eyes of Frank Bridge? There is a glittering fantasy here that Britten never quite recaptured: "J'ai seul la clef de cette parade, de cette parade sauvage."

Many musicians of distinction had been drifting west ever since the Bolshevik revolution. Rachmaninov, Stravinsky and Prokofiev were the first to leave Russia, and of these only Prokofiev returned. The Nazi terror added its quota; Bruno Walter, Schoenberg, and Bartók went to America, Egon Wellesz, Hans Keller and Mátyás Seiber came to England. The effect on the host nations, first France and then America and England,

---

* During the early part of the war the musical press was full of intemperate letters from musicians whose purpose apparently was to hound Britten out of English society altogether; see, for instance, the letter columns of *The Musical Times* during 1940 and 1941, and the writings of one Dora Bright in *Musical Opinion*.

was inevitable. It is doubtful if American orchestras would have reached such a pitch of efficiency if they had been forced to rely exclusively on native conductors. Any country that received Toscanini, Koussevitzky, Leinsdorf, Reiner and Walter was bound to have its orchestral standards raised. In America the influx of composers had a mixed effect. I have always thought that the influence of Stravinsky on American composers has been exaggerated: there is no American *Le Sacre du printemps*. Schoenberg had a more subtle effect. With the possible exception of Elliott Carter, most avant-garde American composers seem to have skipped a generation. They tend to be post-Webern with undigested Satie and Ives, a curious combination seen at its most typical in John Cage.

The phoney war came to an end in May 1940, when the Nazis invaded the Netherlands. A British expeditionary force, cut off, was evacuated from Dunkirk; shortly after France surrendered, and air raids on England began in earnest:

On Sunday, December 8th 1940, Queen's Hall was damaged by 'blast', nearly all the doors and windows being blown out. Temporary repairs were carried out and the Hall was opened for the concert advertised for the following Saturday. On Saturday afternoon, May 10th 1941, the Royal Choral Society (which had migrated to Queen's Hall owing to the closing of the Albert Hall) gave a performance of Elgar's *Dream of Gerontius* with the London Philharmonic Orchestra. The conductor was Dr Malcolm Sargent; Miss Muriel Brunskill, Mr Webster Booth, and Mr Ronald Stear were the soloists. To these artists falls the melancholy distinction of having taken part in the last concert to be given in Queen's Hall. On that night, to quote the official account, "came the Luftwaffe's final fling before its journey to—or towards —Moscow. For five moonlight hours over three hundred bombers dropped great numbers of incendiaries and high explosives. . . ."
At ten o'clock on the morning of Sunday, May 11th, the members of the London Philharmonic Orchestra arrived for the rehearsal of a "Summer Sunday Concert" due to be given

that afternoon. They found clouds of smoke pouring from
the ruined building. . . .*

In fact, Queen's Hall had been destroyed beyond rebuilding,
and many of the London Philharmonic's instruments, left
overnight in the band room, had been destroyed with it. Sir
Henry Wood stood among the ruins and wept. Queen's Hall
was an ugly, beloved building whose acoustics—unlike those
of its notorious sister, the Albert Hall—were among the finest
in the world. Ugly though it was, it had mellowed into that
odd little corner at the top of Regent Street, tucked in beside
Broadcasting House, where it had sat for a hundred years. Its
place has been taken by a nondescript hotel.

The Queen's Hall had been a part of the English renaissance,
the background to so much of our best music. Here many
young composers who were to become famous came to hear
their earliest music performed; here Elgar had conducted,
Vaughan Williams, Frank Bridge and Walton; here Delius
had sat surrounded by flowers. In this hall Bax's symphonies
had been heard for the first time in England; Rachmaninov
and Busoni had played here, and Toscanini, Furtwängler,
Weingartner and Beecham conducted. At the start of the
Proms on a hot and glamorous summer evening the place had
exuded a charm, a happiness, a sense of expectant grandeur,
that we who knew it would never find again. Eternal summer,
and eternal youth, lingered in its walls, and even in bitter
winter, after a Beecham concert, the sun seemed to shine in
Regent Street outside.

The death of Frank Bridge in January 1941 passed with
very little comment. For some time a cold breeze had blown
over his reputation. Even his middle-period works were patro-
nised as "eclectic" and "smooth and well written", and the
fact that these terms were regarded as pejorative is revealing.
In fact, in the hands of some critics, "effective" became a term
of abuse; but it was not a critic, but a very well-known fellow
composer who wrote of him: "Of course, the deepest abyss of
the result of writing 'effectively' is Frank Bridge." Very un-
selfishly, Bridge tried to send his distinguished pupil, Benjamin

* Robert Elkin, *Queen's Hall, 1893–1941* (1944).

Britten, to study with Alban Berg, and the fuss that was made about this is astonishing. Britten himself wrote that the objection to Berg on the part of the English academic establishment was so strong that it was felt that his radical music was actually immoral. After the death of Berg in 1935 the obvious influence of his music on that of the latest works of Frank Bridge resulted in hostility to the English composer on the part of a section of the profession, and indifference on the part of the public. In fact Bridge retained tonality to the end, and his music never became more radical than the Bartók of the Third String Quartet or the Berg of the tonal parts of *Wozzeck*. In spite of teaching at the Royal College of Music, and participating fruitfully in English musical life, Bridge became increasingly an outsider—not by his own choice, for he was a most friendly man.

He was a complete professional, a professional of genius, a fine string player, pianist and conductor, and in his compositions he went his own way because he could no other. There was no question of open defiance—he accepted the bigoted decision not to send Britten to Berg when he could have made a lot more fuss. But as he was, so he was, and he was incapable of insincerity. He died at the blackest period of the war, and it was noted, with the business of Berg unforgotten, that his pupil Britten was a conscientious objector. He became the recipient of all the dislike of which the academic establishment was capable. These people did not understand Bax, but in a sense they understood Bridge only too well; they guessed that he was not only radical, but right; that in the end music would go his way, not theirs.

English composers tend to be forgotten for a while after their deaths, but in no other case was the eclipse so total as in the case of Bridge. Quite recently I was told when enquiring about the Frank Bridge Trust: "There are still people who do not like him"—nearly forty years after his death. But many composers paid tribute to him, and the 1970s, in which so many prejudices died and unjust verdicts were reversed, have seen Bridge's dramatic return to our musical life. In particular, much of his music has been recorded. His eclipse was not inexplicable; it was due to the endemic disease of English musical life that it is a part of the purpose of this book to diagnose and analyse.

His early music was an attempt to escape from the overwhelming influence of Stanford, and also to make his way in the world; if some of it suggested the popular music of the time, that may well be an attempt, after Stanford, to be cheerful at all costs! His first characteristic music was full of delicate poetry and, before the 1914–18 war broke his heart, a fresh and unfeigned gaiety. His radical temperament, in art as in life, refused all pretence. He would not shut his eyes to what was there. At the end he was rewarded with a unique vision, the vision of one who looked, like Blake, not with but through the eyes.

Bridge's music has survived because its technique is impeccable, its vision individual and unique, its integrity complete. Its flavour is hard to define. The last works are uncanny, powerful, as if grief were transmuted into eerie clairvoyance. But the middle-period music, *The Sea, Summer, Two Poems*, the first two String Quartets and the rest—these belong to the landscape of England just as much as the works of the folk-song movement, only this is the vision of the vagabond and the artist rather than the farm hand. Bridge was born in the same county as Shelley, and shared Shelley's hope for the other England. In those last works you may feel an England that only appears when the crowds have gone, and the furtive hedgehog slips across the road; the England of moths, when the scent of flowers grows strong in the gathering dark, and small sounds are suddenly eloquent.

In 1942 Benjamin Britten produced his first large-scale work for orchestra, the *Sinfonia da Requiem*. It is in three movements, "Lacrymosa" (Andante ben misurato), "Dies Irae" (Allegro con fuoco) and "Requiem Aeternam" (Andante molto tranquillo). It is dedicated to the memory of his parents. Mahler had always been a strong influence on Britten, perhaps the first sign of Mahler's subsequent triumphal conquest of England, and Mahler presides over the *Sinfonia da Requiem*. But Purcell, surely, is the origin of the bass pedal and chromatic figure in the cellos with which the work opens; Dido's lament is never far from Britten's imagination. The first part of the "Lacrymosa" suggests an extraordinary amalgam of Purcell with the opening of Mahler's Second Symphony. The movement is a unified build-up to a climax of massive power, with the bass ostinato prominent throughout. It leads straight into the "Dies Irae", with Mahler still presiding, the Mahler of the Rondo Burleske of the Ninth Symphony, but he is joined by Stravinsky. The ending of this movement, in which the music simply disintegrates, is masterly in the extreme, and proved too much for some contemporary critics. The last movement, another slow build-up, is based on a melody of more explicit emotion than Britten usually allowed himself, especially later in his career, but it ends in quiet peace. The work had a rough reception; but Britten's time had not yet come. At least he had recognised the seminal importance of Mahler, as against a mixture of Brahms and folk-song.

From 1940 to 1942 Bax wrote nothing, his longest period of silence since he began to compose. What was the reason? He did somewhat tentatively resume composition; he had not quite "retired like a grocer". Was it perhaps the unsettling effect of the first years of the war? The silence was broken in 1942 by music for a film, *Malta G.C.*; and then in 1943 he began, somewhat spasmodically, to compose again. The year 1943 saw the Legend-Sonata for cello and piano. Its textures confirm that Bax was writing with greater economy, a quality English and laconic, that he developed with his Third and Fourth Piano Sonatas and Seventh Symphony; but the quality of the material, although not Bax at his best, is higher than in the last piano sonatas. It is an attractive work.

Vaughan Williams was also writing film music at this time, and in 1942 he wrote the music for *Coastal Command*. But on 24 June 1943, at a Promenade Concert in the Albert Hall (which had taken over from the destroyed Queen's Hall), he conducted the London Philharmonic in the first performance of his Symphony No. 5 in D. For the greater part of his career—since 1909, in fact—he had been working on an opera on the subject of *Pilgrim's Progress*; *The Shepherds of the Delectable Mountains* of 1922 was an excerpt from this work, and when the opera was eventually completed it was incorporated into the score. When war broke out Vaughan Williams was doubtful that the opera would be finished, and a certain amount of the material was used in the Fifth Symphony, which bears the same relationship to *Pilgrim's Progress* as the Fourth Symphony bears to *Job*. The Symphony is in four movements, and is dedicated to Sibelius. Generally speaking, those who, privately or openly, disliked the Fourth appreciated the Fifth, while those who, like myself, had seen the Fourth as a liberation from an impasse for Vaughan Williams, and a possible new development, were disappointed that the Fifth regressed and did not follow it up. I have a suspicion that some of Vaughan Williams's followers value his Fifth above the other symphonies not just for its sentiment, but also for its refusal of the more difficult, radical path outlined by the Fourth.

Vaughan Williams was never really a radical. The Fifth is a mild, soft-centred work that borders dangerously on sentimentality. It is beautifully scored, clearly constructed, but its materials and textures reveal a slackening of grip, and the work as a whole is painfully anachronistic for the time in which it was written. It is nothing like the *Pastoral*, for the *Pastoral* is a singularly hard and unsentimental work, and far more contemporary in feeling, in the early 1920s, than the Fifth was twenty years later. Although it is dedicated to Sibelius, the Fifth reverts in many things to Hubert Parry. The discords lack the hard edge of those in the *Pastoral*, and are warm and bland, very much in Parry's manner; the music lacks the original polyphony of streams of chords in contrary motion which makes the *Pastoral* sound strangely timeless even today, substituting conventional, emotional progressions. As a purely personal view, I see the Fifth as a loss of nerve; and after the Sixth Vaughan Williams never quite regained the powerful inspiration that makes the Fourth the climax of his achievement.

The year 1943 saw the turning point of the war. It was to continue for another two years, but its decisive battle was fought at Stalingrad. When the Americans and British invaded Europe they met with greatly depleted German forces. But in England for the rest of the war all civil events took place against a background of constant air raids.

Rawsthorne, Moeran and Bliss produced characteristic work in 1944, although the most important event was the evolution of Michael Tippett into a major composer. Rawsthorne's piece was his overture, *Street Corner*, which was widely played for some years. It is a surprisingly radical work to have become so popular at the time, with a decidedly diffuse tonality, and it is interesting to observe how he creates the elements of popular success—including a barking dog that is entirely musical and a part of the texture and argument—out of his austere idiom. A brilliant and endearing work. E. J. Moeran was in his neo-classical phase; his early work had revealed a delicate or robust romanticism, but the Sinfonietta and later Serenade for orchestra are neo-classical in style. The Sinfonietta is pawky, extrovert and rather simple-minded, with lyrical interludes which reflect Moeran's partially Irish ancestry. Very different is Bliss's ballet *Miracle in the Gorbals*, put on in spite of the raids by Sadler's Wells. It is a powerful and serious score, based on a sombre story about a Stranger in the Gorbals who brings a suicide back to life; the crowd in superstitious awe lynch him. He is a Christ-figure of course, set against the heartbreaking background of Britain's most squalid urban area. For this tale Bliss provided a violent nocturnal score, full of grief and menace.

In March 1944 a new oratorio by Michael Tippett was performed. It was a secular oratorio, inspired by the assassination of a German official by a persecuted Jewish boy, and the Nazi vengeance that followed. It was given by the Morley College Choir—Tippett was now musical director of this workingmen's college—the London Philharmonic Orchestra, now composed of near-amateurs and at a very low ebb, and four eminent soloists, Joan Cross, Margaret McArthur, Peter Pears and Owen Brannigan. Tippett had written the words himself, and they were reported to be nonsense. In practice, the work struck like a thunderbolt, and England awoke with the realisation that there was another major English composer. It was a long time before this initial impression was confirmed and made certain, and years of misunderstanding and doubt still lay before Tippett, but *A Child of Our Time* kept his name alive until the next major works came along.

The basic shape of the composition is that of a Bach Passion, with narration, solo comment, and chorales. One stroke of genius was to use Negro spirituals to take the place of the Lutheran hymn-tunes in the chorales; they are used with great skill, and have tremendous emotional impact, the words and mood of each spiritual suiting the situation as in Bach. For the modern audience there is a combination of the unexpected, the familiar and the harrowing in this device which cannot be found elsewhere in the music of our time. "Steal away to Jesus" is used after the opening narration of persecution, and "Go down Moses" after the account of the Nazi vengeance. For the rest, the music and the words are gawky, impassioned, painfully sincere, and often of a sudden, stabbing beauty. The whole personality of the mature Tippett is here, as it were in a roughly shaped marble before the finishing. The emotion of the piece, with its call to compassion and sense of universal brotherhood, was a challenge to the public mood of the time, but its appeal to private emotions was immense, and it struck some sort of spark in most people. In some ways it divided the nation. This is inherent in the words that are almost the last in the work: "I would know my shadow and my light, then shall I at last be whole."

Dame Ethel Smyth died in 1944. The Overture to *The Wreckers* is the only music of hers that survives her, and that but fitfully. In her youth she had known Brahms, and many of her works, including large-scale ones like operas, had been performed in Germany; her style was vaguely Brahmsian, but with interjections from things like *The Flying Dutchman* and *Das Rheingold*, but nothing so daring as *Götterdämmerung*, let alone *Tristan*. She wrote several operas as well as *The Wreckers*, including *The Boatswain's Mate*, based on a story by W. W. Jacobs. She also wrote a Mass in D. Why women should not be great composers is one of the mysteries, but, although in the latter half of the twentieth century there are many women composers, none of them is in the front rank; and neither, alas, was Ethel Smyth. It was her ferocious energy rather than her talent that gained her so many performances during her life, but with her death they ceased.

The year 1945 saw the deaths of two of the great figures of music: Béla Bartók and Anton Webern. Bartók died in New York, after a long illness. His heroic defiance of the Nazis had been such that his friends had almost to kidnap him to save his life, and he arrived in America stunned with homesickness.

For some time he was too dispirited to work, but after a while the old drive returned, and he was graced with a last period of glory: the Second Violin Concerto, the Third Piano Concerto, the Concerto for Orchestra and the Viola Concerto. The last work was left in confusion, and was finished by Tibor Serly. Before he died Bartók's music was considered "difficult", and this added to his poverty. Today he is a classic, one of the greatest of composers, and not only in this century.

Webern was shot accidentally at the end of the war. More even than Schoenberg he was the father of twentieth-century music. Shortly after the war there was a reaction against Schoenberg, not by conservatives, who had never accepted him anyway, but by radicals. Led by Pierre Boulez, their slogan was "Schoenberg is dead!", and they took Webern as their point of departure. It was the romanticism of Schoenberg's music they reacted against; against this the pure classicism of Webern stands out with all the more clarity and poise. Moreover, his scores are models of concision and economy.

Here in England there were some small things afoot in 1945 and the stirrings of something greater. Bax published a Suite for Fauré, for piano; Moeran had married the cellist Piers Coetmore, and wrote a Cello Concerto for her. It was a return to his Romantic style, and emphasised once more his uncertainty of direction. After Tippett's *A Child of Our Time* it seemed appropriate that the air should be full of rumours concerning his friend Benjamin Britten; a big work was expected of him, but when it came it exceeded all expectations.

Peter Grimes was given for the first time at Sadler's Wells on 7 June 1945, with Peter Pears in the title role. It was a turning point in both Britten's career and the history of English opera; for after the first night it was realised that England, after two hundred years, had an opera that would be an international success. It was a perfectly viable, indeed great, opera on a grand scale, yet modern in psychology and conception; there was plenty of drama, but no old-fashioned heroics; there was magnificent character-drawing and magnificent music. It was neither Wagnerian music-drama nor Verdian grand opera, but, learning from both, and with Berg's *Wozzeck* somewhere in the background, authentic English opera. Britten had conceived the idea while reading Crabbe in exile in America, which gave him an intense nostalgia for his native Suffolk. Crabbe was an ideal source, and the libretto that was fashioned from his poems by Montague Slater gave Britten several of his most potent archetypes for music: a visionary but flawed individual pitched against a "normal" but limited society (Peter Grimes himself); innocence at the mercy of a corrupting world (the apprentices); and the sea. It was not recognised at the time, but the music of Frank Bridge coloured much of the orchestral part; Bridge's *The Sea* was a mine from which Britten quarried much. The vocal parts are written with all Britten's skill in setting English words, and, in the midst of highly coloured recitative set in an eloquent orchestral web, contain many haunting lyrical inventions.

The sombre power of the score, the compassion of the telling, and the realistic, almost contemporary tragedy of the story, marked the end of the "smart alec" label that had been attached to Britten from the beginning, a label somewhat eroded by the *Michelangelo Sonnets* and the lovely, popular Serenade for tenor, horn and strings. There has always been a certain criticism from the avant-garde, for *Peter Grimes*, for all its power, is largely pre-*Tristan* in harmony and the handling of tonality, and it remains one of his most advanced scores. One curious thing about Britten's harmonic idiom is that it is at once Mahlerian and pre-*Tristan*—the scoring and counterpoint suggest Mahler, but there is nowhere any trace of those tonality-destroying suspensions. Britten's music throughout has been not only tonal but diatonic.

The end of the war in Europe, in the spring of 1945, was very different from that of the war of 1914–18. For the greater part of five years the main body of the English conscript army had not been engaged with the main body of the enemy; and when that engagement came, with what was left of the German army after Stalingrad, it was brief and almost entirely victorious. Penned in between Russia and America, the two most powerful nations in the world, the Germans swiftly surrendered. Whereupon the opening of the concentration camps brought revelations so sickening that no one could quite take them in. From

1914 to 1918 mankind had been forced to confront its own blind folly, but this was worse than folly. Mass air raids on civilians, and then the revelations of the camps, forced mankind, for perhaps the first time, to confront the full horror of the dark side of its own nature. Cold and conscious cruelty on a monstrous scale shattered the mind of Europe. Then, after a pause in which the war in the East went on, and seemed to be turning in favour of the Allies, the first atomic bomb was dropped on Hiroshima. Whether or no the Japanese had surrendered, a second bomb was dropped on Nagasaki a few days later.

H. G. Wells was an old man, and dying, but he voiced a feeling shared by all who were reasonably well informed when he wrote, in 1945: "this world is at the end of its tether. . . ." Wells, it should be realised, had pinned his whole faith on science, that should save mankind from superstition and ignorance, and herald a golden age. But science had betrayed mankind. Later, when the bruised mind of man had made its adjustments, science was questioned as never before in modern times, and there was a reaction against materialism which took some peculiar forms; there was a spread of strange cults, half-understood Eastern religions, and sheer superstition. But in 1945 joy in victory was tainted by disgust, guilt and shock. The victory celebrations, unlike those of 1918, were muted. A mood of disorientated confusion was common to all England.

8

AFTERMATH
1945–1958

THE FIRST ACT of the English people after the war was to turn in revenge on those who had been in control during the crucial years in which war had become inevitable. For the first time a Labour Government was elected with not only a working majority but a huge one. It was a cold, drab, disheartened country after the war, however; rationing continued, and there were fuel crises that plunged even London into darkness. The austerities were no fault of the Government, but they were resented; and many curious attempts were made to cheer us up. One of the most curious of these attempts was the founding of music festivals. Of these, and there were several, the Edinburgh Festival was the most successful, but the Cheltenham Festival was the most profoundly significant. Our native music was in disarray, to put it mildly. For five years we had been insulated from world music, and we had ceased to know what good orchestral playing was like; Beecham was in America, conscription had depleted our orchestras of professional players, and orchestral standards had sunk to an abysmal level. The Cheltenham Festival, intended to provide a platform for English music, had been mooted as early as 1944, and six weeks after the ending of the war in Europe the first Festival duly took place.

Musical chauvinism had by now reached a pitch of utter unreality in England, and had the Cheltenham Festival programmes included nothing but the best of the English music of all idioms, including the avant-garde, we could have turned our natural pride in native genius to splendid advantage. But an examination of the programmes, and especially of the first performances, for the first ten years makes alarming reading, and the complacency with which these recitals of retrogressive mediocrity were greeted is even more alarming.

The phrase "Cheltenham symphony" was coined, to describe a work in simple-minded sonata form, simple-minded tonality, and simple-minded faith in a scissors-and-paste method of composition. A certain division in English music became apparent at this time; young progressive composers were arising in England, and they saw what was happening; on the other hand, the conservatives saw them, and hated what they saw.* The Hallé Orchestra became the chief band to play at the Festival; its much-loved conductor, Sir John Barbirolli, had very conservative tastes, and was said to have influenced the Festival programmes in the direction of 'safe', academic works. But the nature of these programmes was the result of not one but many reactionary forces working together; there is no doubt that for many years they did not remotely reflect the facts of contemporary compositional practice.

Vaughan Williams came to dominate English music after 1945 in much the same way as Elgar had dominated it before 1914. But the man, and the atmosphere, could not have been more different. Elgar was a progressive in the awakening renaissance; after 1945 English music was in stagnation, and Vaughan Williams was a conservative force. Elgar's output of salon and state music has often been criticised as unworthy of him, but in fact it constituted his link with the common people. He hated the words of "Land of Hope and Glory", but perhaps we may bow to his ghost when we say that the trio of the First *Pomp and Circumstance* March quickly became something like a folk-tune. The only tune in Vaughan Williams with which the common people were vaguely familiar *was* a folk-tune, and Vaughan Williams had no possible claim to it—"Greensleeves". When Elgar said "I am folk music" he spoke the truth, for many of his small pieces had entered the public mind to such an extent that they might not have been able to put a name to them. Elgar bridged the gap between the man in the street and the complex, sophisticated symphonic art of Europe at the end of the nineteenth century in a way that

* When at last a work by Peter Maxwell Davies was performed at Cheltenham, the *St Michael Sonata* (see below, p. 215), Frank Howes, in his booklet on the Festival (1965) wrote of it: "no one could determine whether the notes were right or wrong (this is literally true)".

Vaughan Williams did not do in the years following the Second World War; "RVW" never became a household word, as the name of Elgar did, and his music was much less contemporary in the 1940s and 1950s than Elgar's was in 1910. He found his place very comfortably among the unadventurous concert-goers, and appealed strongly to the deeply conservative strain in English musical life.

His pupils were also hardly avant-garde. Gerald Finzi (1901–56) and Herbert Howells (b. 1892) were the two best-known of them. Howells was a familiar name at the Proms between the wars for his two short orchestral pieces, Puck's Minuet and Procession, and the Elegy for Strings, which was recorded by Boyd Neel for Decca. Towards the end of his life he turned more and more to organ and church music. Finzi composed many songs, and those to words by Thomas Hardy are sensitive, and stronger in idiom than his large-scale works, his choral setting of Wordsworth's *Immortality Ode*, and his Cello Concerto. These things suffer from the endemic insipidity of minor English music. His best work was probably *Dies Natalis*, to words by Thomas Traherne, for high voice and string orchestra (1939). Both Finzi and Howells were too close in style to their teacher, and to the pastoral style which had long since lost what force it had.

Another aspect of the musical atmosphere of England in the 1940s and 1950s was the cult of the Danish composer Nielsen, who for a while was in fashion as Sibelius had been in the 1930s. This was in part another attempt to put the clock back, and raise an anti-pope to Schoenberg; Nielsen's habit of ending his symphonies in a different key from the one in which they began was seriously put forward as more important historically than Schoenberg's atonalism—an argument which hardly affected Schoenberg's world stature.

After *Peter Grimes*, what could Britten do for a new opera? The answer may have been a reaction against the traditional aspects of *Peter Grimes*, since his next opera, *The Rape of Lucrece*, is experimental in form, a chamber opera resembling in some respects more radical chamber operas of the twentieth century. It is based, moreover, on a classical subject, far removed from the realism and the almost modern setting of *Peter Grimes*. Its whole atmosphere is at an extreme remove from Britten's successful first opera. Latin, sensuous, almost sensual, but with an embarrassing insistence on a Christian moral, it is ambivalent in atmosphere; the basic subject is the usual Britten one of the helplessness of innocence. The libretto is by Ronald Duncan after André Obey's play *Le Viol de Lucrèce*, and it was first given at Glyndebourne in 1946. The presence of two Chorus figures, male and female, adds to the ambiguity of this curious work; they comment on the action and draw morals. Some of the music is masterly: the passage known as "Tarquinius's Ride" is a superb firework; the opening atmosphere of the Roman military camp under sweltering heat, with the men bickering about women, is also gripping and pungent. On the other hand, some of Lucretia's music suggests Puccini, and that is not meant as a compliment. A curiously flawed opera, an interesting experiment rather than a realised work, it has too much powerful and beautiful music to be a failure. *Peter Grimes* was hard to follow.

Britten's next opera was a comic one, *Albert Herring*, based on a short story by Guy de Maupassant, "Le Rosier de Madame Husson", with a libretto by Eric Crozier; it marked Britten's break with Glyndebourne and the founding of the Aldeburgh Festival. *Albert Herring* I find a peculiar piece, compound of French cynicism and English humour at its most naïve, an indigestible mixture. The English humour is at times so unfunny that it becomes funny in its ineptitude. Episodes like the spiking of the innocent's lemonade, or the humour to be derived from a village schoolteacher or policeman, are the beloved staple of rural humour and have been for centuries. But when a sophisticated composer of world stature sets them to music the result is culturally peculiar. Gilbert and Sullivan are not far off; it must be said that Britten is a better, and wittier composer than Sullivan, but Gilbert's superior and occasionally mordant wit is absent from the libretto. The music has its moments; after all, it is by Britten. A typical touch is the ominous stroke on the gong whenever Foxe's *Book of Martyrs* is mentioned. The French original rested on the gambit that no girl in the village can be found to be a virgin, so they have to crown the village idiot as May king. In Britten's opera

Albert Herring is by no means an idiot, although he is sheltered, simple and naïve, and very much bullied by his mother. One very curious aspect of Britten's choice of this story is connected with his concern for outraged innocence. Sometimes, as in *The Turn of the Screw* (1954), his quivering horror at the idea of growing up becomes somewhat exaggerated. In a sense, we all lose our innocence, and are the better for it. This is the motto of *Albert Herring*, a commendable one. But why, in this opera alone of all his works in this form, did he celebrate the loss of innocence with such fearful glee? He could have avoided setting a treatment of his usual subject which reverses all his usual values.

The number of composers active in England began in the late 1940s to increase dramatically. Alan Rawsthorne continued to produce distinguished works, although he never quite fulfilled the promise of his Symphonic Studies. He was joined among composers of his kind by Lennox Berkeley (b. 1903); attention was focused on them both rather late in their careers, not an unusual thing for English composers. Elizabethan Lutyens continued to compose with little recognition for her advanced style, but a measure of recognition was to come. Other women composers working at this time were Thea Musgrave (b. 1928), Priaulx Rainier (b. 1903), and Elizabeth Maconchy (b. 1907). Elizabeth Maconchy had won a prize for a string quartet in the 1930s; she followed this with eight more by 1969. Her style is somewhat crabbed; like many women composers she seems to be trying to outdo the men in stern and dry music. Thea Musgrave was only just beginning to be known in the late 1940s. She was another pupil of Nadia Boulanger. Priaulx Rainier, born in South Africa, was another product of the "Boulangerie". Her music tends to be athematic.

Vaughan Williams's Sixth Symphony was first performed on 21 April 1948 by the BBC Symphony Orchestra under Sir Adrian Boult. The three central symphonies, Nos. 4, 5 and 6, are strongly contrasted, as if by design. The Sixth shares with the *London* a picturesque atmosphere, some harmonic procedures, late-Romantic technique, and dark orchestration. In the intervening years, however, certain harmonic formulae had become overworked. As in the Fourth Symphony there is a "machine-age folk-tune" for second subject. But the extreme concision of form of the Fourth is not repeated in the Sixth. The four movements are played without a break, and the second section, Moderato, contains the greatest inspiration of the piece: the menacing rhythm that persists throughout, growing nearer and receding with the effect of nightmare. The Scherzo, revised in 1950, has a typical Vaughan Williams saxophone tune, and at times sounds like a speakeasy in Hades, Vaughan Williams being not quite the man for a depiction of hell. The finale depends for some of its effect on its power to surprise. It is moderately slow and very quiet throughout, desolate in colouring and composed of a few snippets of thematic material; its contrast with the noisy first three movements is extreme. This is a dramatic, powerful symphony, and if I feel that it is not quite the masterpiece that the Fourth is, it is due to the work relying more on drama than on development. The effects that suggest film music were prophetic, since Vaughan Williams's next symphony was to be a reworking of such music.

During 1947 to 1949 there were signs that, although our own orchestral standards were only slowly recovering from the effects of the war, these islands were about to become a great international music centre. The first Edinburgh Festival took place in the late summer of 1947. Unlike the Cheltenham Festival it had no axe to grind, but was simply an international festival in a most beautiful setting. When the Festival first began there were two main disadvantages; the first was that the acoustics of the Usher Hall and the Freemasons' Hall are poor, and the King's Theatre, with its fine acoustics, is too small. The second disadvantage, very obvious at first, has been put right. This was Edinburgh's puritanism: when the Festival started the few restaurants closed on Sundays, children were turned out of the parks for playing ball, and the Festival was preached against as Sin from many pulpits. The situation was rather peculiar. But the Festival has by now exercised its benign influence; the city of John Knox has accepted operas and plays, and has even become mildly permissive, to judge from the book-stalls.

186

The first Festival was notable for the formation of the Szigeti–Fournier–Schnabel Trio, and the second for the visit of Wilhelm Furtwängler; the old, glorious order of European music-making lit the young Festival with a sunset glow. In 1949 Bruno Walter and Kathleen Ferrier gave their famous performance of Mahler's *Das Lied von der Erde*, which was the first glimmer of recognition for Mahler in Britain, apart from some limited-edition records issued at the beginning of the war. Up to this time the English press had hardly taken Bruckner and Mahler seriously, and even after this it was not until the 1960s that opposition was finally overcome. Edinburgh anticipated London in the forging of great international seasons; but such seasons were to make Britain one of the musical centres of Europe in the 1960s and 1970s.

In 1948 Arnold Bax was still composing in a desultory manner; his music for the film *Oliver Twist* captured the public imagination for a while, and two of the episodes were published for piano solo. More important was the Concertante for three wind instruments and orchestra; Elegy, Scherzo, Lento and Allegro ma non troppo. These are delicate and gnomic movements, of sombre orchestration, bronzed and autumnal in colouring. The year 1949 saw the production of Bax's last substantial music: the Concertante for piano (left hand) and orchestra, and the orchestral Variations on the name Gabriel Fauré. Bax's interest in Fauré seems to have been a late one. Elgar too admired the reticent French master, and it is intriguing to observe these two flamboyant and highly emotional manipulators of the full orchestra paying homage to the master of understatement, whose most important works were for solo piano, voice, and chamber group. Bax's Concertante was written for Harriet Cohen, who had fallen while carrying a tray of glasses and severed the tendons of her right wrist. The Concertante does not amount to much, but it was a last tribute to a woman who had been Bax's companion and inspiration for most of his life as a mature artist—though in the end this association had turned rather sour. An air of disillusion, of the souring of old loves and enthusiasms, surrounds Bax's last years.

Alan Bush (b. 1900) is isolated in English music, for the

reason that his music, centring round his Communism, is dedicated to furthering the class struggle. His operas are *Wat Tyler* (1953), *Men of Blackmoor* (1956), *The Sugar Reapers* (1966) and *Joe Hill* (1970), all of which have been produced in East Germany—thus continuing a tradition established by Ethel Smyth and Joseph Holbrooke, but for rather different reasons. Indeed, Bush's music is much like theirs: diatonic Wagner with a social message. William Wordsworth (b. 1908) is another, different minor late Romantic. A descendant of the poet's brother, he was writing in the 1960s in a style not more advanced than that of the nineteenth century. It might have been possible, in 1949, to confuse William Alwyn with such composers; his First Symphony was performed at Cheltenham, ominous fact! But that First Symphony contained just enough bloody-mindedness to raise it above the usual Cheltenham symphony, and his later works became more and more distinguished. He was born in 1905, and studied with J. B. McEwen (1868–1948), who had the sense to tell Alwyn to throw away his textbooks and buy the scores of Strauss and Debussy; which was probably Alwyn's salvation.

Edmund Rubbra's Fifth Symphony does not sound to me any better scored than his others, although it has been said that it has "chamber-music textures". We are used to the brilliant scoring of Bax and Bridge, and Elgar's triumphant normality, but when we think of Rubbra we have to remember Schumann's scoring in his Fourth Symphony. However, I do not think that Rubbra's orchestration is anything external; it is his textures, the result of his actual musical thought, that result in his characteristic sound.

Britten's Spring Symphony was his second full-scale symphony, and choral throughout. He uses a number of poems, by Spenser, Nashe, Peele, Clare, Milton, Herrick, Vaughan, Auden, Barnfield, Blake, and Beaumont and Fletcher. It is scored for three soloists, chorus, boys' chorus and large orchestra. I suppose that the name that lies behind the Spring Symphony is Gustav Mahler, especially *Das Lied von der Erde*. Yet it is one of Britten's most English works, and in many a phrase and turn of harmony may be discerned the genial ghosts of John Ireland and Frank Bridge. In spite of their diverse natures Britten integrates these poems with great skill into a convincing symphonic structure. The scoring is fresh and clear, glittering and masterly. It has a rousing finale, "London, I do to thee present", which makes a completely convincing end to the work.

Two distinguished compositions by European composers in 1949 were Prokofiev's Sixth and penultimate symphony and Messiaen's *Turangalila*. The Sixth was Prokofiev's most "contemporary" symphony since the only partly successful Second, which was written in sincerest flattery of Stravinsky's most dissonant period. An air of anxiety pervades the Sixth, and the material alternates between the tragic and the brutal. It is almost certainly Prokofiev's finest symphony, a magnificent and rock-like work. The heavy, stamping rhythm that pervades it surely suggests tyranny. The first performance of *Turangalila* was in Boston on 2 December 1949. Messiaen was emerging as a world figure, and his pupil Pierre Boulez was to become one of the outstanding composers of the second half of the twentieth century. *Turangalila*, a love-song in ten movements, is scored for enormous forces; the huge percussion section marked the beginning of a concern with this department of the orchestra on the part of contemporary composers. The work has a tremendous, if slightly monotonous impact; it marked the climax of one of Messiaen's three central compositional motivations: the erotic, the religious, and bird-song.

Richard Strauss died in 1949, aged eighty-five. He had conducted in London only a few years before, and had enjoyed an Indian summer in composition after a long period of decline. His operas after *Die Frau ohne Schatten* were hardly memorable, though we may except *Arabella*; but after 1945 he had a sudden resurgence of his old power. The ravishing *Four Last Songs* (perhaps his finest work in the medium), the gay and infectious *Capriccio*, and above all *Metamorphosen* for twenty-three solo strings, revealed that he was still capable of masterpieces. *Metamorphosen* is a lament, eloquent and full of pain, for the glory of German music that had passed away. It ends with a quotation from the Funeral March of the *Eroica*, with the words "In Memoriam!" written under it. As a composer Strauss, like Wagner, has a slightly ambiguous reputation. In both composers the last great challenge, which was accepted by Bach, Beethoven,

Mozart, and—with results that are not yet quite plain—by Schoenberg, was evaded. Both were cynical realists, and it shows in their music. Yet technically and musically both were giants; Strauss's shrewd assessment of himself as a "first-rate second-rate composer" only needs to be amended to a second-rate first-rate composer. We criticise Strauss for an opportunism, a lack of idealism, which limits our admiration for his music. But in spite of some absurd claims, has England ever produced a composer of his world stature?

The Three Choirs Festival continued on its course, a conservative institution with occasional excursions into the mildly radical or the simply quaint. The Festival at Worcester in 1950 saw the first performance of *Hymnus Paradisi* by Herbert Howells. This work was a major effort and *tour de force* by a Vaughan Williams disciple who for long had produced nothing of consequence. Alas, in spite of the attention that was paid to it by a press that was becoming, at this time, more and more conservative and rootedly opposed to all innovation, it was not a very important work. Whatever one may think of Vaughan Williams's more routine bucolic style, few of even his minor works totally escape some flash of imagination, a scrap of tune, a turn of invention, that conveys at once who it is. The absence of any such moments in a lengthy work that sounds as though it might have been written by Vaughan Williams is disconcerting. It is hard on Herbert Howells that his patently sincere work should have been seized upon by some people as a counterblast to "new" music which in fact was by composers who were actually dead (Schoenberg, Berg, Webern).

Rawsthorne's First Symphony was written for the Royal Philharmonic Society in 1950; less individual than the Symphonic Studies, it is a comparatively conventional work, but saved by its composer's taut strength. Lord Berners, who died this year, was a very minor composer, but a picturesque figure, and a vivid part of the English renaissance. He has been described as "the English Satie" but he wrote no masterpiece like *Socrate*; the wit in his music is less dry and pointed than Satie's and more robust and absurd. He was interested in ballet, and wrote two notable examples, *The Wedding Bouquet* and *The Triumph of Neptune* (mentioned above). His funeral marches for piano (including one for a rich aunt) attracted attention when he was young, and he was a deft hand at parody. He was an amateur; but although his gift was slight, it was more professional than that of some of our academic composers.

Mátyás Seiber (1905–60), one of the refugees who came to live in England as a result of the Nazi terror, composed a few works, and taught extensively. At one time he was hailed, somewhat optimistically, as the saviour of English music. But in fact the only composer of any distinction who emerged from his teaching was Peter Racine Fricker (b. 1920). Fricker's music is an amalgam of mildly progressive harmonic tendencies and the usual academic forms, mostly string quartets and symphonies, short and well-constructed, but revealing few original features of form. His First Symphony of 1948–9 was awarded a Koussevitzky Prize, his Second was written for the Festival of Britain in 1951, and his Third came in 1960. The Fourth (1967) is in memory of Mátyás Seiber, and showed Fricker was moving away from the classical four-movement sonata style; it is in one movement of ten sections. By this time he had moved to America, and this move isolated him from English musical life. His music has personality and colour, and is by no means as limited as that of the typical Cheltenham symphonist; he uses modified serial technique and free tonality. Of his work in other forms, *The Vision of Judgement*, a large-scale choral piece, is important.

E. J. Moeran was only fifty-six when he died, on 1 December 1950, and his output up to this time was uneven and rather scrappy. His style changed restlessly; or rather, he seemed to have two or three styles running concurrently. His neo-classical style, that of the Serenade in G and the Sinfonietta, was not convincing; his piano music and songs, mostly early, were in the Ireland tradition, and very pleasant. The Two Pieces for Small Orchestra, Overture for a Masque, and above all the Symphony in G minor are his best works; the Cello Concerto and Violin Concerto lack the Symphony's intensity and imaginative power.

In 1951 the Festival of Britain took place. The South Bank

emerged as an entertainment centre, dominated by the Royal Festival Hall, to which was added later the smaller Queen Elizabeth Hall, and the still smaller Purcell Room. The acoustics of the Royal Festival Hall aroused considerable controversy. The war-destroyed Queen's Hall had perfect acoustics, clear and true, with perfect blending, no major resonances, an ideal decay time, and was suitable for all kinds of music. The Royal Festival Hall revealed itself as having frightening clarity, an ambience which meant that a singer felt his voice to carry no further than his mouth (although in fact a whisper could be heard in every part of the hall), a high resonance which produced a somewhat glassy sound, and a thin, dry bass. Scientific perfection of acoustics had been the aim, and ironically it might be said that the original hall achieved that aim; but scientifically perfect acoustics do not guarantee a musical result, and romantics like Sir Thomas Beecham immediately denounced it. Sir Thomas, after a fiery youth, was beginning to become tiresomely reactionary in his old age, for he also denounced the appearance of the hall. From the outside it is almost ordinary, certainly conventional and in no way surprising; in its massive solidity relieved by a neat touch here and there it belongs to its time as surely as Coventry Cathedral. But inside all changes. The RFH has one of the most beautiful interiors of any modern building, and the hall itself, with its mellow colour and "flying" boxes which do not seem to be attached to the walls, is no anticlimax. The acoustics have mellowed through the completion of the organ and the use of certain built-in devices, but still only suit such brilliant and glittering scoring as that of modern French and Russian composers. Anything romantic and melting, or the music of Delius, Bax and Vaughan Williams, almost certainly written with the gentle acoustics of Queen's Hall in mind, suffers most, along with the cathedral spacing of the scores of Bruckner.

Alan Rawsthorne's Second Piano Concerto—the First dates from 1939, revised 1942—was one of the Festival of Britain commissions. The brilliance of Rawsthorne's piano writing dominates this concerto as it did its predecessor, but this time there are four movements, the additional movement being a scherzo.*

* Rawsthorne's note for the HMV recording of the concerto describes

The most significant contributions to 1951 were two strongly contrasted operas. Vaughan Williams's *The Pilgrim's Progress* was performed at Covent Garden on 26 April 1951, having been completed at last in 1949. He had been at work on it since the end of the First World War, although he had been considering the book, and writing odd bits connected with it, for years before that. This work, then, had been its composer's constant preoccupation for over forty years, throughout his entire career, and all his other works had been written in this context. Once more the agnostic composer was obsessed by a Christian theme; his one concession is that Pilgrim, who is called Christian in the book, remains Pilgrim throughout the opera. The book, *The Pilgrim's Progress*, was written in Bedford jail, and its argument is one for which Bunyan, the poor tinker, would have died; for it concerns not so much our brief passage through this world as the way that passage affects eternity. It is a national monument, and monuments tend to lose their original message, and to become sentimentalised with time. *The Pilgrim's Progress* has taken on some of the aspect of a fairy-tale. But a composer of sensitivity, concerned to probe beneath the surface of things, should, one would think, come up against the deep import of this tale, the things that still trouble us, believer and non-believer alike, imparted here as allegory.

In my view, Vaughan Williams saw the book through Victorian eyes rather than through Bunyan's. The story, in spite of language which the distance in time has rendered quaint, is serious and troubled, and at times redolent of nightmare. Vaughan Williams tends to set the picturesque rather than the probing episodes; and although the theological disputes therein have lost their force, the story still speaks to our desperate times, and I suggest that a composer should be committed to the extreme spiritual implications of it—not necessarily from an orthodox point of view, but from the stance of one who has been troubled, and who cares. Vaughan Williams set it as a masque or charade, and I am afraid that his music is amiable,

---

the slow movement in these amusing terms: "The third movement has about it that nostalgic character so much disliked by the immobile intelligentsia of today, who confuse this quality with the emotional mess of the last century."

and even sentimental. One remembers Bernard Shaw's mordant words about Parry's *Job*; Vaughan Williams does not come within a million miles of the imaginative power of Bunyan's text. The music is patchwork, as one might expect in a work with so long and so troubled a history. Walton's *Belshazzar's Feast* is almost quoted in the "Vanity Fair" episode (but where is Giant Despair? was he too real a figure for Vaughan Williams?), and Pilgrim fights Apollyon to a tune resembling "Albert the Good, long may he reign" from Britten's *Albert Herring*. The recitative lacks grace, the hymn-tune-like passages are weak rather than inspiring. But the work does contain one example of the great Vaughan Williams, written nearly thirty years before: *The Shepherds of the Delectable Mountains*. This pure, accomplished, heartfelt music stands out in the score.

The Pilgrim's Progress sharply divided the critics. The more progressive of the younger critics condemned it out of court, and some of those who defended it did so as a rear-guard action against such composers as Peter Maxwell Davies, who were coming to the fore at this time. But English music has an odd habit of redeeming itself whenever it is at a low pass, and the other opera of the year comforted many for whom the Vaughan Williams was a sad disappointment.

The first performance of Benjamin Britten's *Billy Budd* took place at Covent Garden in December 1951, within the same year as *Pilgrim's Progress*. It was in four acts.* The libretto is by E. M. Forster and Eric Crozier after the novel by Herman Melville. *Billy Budd* must be the only surviving opera with an all male cast. Its initial reception was warm; but subsequent performances have confirmed the opinion, held by others as well as the present writer, that this is one of the two or three finest of Britten's works.

I profoundly disagree with the view that the subject of the opera is pagan and concerned with Fate; this would be unlike Melville and there is no warrant for it. At any rate the subject as it is presented by the librettists is religious and concerned

* A decade later, on 13 November 1961, a version in two acts was broadcast in the Third Programme. This two-act version is definitive and was recorded by the composer.

with redemption; this would appear to be the matter of the prologue and epilogue, sung by Captain Vere as an old man. Billy comes near to being a Christ-figure, only his single flaw, his stutter, hinting at something subtler and more complex— that there is always some imperfection; but it should be noted that the imperfection is physical, not moral, and seems to imply the intrusion of our mortal state on the spiritual. Billy is impressed from the merchantman *Rights o' Man* (in itself a significant name) by the naval vessel *Indomitable*, and confronts Claggart, the Master at Arms. Billy is perfect good; Claggart absolute evil. Absolute evil sets out to destroy perfect good, since it cannot tolerate it. Claggart accuses Billy of mutiny to the Captain, Edward Fairfax Vere (Fairfax: good-maker; Vere: truth). Vere brings them together, and Billy, confronted by the accusation, falls into a stammer he cannot control. Unable to answer, he strikes out and kills Claggart. Vere is a good and just man, and an extremely intelligent one; the tragedy is his, forced to make an impossible moral decision. But before he is hanged Billy cries out, "God bless you, Starry Vere" and Vere, the recipient of perfect love, is redeemed.

From beginning to end Melville's haunting prose is matched by Britten's music. The music to the first scenes has a breeziness and rhythmic pounce suggestive of Boyce; both Billy and Claggart are sharply defined by their music, but the part of Vere is so subtle and psychologically profound that only that masterly actor-singer Peter Pears could have been in Britten's mind when he wrote it. As the story unfolds the orchestral commentary moves closer to the drama, and ceases to reflect only the sea; it culminates in the unheard interview between Vere and Billy after the verdict; 34 bars, one of the most expressive passages in the orchestral part of any opera. Another powerfully projected scene is that of the beginnings of mutiny when Billy is hanged: the sullen murmur of the crew, and the frightened barking of the officers which quells it. Every detail of this score is economical, vivid, brilliantly composed, and it projects the drama, physical, moral and psychological, with unflinching power. In sheer compositional virtuosity it is in a different world from *Pilgrim's Progress*; it also confronts where the Vaughan Williams evades; in its refusal to shirk any of the moral problems and artistic responsibilities of its situation, it redeemed more than Captain Vere.

The fact that Alban Berg's *Wozzeck*, that other great opera of compassion, was also given at Covent Garden in 1951, under Erich Kleiber, was a ray of light in a dark year, in which another English composer came to a tragic end.

The story of Constant Lambert's last work and his death are inextricably interwoven. Lambert was always involved with ballet, and this last work was *Tiresias*, a ballet based on the Greek legend of the blind prophet, which was performed for the first time at Covent Garden during July 1951. The subject is not at first sight ideally suited for treatment as a ballet. Tiresias killed two snakes who were copulating, and was changed by the gods into a woman. Later he again saw two copulating snakes, and killed them, and regained his original sex. The gods, since he alone had experienced sex both as man and woman, asked him whose was the most rewarding experience, and he replied, woman's. Whereupon Hera, somewhat strangely, struck him blind; but Zeus, in compensation, gave him the gift of prophecy.

There has been some speculation as to why such a curious and unballetic story should have appealed to Lambert. The ballet in any event was a failure, and under unusual circumstances. It was not a flop in the theatre, but it was most cruelly and intemperately attacked by the critics, or some of them. Musical politics were not in question, since the chief attackers were not involved in such politics. But English musical criticism had sunk to such a level that incompetence would seem to be the only explanation. *Tiresias*, although still tonal and largely traditional, is rather more astringent and austere than Lambert's previous music, and that alone would puzzle the usual ballet hacks of this time. Though he was stoutly, and justly, defended by the Sitwells, Lambert was badly hurt by the notices. He had for years drunk to excess, and now he began drinking still harder. He became more and more seriously ill; he went into delirium tremens on the night of 20 August, and was rushed to hospital, where, on the morning of 21 August, he died.

From this time on his music fell out of print, and his work from memory—even *The Rio Grande* vanished from the Proms—

though at the time of writing he is sharing the current revival of all the composers of his period. Lambert was a little master of great individuality and skill, and his best music has a poignant beauty. He would, I think, have appreciated that assessment, since he was himself a great champion of little masters of the past, Borodin and Chabrier among others. *The Rio Grande*, the Piano Concerto, Music for Orchestra, *Horoscope, Summer's Last Will and Testament* and the Piano Sonata are works of such distinction that any country would have been proud of them; especially perhaps France, since Lambert's spirit was so Gallic that some people in the 1920s tried to pronounce his name as if he were a Frenchman. Virgilian, I think, best describes the Mediterranean melancholy of his music; a basically heroic enjoyment of the sweets of life in full consciousness of life's end. The Latin transparency of his scores—the result of a fastidious aesthetic—and the skill with which he utilised so many different idioms, including that of authentic New Orleans jazz, and integrated them into a very personal style, attest his consummate musicianship.

Arnold Schoenberg died in 1951, leaving an unfinished opera, *Moses und Aron*, which England would not hear for some time. When he died his effect on English music had been minimal, only Humphrey Searle and Elizabeth Lutyens among native composers acknowledging his example or his influence. But in Europe he had a large following; Boulez, Stockhausen, Henze, Berio and Nono, among others, used the methods of the Second Viennese School, but at this time these composers were little known on the Continent and quite unknown, except to specialists, in England. Schoenberg, when he died, was on the point of being acknowledged as the great figure he has now, in the 1970s, become; he felt that it was his mission in life to watch over the emergence of music that was not bound by the old systems of tonality. It was a daunting task, and he believed that he was the only composer who would volunteer for it. As a consequence he is better known, even today, as a great revolutionary theorist than as the classical composer in the great German tradition that he wanted to be. But it is sufficiently obvious that purely as a composer he was one of the outstanding figures of twentieth-century music.

For all its alarming symptoms for English music, 1951 was a year packed with event; 1952 was less eventful. Cheltenham produced a symphony by John Veale, who made no further mark, and an overture, *The Spanish Rivals*, by another Bush, Geoffrey this time (b. 1920), who did continue to compose, writing two symphonies. There were also pieces by Richard Arnell (b. 1917), William Wordsworth, John Gardner (b. 1917), Finzi and even Eric Coates.

Towards the end of the 1939 war various pieces by Humphrey Searle (b. 1915) began to percolate through, notably the *Night Music* for orchestra, performed by the Society for the Promotion of New Music, a body which had been formed during the war, largely by refugees from Europe. Searle is a serialist, deriving from Liszt and Schoenberg. He studied for a while with Webern, having begun his studies with John Ireland. To 1953 belongs Searle's First Symphony, written for the conductor Hermann Scherchen, which uses serial technique in a conventional symphonic framework, yet uninfluenced by the revolutionary inroads into form and orchestration of Gustav Mahler. Mahler begins to emerge as a key figure, some of his innovations overriding even those of Schoenberg, and nowhere so much as in form. Attempts to equate atonal or serial music with the neat Viennese classical sonata forms have not so far been successful; Benjamin Frankel (1906–73) was another victim of this idea.

William Alwyn's symphonic poem *The Magic Island* of 1952 was an interesting, if hardly original, essay in the tradition of Bax's symphonic poems—the Allotment of Fand, almost. The Second Symphony of 1953 revealed that he was developing, and rising out of the general rut of "Cheltenham symphonists". It is in two movements, each in three parts; it established that Alwyn's material was imaginative, his creative urge positive.

Malcolm Arnold (b. 1921), whose Second Symphony also dates from 1953, is one of the most curious phenomena of the postwar years, and remains a composer to be reckoned with. If he had not existed it might have been necessary to invent him. How shall we classify a composer whose lapses of taste are so frequent and so crass that he erects the principle of the banana-skin into an artistic canon, yet whose compositional

skill is the equal of some of the greatest composers of the twentieth century? Who throws everything handy into his symphonies, and switches with nonchalant ease from blush-making
bathos to invention instinct with the fire of genius? In spite of
faults so glaring that even to mention them is a trifle naïve,
Arnold has a gift that has been denied to all the solemn academic symphonists in England in these later years of the century.
It is not unknown for a new work of his to raise an easy laugh,
followed by the uncomfortable realisation of its quite remarkable power. Mahler is once more relevant; but Mahler's muse
is essentially cosmic and tragic, while Arnold's is cheerful (alas,
that commonplace word is the only possible one) and domestic.
Certainly his scoring suggests Mahler most of the time, but also
on occasion Stravinsky, while his hero is Sibelius.

Arnold burst upon us in 1945 with his overture *Beckus
the Dandipratt*: it aroused the enthusiasm of the great Dutch
conductor Eduard van Beinum, who recorded it. It is a marvellously cocky affair, in the great English comedy-overture tradition of *Overture to a Picaresque Comedy*, *Portsmouth Point* and *Street
Corner*. Incongruously, it seems to be based on "A Life on the
Ocean Wave". There is another equally hilarious comedy overture, *Tam O'Shanter*, which is a kind of Scottish Witches' Sab-
bath. Arnold's First Symphony of 1951 made little mark, but
his Second Symphony of 1953 created a sensation. It was written, characteristically, for the Diamond Jubilee of the Bournemouth Symphony Orchestra and was given its first performance
by them under Charles Groves. It is in four movements; a
lyrical Allegretto which is famous for the exquisite tune that
has become Arnold's "signature tune"; a brilliant Scherzo; a
curious Lento, music of haunting melancholy with some
peculiar interludes; and a finale which is famous for its grotesque and indeed alarming fugue. This fugue, which uses
Mahler's dinosaur orchestral effects, is a black comedy so
strange that the fugue has never been the same since. The
world of music accepted this curious offering with astonishment
and affection, and even the more advanced musical journals
solemnly analysed it. The extraordinary thing is that it is so
impressive a symphony.

Questions of taste are indeed raised when we consider that

the other major symphony of 1953 was Vaughan Williams's Seventh. It was first performed by Barbirolli and the Hallé Orchestra on 14 January 1953, and in the same year came Vaughan Williams's choral miscellany, *Hodie*. The symphony is an arrangement of some incidental music for the film *Scott of the Antarctic*, and bears the title *Sinfonia Antartica*. Symphonies have been arranged from operatic music before now, by Haydn and Prokofiev among others, but opera is not like film. For an opera the music is the most important part of it, and is continuous in coherent forms. Film music is no more than a background, and consists of snippets only; it is at the furthest remove from symphony, which is wholly musical, composed of foreground music exclusively, and which is the most logical, coherent and disciplined of all musical forms. The music for *Scott of the Antarctic* was concerned with depicting wind and waste, the walk of penguins and the spouting of whales, and it was largely onomatopoeic; it makes some very impressive noises, and is entirely fitting in its place, but does not suggest anything like symphonic treatment. In the end, the objection to *Sinfonia Antartica* is that its musical content, in the form in which it has been moulded, remains travelogue music, while Webern's chamber textures are nevertheless rigorously symphonic. Beethoven's "More an expression of feeling than painting" defines the limits of absolute music, even today. As for *Hodie*, it is perhaps Vaughan Williams's least successful large-scale score; made up of pieces that do not fit very well, and sentimental in content, Malcolm Arnold obviously has a long way to go before he equals the composer of the F minor Symphony, or even the *London Symphony*; but his rather peculiar Second is more like a symphony than Vaughan Williams's Seventh.

The year 1953 saw the coronation of Elizabeth II, and this affected the music in it to some extent; two composers of the middle generation each produced an opera, of very different kind and fate. Britten's opera was called *Gloriana*, and it was about Elizabeth I, appropriately enough. It was Britten's only operatic failure. The music is warmer and more immediate than that for his *A Midsummer Night's Dream* of 1960, but the opera is dramatically inept; it has no real central situation, and the long final monologue for the dying queen is in a different dimension from the rest of the work, and provides no dramatic climax. It has hardly been performed at all since its première, and is the only Britten opera, at the time of writing, that has not been recorded.

Michael Tippett's first opera, *The Midsummer Marriage*, produced at Covent Garden under John Pritchard in 1955, had been completed a couple of years before.* The work was greeted with bewilderment; the libretto (by the composer) was not understood at all, and the music, with the possible exception of the Ritual Dances scattered through the work and arranged by the composer as an orchestral suite, was no better comprehended than the words. A certain respect for a composer of formidable integrity was registered, the old cry of "Tippett the muddled thinker" was raised, and the work was forgotten until it was given again in the musically more enlightened atmosphere of 1968.

The Midsummer Marriage is in fact a great cry of joy, a hymn of praise to the earth and its creatures, and to the mystery of human love, by one of the deepest and most compassionate tone-poets of our time. It was born out of Mozart's *The Magic Flute*, and those passages in the Book of Job in which God answers Job out of the whirlwind; the singing of the Morning Stars and the shouting of the Sons of God. The psychology of Jung informs the action, and the whole is permeated with Tippett's knowledge of mythology. It is a midsummer ritual of the ordeals and marriages of two couples, Mark and Jennifer (Guinevere), both royal names and associated with Tippett's native Cornwall, and Jack and Bella who are the Papageno and Papagena of the piece. The dark or daemonic element, symbolised by Mozart in the Queen of the Night, is here personified by a character—a businessman—called, with deep significance, King Fisher. King Fisher's function is to hinder and obstruct; the lovers begin by being in his power, but during their ordeals Mark and Jennifer grow in strength until they can

---

* The work belongs to the years during which it was written, and that is why I am dealing with it here, rather than in the year of its first performance, or that of its ultimate recognition, 1968; it belongs to a certain stage in Tippett's development.

dismiss him from the action. The Ritual Dances symbolise the sacrificial aspects of human mating, and also the progress in enlightenment of the lovers, for Tippett has said that this opera is also about enlightenment. The action takes place during Midsummer Day, from dawn through the day and night to the subsequent dawn. In the words of Mark in Act I: "On this day, this day,/Anything can happen and everyone shall dance for me."

The music has an enormous emotional range and colour, a pervasive lyricism and orchestration which anticipates the "magical" Tippett of his latest phase. The chorus is very fully used, sometimes with dancing gaiety, sometimes with massive and cumulative power. The story, and the music, move inevitably towards the great climax of the Fourth Ritual Dance in Act II, Fire in Summer: "Carnal love through which the race/ Of men is everlastingly renewed/Becomes transfigured as divine/Consuming love whose fires shine/From God's perpetually revealed face. . . ." *The Midsummer Marriage,* as was realised when it was given again in 1968 and then in 1969, has a magic and a power which place it high among operas of the twentieth century.

Arnold Bax died on 2 October 1953, a few days before his seventieth birthday; he had been adjudicating in Cork, and was buried in St Finbarr's cemetery there. For a long time he had been supremely unfashionable, in spite of the lazy acceptance given in the 1950s to composers who were his inferiors, but who accorded with the taste of the time for easy music. The eclecticism of his style, and his mildly radical bent, told against him in an atmosphere of self-conscious nationalism, easy sentiment, and deep conservatism. The progressive critics and composers, now thoroughly militant, and justifiably resentful of the way our young composers were dismissed by the critics of the most important journals, in their scorn and contempt, lumped Bax with composers utterly unlike him. He fell between two stools; in spite of his official position as Master of the Queen's Music he was never a man of the establishment, yet he could not adapt his style to that of the Second Viennese School. Not long after his death the premises of his new publishers, Chappells, burned to the ground, and their entire stocks of his music were destroyed. It seemed a last gratuitous blow.* But the fact that all Bax's major works were out of print, and his publishers reluctant to reprint them, told against him when his reputation had reached nadir.

It is still difficult to come to any definite assessment of Bax's stature and achievement, though one has only to compare any symphony of his with the average Cheltenham offering of the 1940s and 1950s to realise that he stands head and shoulders above such composers. It is not insipidity or lack of invention that has been responsible for Bax's troubles, but the strength of his personality, which repels some people as much as they used to be repelled by Liszt. He is what he is with such force. Until very recently the English have reacted strongly against the music of strong emotions, vehement music, expressionist in style (and this means most of the great music of the last seventy years or so); but the acceptance of Mahler has swept all that away. Something of Mahler's lack of emotional restraint can be found in Bax; his gestures are violent, often sudden, always powerful, and they are interspersed with a wild and dreamy beauty which sometimes stops the breath. Moreover, he was technically brilliant, and, like Bridge, "effective". No wonder the England of before 1960 rejected him! He persisted in his madness, like Elgar; he had something of Blake's vision.

The complexity of Bax's textures—they are often complex but seldom thick or muddy—makes his music almost as difficult to grasp as that of Schoenberg, at a first hearing, and for the same reason.† It is only with familiarity that the salient, vital lines begin to emerge. His First, Second, Fifth and Sixth Symphonies are satisfactory wholes, his Third and Fourth contain sufficient incidental beauties to offset the effect of their bungled form, and his Seventh is a low-key work that aptly sums up his life's achievement. Scattered around the symphonies are other

* It was discovered in the end that no unique manuscript had been lost, although it was thought at first that the only copies of *Spring Fire* and the Symphonic Variations had been burned; other copies were found.

† When the Fourth Symphony was recorded, the first of the seven to enter the catalogues, his music had been forgotten for so long that the young critics were bewildered; some of them accused him of plagiarism on the strength of passages in his music written long before the better-known music he was supposed to have copied.

fine works, the symphonic poems and the overtures, the Piano Quintet, Piano Quartet, Nonet, Third String Quartet, late Piano Trio (1946) and Viola Sonata. Vaughan Williams in his old age so fitted the contemporary English idea of what a great composer ought to be that Bax was almost extinguished. Yet I do not believe that Vaughan Williams towers above Bax, who by reason of his unique vision and technical brilliance was one of the great figures of the English renaissance.

Serge Prokofiev died in 1953. His particular style has been cited as the mainstream of conservative music in the twentieth century, rather aptly I feel. Overshadowed by the more radical Stravinsky, he nevertheless composed seven symphonies, five piano concertos, two violin concertos, and many ballets and operas, all of which music remains in the repertory. Both his compatriot Shostakovich and Benjamin Britten belong to the same broad compositional stream, and both Prokofiev and Shostakovich suffered from Soviet intolerance of even their mild modernism.

Back in England, Rawsthorne's Second String Quartet appeared in 1954, in four movements, none of which is in slow tempo. In spite of this it remains lyrical and it is idiomatically written for its medium. Also this year came Edmund Rubbra's Sixth Symphony. Britten's chamber opera, *The Turn of the Screw*, based on a story by Henry James, was produced in Venice. This is a brilliant opera, formally dazzling, since it is constructed in the form of a series of variations on a serial theme; this has the classic twelve tones, but they form a series of six-four chords, so the work remains tonal. Britten's preoccupation with innocence and its loss, and his sympathy with children, here assume a pungent but ambiguous form: Are the two children possessed by the ghosts of the former servants, or are they the victims of the new governess's neurotic delusions, which may have driven one of them to his death?

Subjectively one feels that Britten accepts the obvious reading that the governess is a normal person struggling with the posthumous influence of the two corrupt servants, Peter Quint the footman and Miss Jessel the former governess who was his mistress. But the music seems to fight the stage action every step of the way. It tells me, at any rate, that the governess is an impossible prig, sanctimonious and hysterical, while the music for the two ghosts is eerie, but ravishingly beautiful. "You heard the terrible sound of the wild swan's wings"—it might be initiation into the wild beauty of the world, or a description of genius itself, or almost anything but the kind of evil the living servants talk about with bated breath. The ambiguities—and there are many—in part stem from what was possibly an unconscious complexity in Henry James's plot. It remains a splendid opera.

There were two more English operas in the next year, 1955: Lennox Berkeley's *Nelson* and William Walton's *Troilus and Cressida*, the latter in its first version. The Berkeley is, alas, quickly dealt with. Gentle, Gallic, graceful music, hardly suitable for its theme, and an opera that is only too easily forgotten. But the badly flawed Walton refused to die, and was revised many years later and given in 1977 at Covent Garden with the part of Cressida lowered for a mezzo to suit Janet Baker. Even in this version it lacks vitality, and a sense of the theatre: one might guess that before 1939 Walton would have shown more stagecraft.

The piano has played a marginal part in Michael Tippett's output,* although he is fascinated by some aspects of its sound. The Piano Concerto of 1955 derived from his memories of Gieseking's performance of Beethoven's Fourth Piano Concerto, a singularly light and transparent reading, full of tender joy; but the romantic textures and the material of Tippett's Concerto are full of memories of *The Midsummer Marriage*. Its opening is rhythmically so complex that it presents a challenge, not so much to virtuosity as to sheer understanding and control. Typical of Tippett is his own, most apt description of the first tutti as "streaming lines of sound". The first movement is a long one, and balances the slow movement and finale. The horns of the slow movement derive from Schubert, Weber, Wagner and Bruckner, and are full of the remote mystery of the romantic forests. The finale is a very perky rondo, embodying

* One of the first of his works to attract attention was the First Piano Sonata of 1938, which had been recorded by Fred Smith of the record shop Rimington's.

elements of sheer play unusual in Tippett, the entry for piano and celesta being a favourite passage of the composer's.

Romantic but linear, the Concerto's thematic material speaks uncompromisingly of its composer: a strange and gawky, but very convincing voice. People were by now comparing Tippett in stature with Britten. The two are very different. Britten is fluent, lucid and original, in spite of the unoriginal nature of his technique; Tippett's originality stems from, indeed is, the unique nature of his technique and methods. Britten's music is atavistic and suggests music before *Tristan*; but Tippett is divided between the nineteenth century and the twentieth.

Arthur Bliss, never a fast worker, and now Master of the Queen's Music in succession to Arnold Bax, was beginning to slow down. But in 1955 he produced a large-scale work for orchestra, *Meditation on a Theme of John Blow*, which is one of his best pieces, comparable to the Introduction and Allegro and the Colour Symphony. The slightly archaic nature of the tune, and Bliss's own natural idiom, produce a sonority rich in English antiquity. A stylish and well-shaped work, with typical fluent scoring.

The Eighth Symphony of Vaughan Williams was given its first performance in Manchester on 2 May 1956 by the Hallé Orchestra conducted by Sir John Barbirolli, to whom it is dedicated. There is no saxophone, but a vibraphone, an unpleasant instrument to which Vaughan Williams was addicted at the time, and a huge array of percussion, including "three tuned gongs, as used in Puccini's *Turandot*". It all sounds ominous; and it is. The Eighth is a short work, in four miniature movements, and some of its peculiarities, scoring apart, suggest that it was modelled on Beethoven's Eighth. But Beethoven's Eighth is a miracle of form, even among his formally magnificent symphonies: the four short movements are each constructed with jewel-like concision; the material and its treatment alike argue brevity. The four movements are linked, not thematically, but by every other compositional device. Each movement of Vaughan Williams's Eighth starts as though it is going to be a full-length movement, and then just lamely ends. He lacks Beethoven's genius for brief forms that are perfectly self-contained. Moreover, the four movements have no relationship to each other, they are just four odd pieces. Without wishing to be a kill-joy, the orchestration is merely reckless. The vibraphone is just nasty, and the concatenation of "spiels and phons" in the last movement provides an aura of overtones which prevents one from hearing either theme or shape.* All the evidence is that Vaughan Williams's scoring is simply miscalculated.

The year 1956 was that of Robert Simpson's Second Symphony and William Alwyn's Third. The Simpson was predictable. It raises the question of material and form in an acute degree; it is greatly admired in certain circles for its neatness of form, and, one might add, for its extreme conservatism; but whether the cleverness of the former and the desirability (if that is how you feel) of the latter make up for its wooden and unmemorable material depends on your point of view. Alwyn's Third Symphony gives the immediate impression of being a work of more imagination and creative urge than Simpson's Second; yet one has the feeling that Bax wrote this sort of thing with more commitment. Alwyn's personality, for all that he writes nature music close to Bax's, is more austere and athletic; and he is in closer intellectual control of his material. His Third Symphony, in three closely argued movements, is impressive.

After a silence of some 33 years Sibelius died at his home in Jarvenpaa in 1957. In a few years from his death his reputation was to be torn to shreds by the new young critics of England, who regarded him as the arch-enemy, the composer who had been inflated into a major figure solely to dish Schoenberg. He survived this onslaught; with the general public he was firmly established, and had become a classic. During the 1930s his extreme popularity had been confined to England and America; the Germans regarded him as a kind of inferior Grieg, the French held him in contempt, the Italians had probably never heard of him, and the Dutch were only slightly acquainted. In the 1960s his music became more widely known than ever before, and even the Germans began to play

---

* Boulez's handling of the more resonant percussion is a model here. In the main, he gives each sound time to die away, and only employs the aura of conflicting overtones of several instruments playing together when he intends that effect.

him; after a while he was back in what was probably his true position.

It is a thing that it is impossible to define objectively, but Cecil Gray was probably right when he wrote of the magic in Sibelius's music. A formally convincing symphonist of great originality whose music has an extra dimension of magic is a formidable proposition. Moreover, although technically Sibelius appears to be a conservative, his music has an inexplicable twentieth-century sound; it could not possibly belong to any other time. This is because of the utterly individual use to which he put the most ordinary progressions. His formal procedures are quite different from those of the academic manipulators of uninspired themes. Sibelius's themes are different, pungent, magical. This is one of the mysteries of creation; Arthur Koestler's definition of genius as the sudden leap that connects things believed to be unrelated applies with precision to Sibelius. He was a genius; it is improbable, after all, that he was not a great composer.

Malcolm Arnold's Third Symphony, written in 1957 for the Royal Liverpool Philharmonic Orchestra, sounds like an attempt to be serious. It is an altogether graver affair than the Second; there are the same grotesque noises, but much more subdued; the form has the appearance of being better thought out. "Towards the end of the movement the tempo abruptly changes, and the same material is developed as a scherzo," writes the composer. The slow movement is very nearly solemn, and of sombre colouring; an almost unique phenomenon in Arnold's music. The finale, a more or less rondo, is also more serious than anything of the kind he had written before. There is the same sense of comedy material used to dramatic purpose that we find in Prokofiev. Less popular than some of his other symphonies, this is an impressive work. The personality is as strong here as it is in any other piece by him.

Nothing could better illustrate the strange withdrawal of creative power from William Walton than his Cello Concerto, which was first performed by Gregor Piatigorsky and the Boston Symphony Orchestra under Charles Munch on 25 January 1957. It is constructed on much the same lines as the superb Viola and Violin Concertos: Moderato, Allegro appassionato, and a finale with a slow introduction. But every trace of Walton's personality has vanished from the music. The thematic material is weak in the extreme, the harmony trite and dull, the rhythms emasculated. Part of the trouble, at this low ebb in English music, was that our two greatest senior creative talents, Vaughan Williams and Walton, were both simultaneously undergoing a compositional crisis, and the conservative press refused to notice.

Edmund Rubbra's Seventh Symphony also dates from 1957; after his Third Rubbra ceased to develop very much, and each subsequent symphony reveals nothing much that is new or original. Lack of originality is Rubbra's prime failing; only his opaque orchestration marks his music off unmistakably from half a dozen other minor English symphonists, or indeed, as each new work appears, from his First Symphony, the most cleanly scored of them all. The future of the symphony would appear to lie in advancing its form from the pre-Brahmsian model to something more contemporary, and utilising in it the harmonic advances that have occurred since Mahler. There are symphonists working in England for whom nothing has happened since Brahms.

Stravinsky had been for so many years Schoenberg's antithesis in modern music that it came as a shock when in 1957 he began to adopt twelve-tone technique. Schoenberg had never concealed his scorn for Stravinsky, whom he called "Little Modernismus", and Stravinsky had never been attracted to Schoenberg's Germanic Expressionism. But Webern was different; Stravinsky was converted to his music, perhaps through the persistence of Robert Craft. Stravinsky's serial music proved to be entirely valid. It began with the ballet *Agon*, an austere work rather like the Mass, not particularly frightening, although disliked by the old school of English critics.

Among the new works performed for the first time in 1958 was Humphrey Searle's Second Symphony. Liszt is as much in evidence in it as Schoenberg; and perhaps the first performance, at the Berlin Festival, conducted by Scherchen, of his first opera, a one-acter based on Gogol's *The Diary of a Madman*, was of more moment. In this work Searle's relationship with the sense of alienation common to late Romanticism, which had achieved notable things in Schoenberg's *Erwartung* and Berg's *Wozzeck*, is evident. Searle's Expressionist atonalism is ideally suited to his subject.

Tippett's Second Symphony was performed for the first time in February 1958, at the Royal Festival Hall under Sir Adrian Boult. So many of Tippett's works take their departure from some piece of eighteenth- or early nineteenth-century music: the First Sonata from Domenico Scarlatti, the Piano Concerto from Beethoven's Fourth Piano Concerto, the Third Symphony from Beethoven's Ninth. The Second Symphony owed its beginnings to a performance of Vivaldi, overheard in a studio of Radio Lugano, overlooking the lake. The opening of the first movement derives its impulse from the pounding Cs in the bass at the beginning of the Vivaldi. The Second Symphony is far more original and powerful than the majority of symphonies being written in England during these years; this is in part due to Tippett's original concept of form. The Scherzo is in additive rhythm and the finale, to quote the composer, "is a fantasia in that its four sections do not relate to each other, like the four sections of the first movement of sonata allegro, but go their own way". In spite of such touches, there is no hint in the Second Symphony of the sudden new direction Tippett's music was about to take.

Britten's Nocturne for tenor solo, seven obbligato instruments and string orchestra received its first performance on 16 October 1958, at the Leeds Festival. The poems are by Shelley, Tennyson, Coleridge, Middleton, Wordsworth, Keats and Shakespeare, and a different instrument takes the obbligato for each setting. This is a Nocturne, and the mood and instrumentation are appropriately dark; dreams sombre and uncanny move through the work, and the whole is set in a hazy veil of sleep. Very Mahleresque in some aspects of technique and in the genre of a song cycle with orchestra, this subtle and haunting work is one of Britten's best.

Vaughan Williams's Ninth and last symphony did not fulfil one's awful anticipations and sport a *Schlusschor*. It was in fact a wholly abstract symphony, and marked a last return of its composer's mighty talent. It was composed between 1956 and 1957 and revised in the spring of 1958; its first performance took place at a Royal Philharmonic Society Concert at the Royal Festival Hall on 2 April 1958 under Sir Malcolm Sargent. Vaughan Williams's decline had been long and obvious. It was not a sudden withdrawal of power, as in the case of Walton, but a slow and majestic subsidence. But even in the midst of the general decay there was an underground tide moving, a sense of a third period that was not being allowed to come through; in the Ninth this sombre element takes over, and the result is a final masterpiece.

The scoring of the Ninth is thicker and duller than the rest of his symphonies. This peculiar colour is part of the uncanny atmosphere of the work, which always suggests nightmare to me; consistent report has it that Vaughan Williams frequently dreamed his material while asleep, and this symphony does suggest that this most unconscious of composers had entered the realm of the unconscious mind and it had closed over him. The key of E minor is appropriate; this seldom-used tonality, with its dark yet fiery undertones, was also used for Brahms's Fourth Symphony. There are many places in Vaughan Williams's Ninth that suggest a parody of his early mannerisms in the same way as the parodistic elements in Mahler's last works do. But in Mahler's case the intention was obvious and deliberate; one has the feeling that Vaughan Williams did not consciously will the extraordinary atmosphere of this symphony, that he simply composed as he had always done, and the music came out like that.

It is a symphony by a very old man, and it sounds like it; by that I do not mean that the technique is any more clumsy than usual, but that its strange and twisted atmosphere, with terror always just around the corner, its troubled and haunted mood, like that of a troubled dream, suggests what it must be like to be very old. Fauré's String Quartet, composed at about the same age, has much the same atmosphere, and, strikingly, the same unusual key. The feeble harmony of *The Pilgrim's Progress* has gone, and in its place is a harmonic texture as masterly and radical as anything since the Fourth Symphony and *Job*. The four movements fall into a typical pattern. The main theme of the first movement occurred to the composer when he was playing the organ part of the opening of the Matthew Passion; the music is chromatic, more so than usual, and proceeds in a shadowy, eerie similitude of his other first movements. A slow movement which is perhaps too like the first movement in gait and colour is interrupted by threatening noises like those of the Sixth, but less defined and more shadowy; the Scherzo is a ragged, despairing movement, with the saxophones of Hades well to the fore; the finale is at once darker and more strange, and culminates in three waves of sound which end the symphony, rather surprisingly, in the major.

The only work of consequence that Vaughan Williams composed after the Ninth was the Ten Blake Songs. This was also film music, written for *The Vision of William Blake* for the bicentenary of the Blake Society. For voice and oboe, and somewhat incongruously composed at "Christmastide, 1957", these songs are bleak and bitter, and in a mood unusual for the composer, though derived from the same psychological source as the Ninth Symphony. Blake was the supreme poet of vision, of the spirit's immortality set against the apparency of things, imposed by earthly rulers. That Vaughan Williams should have extracted such bitterness from Blake's poetry in the last year of his life is strange, but significant. Whatever vague consolatory meaning he attached to his ballet *Job* (also from Blake), it had not resolved his questions, and one must ask what meaning he attached, in this last year of his life, to the quotation from Plato on the score of *Sancta Civitas*.

Vaughan Williams died on 26 August 1958, on the eve of the recording of his Ninth Symphony under Sir Adrian Boult, who had recorded the other eight for Decca. On his death a major change took place in the musical climate of England.

Vaughan Williams was a major figure in the context of England in the first half of the twentieth century, but more than any other English composer of our period he belonged to a certain style, a certain place, and a certain time. No other composer, not even Elgar or Sibelius, wrote so many ephemeral, occasional pieces.* The big, stark works of the 1930s on which

* Because these pieces were so ephemeral, and are so completely for-

212

his reputation may ultimately rest were the work of a short
period, a single tremendous creative thrust which started with
the *London Symphony* and reached its climax with the Symphony
in F minor, tailing off abruptly after the Sixth Symphony.
Apart from the big things and the ephemera, there are a number of works in a style that has been called quintessentially
English: *Hugh the Drover*, the Fifth Symphony, *Hodie*, *The Pilgrim's Progress*, and up to a point the Tallis Fantasy, among
many other less well-known compositions. This specific style
was the result of a musical technique which owed almost everything to Parry coming into contact with modal music, in the
shape of folk-tunes and Elizabethan composed works. It is a
style that for a long time so appealed to certain very conservative elements in English musical life, that Vaughan Williams
became the tacit figurehead for those who did not like twentieth-century music. As such, he became the object, during
the 1950s, of the mounting fury of the young progressive
composers and critics, who were apt to include all other
English composers of his generation in their condemnation of,
not just this one composer, but certain works by this one
composer.

Vaughan Williams would appear to have been an almost
purely instinctive artist. The one work that is an exception to
this is the F minor Symphony, which does seem to have been
the result of deliberate and calculated compositional techniques; even its few failings look contrived, as for example the
principal tune of the last movement. His achievement will
probably be seen as the *London*, *Pastoral*, F minor and Sixth
Symphonies, *Job*, *Riders to the Sea*, the G minor Mass, *Sancta
Civitas* and a few more hard, honest works. He was one of the
most uneven composers who ever lived; that the same man
wrote the F minor Symphony and *Hodie* is almost incredible,
and his tragedy, in his last years, was that works like *Hodie*
appealed so strongly both to the not very musical and to the
entrenched conservatism of the times. Those times were about

gotten, that statement may be challenged; but look through the work-list
in Michael Kennedy's book on Vaughan Williams, and you will see that it
is amply justified; the greater part of his huge output consisted of purely
local, small-scale utility music.

to change, and the reaction against Vaughan Williams that then took place was as exaggerated as the praise of him, which at one stage placed him with Beethoven above Elgar and Mahler, had been in the 1950s.

9

REVOLUTION AND REVIVAL
1959–1978

THE LAST YEAR of the 1950s saw sudden, dire changes in English musical life; there was a palace revolution of some magnitude. Several elderly critics retired or died, and younger men took their place; above all, William Glock established an entirely new order of things at the BBC. The change at Broadcasting House was badly needed, but in some respects England had exchanged King Log for King Stork. William Glock was determined to introduce the people of England to the music Schoenberg had been writing decades ago, and he broadcast so much Schoenberg in the early years of his regime that he nearly repelled even the most willing. The Cheltenham Festival almost became a place in which Schoenberg had replaced English music. And, as the young composers were quick to point out, Schoenberg was dead, and they, and their colleagues in Europe, were alive and in need of performance.

But it had to happen, and there were many benefits. The Proms, nearly dead from inertia, suddenly took on an eccentric life; all sorts of exciting (and sometimes peculiar) music was played for the first time. But English music, and Sibelius, were out. The new regime set its face against most English music except Elgar and Britten. The reaction was too great, badly though a change was needed. Whether the great Romantic revival that swept England in the 1970s was a counter-reaction is not clear.

Despite all this, in 1959 there was an event of profound significance for English music, at of all things the Cheltenham Festival; a work by a composer who was to write a new kind of symphony. This was the first performance of Peter Maxwell Davies's *St Michael Sonata* for seventeen wind instruments. Maxwell Davies was born in Manchester in 1934, and studied at the Royal Manchester College of Music under Richard Hall. He went later to Italy to work with Petrassi. His friends at the College included the pianist John Ogden and his fellow composer Harrison Birtwistle (b. 1934), and they became known as the Manchester Group. Maxwell Davies founded the Pierrot Players, a chamber group constituted according to the instrumentation of Schoenberg's *Pierrot Lunaire*. Birtwistle later withdrew, and the name of the group was changed to The Fires of London. Maxwell Davies's style, which has evolved slowly over the years, has never resembled that of the more humourless of Schoenberg's followers. Black humour it has, and in his early years a preoccupation with the foxtrot and '20s dance music. But an interest in medieval and early Renaissance music was evident, and fruitful, from the beginning of his career. His style is deeply serious without being solemn, something the English find it hard to understand. In the 1950s England was going through a bad bout of Klemperer's disease, almost entirely on the strength of that conductor's unutterable solemnity. I wish to end this book with a study of Maxwell Davies's music as a whole; enough at this juncture to write that his radical but not revolutionary style, which has a few hints of late Bridge, is compound of dreadful humour and no less dreadful seriousness and intensity, and concerned with a concern that hurts; technically masterful, and gripping in a unique way.

At the end of the 1950s various progressives were given a hearing at last, among them Elizabeth Lutyens, who is an elusive figure. She was not satisfied with any of her early works, and it is only very recently that she has felt that her compositions represent her. Though after 1960 or thereabouts she stood still while compositional techniques rushed on,* her music is fairly radical, and her prose extremely combative. Her aggressive personality is a disadvantage to her music rather than otherwise; but her work has a steely professionalism, and has survived indifferent performance and the early ridicule of a hostile press. The first of her works to attract attention was the lovely *O saisons, O châteaux* of 1946; and she achieved a certain notoriety by constructing an exceedingly austere motet on some

---

* She confesses in her autobiography *A Goldfish Bowl* (1972) that Stockhausen and Boulez are beyond her.

propositions from the *Tractatus Logico-Philosophicus* of Ludwig Wittgenstein. Music for Orchestra No. 1, written in 1957 and first published in 1959, is a neatly constructed "fantasy" piece for full orchestra, sensuous in appeal, logical in compositional impulse, and substantially conventional in appearance and sound. *Quincunx* came in 1957, and after 1960 her music was more often performed, in the less restrictive atmosphere of the time.

Another progressive composer whose music began to be heard in the 1960s was Alexander Goehr, the son of Walter Goehr, the conductor. Born in 1932, he was at Manchester with Peter Maxwell Davies, and subsequently studied with Messiaen. His style is Schoenbergian; and one writes advisedly, because his music actually resembles that of Schoenberg in sound. It is unlike that of Webern, because it is obviously based, as was Schoenberg's, on late-Romantic harmony and texture. Goehr became known for his vocal work *The Deluge*, and his opera *Arden Must Die* made his reputation. He established a group called Music Theatre, for semi-dramatic performances of short musical works. He has written three such music-playlets himself, *Naboth's Vineyard*, a sympathetic but comic interpretation of the Bible story, and *Shadow Play* and *Sonata about Jerusalem*, which have political significance. His more abstract works include concertos for violin and for piano, a Little Symphony (which is by no means little; it is pungently argued and lasting nearly half an hour) written in 1963 in memory of his father. There was a Symphony in One Movement in 1970.

Still among the progressive composers whose time came in the 1960s, Thea Musgrave's *Triptych* for tenor and orchestra appeared in 1963. It is based on Chaucer's "Merciles Beaute"; the orchestral part uses a Schoenbergian atonal pointillism, overlaying short bursts of colour, but the flowing, lyrical tenor part seems to conflict with this texture, and to have tonal implications. Another Scottish progressive is Iain Hamilton (b. 1922). He has written a number of large-scale orchestral works, including several symphonies, in a rather opaque atonal idiom, but has recently been composing operas, in which he has gradually reintegrated tonality. *The Royal Hunt of the Sun* (1968; first performance 1977) is basically tonal.

Humphrey Searle's Third Symphony of 1960 went almost unmarked. It is strange how his music, which is always distinguished, has attracted less and less attention as time has passed. Among the conservative symphonies of the year were Rawsthorne's Second and Alwyn's Fourth. The Rawsthorne was performed in Birmingham; it is a charming work, lighter in style than the First, and its finale is a setting of a poem by Henry Howard, Earl of Surrey. Alwyn's Fourth was played for the first time at a Promenade concert. It marked a further advance by this imaginative composer. The Fourth Symphony is in three movements, but the central movement is a Scherzo of some power. The finale of this deeply thoughtful work, Alwyn's finest up to this time, is a passacaglia.

During the 1960s the names of Boulez, Stockhausen, Henze, Berio and Dallapiccola, among others of the progressive continental composers, gradually became familiar to the English public. Several Polish composers, following in the footsteps of Szymanowski, produced the only avant-garde school in a Communist country: among them were Lutoslawski, Baird and Penderecki. From America, in addition to the familiar conservatives Aaron Copland, Roy Harris and Samuel Barber, the name of John Cage entered the English musical scene, with Elliott Carter, Milton Babbitt and others of the American avant-garde. Two of their influences, the resplendent but isolated Charles Ives and the eccentric but profoundly musical Frenchman Erik Satie, emerged from long years of neglect into fashionable esteem.

Pierre Boulez first attracted attention in advanced musical circles with his First Piano Sonata and *Structures* for two pianos, works that used total serialisation to formidable, but only partly comprehensible, effect; *Le Marteau sans maître* for orchestra established his much more relaxed and, it must be said, prettified style. He was a pupil of Messiaen, and in some ways *Le Marteau sans maître* is an extension of the techniques used by Messiaen in the *Turangalila* symphony; the age of percussion was dawning, and both works use vast batteries of these instruments; pitchless in the main, they provide a further avenue of escape from the seemingly inescapable meshes of tonality. I would not be surprised if future generations do not regard

Boulez's later works in much the same light as we regard the music of Rimsky-Korsakov—charming but rather superficial. The piano works are another matter, and so are those of Stockhausen. The piano is an intractable beast, and the piano works of both composers strike me as thoroughly obscure. Stockhausen's large-scale music, however, is uneven but enormously impressive.

From 1959 to 1962 Peter Maxwell Davies was the Director of Music at Cirencester Grammar School, and while he was there he composed his *O Magnum Mysterium*, the first part of which is a series of sections for unaccompanied choir with interludes for instrumental ensemble, and the second part an immense organ fantasia on the same theme, one of the greatest things of its kind since the organ works of Liszt. This is a hard saying, utterly without compromise, a vast Schoenbergian structure of tense intellectual strength. He also began work on a composition of the utmost moment, which was to occupy him until 1969: the opera *Taverner*.

There are more operatic settings of Shakespeare than most people realise; most of them are completely, and deservedly, forgotten. In 1960 Benjamin Britten's *A Midsummer Night's Dream* was given for the first time at Aldeburgh; it was written for the opening of the rebuilt Jubilee Hall, and the libretto was adapted from Shakespeare by Pears and Britten. It was adapted with great skill, and sacrifices a minimum of significant incident and preserves a maximum of Shakespearean poetry. It is scored for a large cast, children's choir and full orchestra— this is not one of Britten's chamber operas. One thing that is excised is the opening gambit of the play, the libretto beginning directly with Puck and the fairies. Puck is a speaking part, and Oberon a counter-tenor—a deft stroke this—and the rest of the cast are allotted appropriate voices in a more conventional manner. The work is tightly integrated, to the point where it is impossible to isolate any part or event for comment. It is most brilliantly written, with pouncing invention and great dramatic judgement throughout;* the orchestration is a study in itself.

* In this respect it is interesting to note how Britten uses some of the inventions of Boulez and Stockhausen for the uncanny effect of the orchestral prelude, while preserving tonality. It is obviously intended to convey the effect of falling asleep and beginning to dream.

The writing for voices is, as usual, polished and idiomatic. Why then does the work have so little effect on me, and I gather that I am not unique in this? Perhaps I am looking for something that is not meant to be there; the human warmth, natural magic and intoxicating melody of Mendelssohn's incidental music to the same play. But it appears to me that the music lacks emotional involvement and magic; and the play is the most magical ever written. There are several works by Britten that distance the listener to the point of not communicating, and I feel this effect with *A Midsummer Night's Dream* more than with any other Britten work.

Malcolm Arnold never holds one at a distance; indeed, he seems sometimes to breathe down one's neck. His Fourth Symphony, which appears to have been composed at the same time as the Fifth, marked a low ebb for his reputation, after an auspicious start. After the serious and impressive Third, the Fourth seems a greatly inferior work to the Fifth, and in it Arnold's penchant for pop tunes does rather run riot. The frontier between the characteristic and the blatant is always thin in Arnold's case, and he has always attracted the kind of criticism that is little more than curt dismissal; but he remains a puzzle.

Walton's Second Symphony, which was first performed in 1960, is a very different affair from the First. A light-weight work, it has something in common with the two abstract symphonies of Stravinsky. It sounds neo-classical, and it marked little improvement in Walton's decline. It does not break new ground, and there is no reason why it should. But it is actually less progressive, characteristic and vivid than the First; not an advance, not even a stand, but a retreat. It has no memorable material, and the tension has gone out of the music to the point of deflation. It is not a bore, like the Cello Concerto, but it sounds like the work of a much smaller composer than the author of the First Symphony and *Belshazzar's Feast*.

Arthur Benjamin (b. 1893) died in 1960. This Australian-born composer had taught Britten to play the piano, and Britten was a prodigious pianist. Benjamin had his meed of performances during his lifetime, and his piece for two pianos, "Jamaican Rumba", was a best-seller. All his operas, of which the best-known was *The Devil Take Her*, reached the stage. He was a composer of, frankly, light music, but he became graver in his last years; his Symphony, and an unfinished opera on *Tartuffe*, are serious and well-written works. But he was less original, more conventional, less touched by genius, than his modern counterpart, Malcolm Arnold.

The year 1961 saw the first performance of Malcolm Arnold's Fifth Symphony, ominously commissioned by the Cheltenham Festival. But Arnold is Arnold whatever the circumstances, and this time he did not disappoint. He wrote of this work: "Without wishing to sound morbid, the work is filled with memories of friends of mine who all died very young; Jack Thurston (the clarinet player), Dennis Brain, David Paltenghi (the ballet dancer and choreographer) and Gerard Hoffnung. . . . The references to each of these friends are fairly obvious in the first movement." The first subject of that first movement is a bitterly sad and twisted theme for oboe; quite a surprise for Arnold. More typical music follows at once, just saving itself from bathos by skilful changes of texture and scoring, although including a dangerously "pop" tune. There is more sense of emotional involvement in this first movement, less impression of a neat pattern fortuitously achieved, than in his earlier symphonies. Arnold describes the slow movement as a cliché. This it is not; the initial melody on the strings at once suggests Elgar, and I am not accusing Arnold of lack of originality, but indicating the power of this tune by invoking that great name. The third movement is a fiery scherzo, and the finale opens with some curious fife-and-drum effects like something left over from Arnold's Oscar-winning music for *Bridge over the River Kwai*, but proceeds to a fortissimo statement of the main theme of the slow movement; another perilous moment, but Arnold pulls it off. The ending of the symphony is quiet and serene, which is unusual for Arnold.

John Ireland died in 1962. He was very old, and had been ailing for some time; his last work of consequence was the *Satyricon* Overture of 1946, but that magnificent piece brims with youth and vigour. Ireland's music had a little influence on some conservative composers, notably Benjamin Britten, but no one could imagine a progressive composer taking his departure from it. Yet he is outstanding among the conservative English composers of his time; his music is simply better, with a fresh beauty that derives from an original imagination and sheer inventive skill. All of Ireland's piano music, slight though most of it is, is of haunting beauty, and so are his songs. The two obviously outstanding piano works are the Sonata and *Sarnia*; of the songs, "Sea Fever" has achieved something like notoriety, and "If there were dreams to sell", "Weathers", "Spring Sorrow" and "Santa Chiara" distil the essence of Ireland's gift.

The Cello Sonata, with its powerful themes and sombre colouring, is the strongest of the four duo sonatas, but the two Violin Sonatas display his lyrical gift at its best. The late Fantasy Sonata for clarinet and piano contains some of Ireland's most radical harmony, and is a notable invention generally. The three Piano Trios are all fine works, the Second sharing the mood of the Cello Sonata. The two most accomplished orchestral works are the overtures, *London* and *Satyricon*; *Mai Dun* is less brilliant and rather thick in sound, but the early *The Forgotten Rite* is most poetic. The two works for piano and orchestra, Concerto and *Legend*, are among his finest compositions, and so is the Concertino Pastorale. *These Things Shall Be* should also not be forgotten. It may not be great music, but it is poignant with a wholly English quality, and of the most refined craftsmanship.

Robert Simpson's Third Symphony dates from 1962 and is arguably his best symphony. It is in two movements, and there is a notable precedent for this: Beethoven's Sonata Op. 111. But that sonata was written 150 years ago, and there is little in Simpson's symphony to suggest that music had progressed since that date. It is beautifully constructed, and most learnedly written, but I must say, as a personal thing, that the fugitive beauty of some small piece by John Ireland suggests to me more of the substance of music. Large forms are as dependent on distinction of material as the shortest piano piece; more so, in fact.

Coventry Cathedral was destroyed in one of the most devastating raids on England during the last war, a single night in which an attempt to "take out" the city of Coventry was very nearly successful. It was determined to build a new cathedral, physically joined to the shell of the old, but contemporary in design; Sir Basil Spence was the architect, and many distinguished artists united to provide decorative features. Epstein's mighty sculpture of Michael triumphing over Satan stands by the blank outer wall of what someone has called "this fortress of the church militant".

Benjamin Britten wrote a Requiem for performance in 1962 in this new cathedral, in the spirit that inspired it, that of reconciliation among the peoples, and repentance for the outrages of war. Over the ruined altar of the old cathedral was placed a slab with the words "Father, Forgive", since the militancy of this great church was against the evil in all our hearts, not against our fellow men. Britten took the words of the Catholic Requiem mass, and troped them with the poems of Wilfred Owen, the poet of the 1914–18 war; he designed the solo parts for soprano, tenor and baritone, and for the first performance he asked that they should be taken by Russian, English and German singers, representing the three main combatants of the 1939–45 war.* The other forces are adult and children's choirs, chamber orchestra, and symphony orchestra.

It is possible that Britten's three masterpieces are *Peter Grimes*, *Billy Budd* and the War Requiem. Certainly the War Requiem is one of the peaks of his output, and in common with the other two the sense of "distancing" found in so many of his works is absent; instead, there is an emotional involvement of terrifying intensity. With a literary and dramatic skill almost equal to the music itself, Britten has matched Owen's poems to the tremendous poetry of the Roman rite for the dead, so that Owen's denunciation of war comments, sometimes with fearful irony, on the words of the rite.

The Requiem begins, conventionally enough, with tolling bells over elegiac orchestral music, in a setting of the "Requiem aeternam"; but it is followed by Owen's poem "What passing bells for these who die like cattle?" as a tenor solo, and at once the premises of the work are established; the tolling bells are

* The solo parts were taken at Coventry by Galina Vishnevskaya, Peter Pears and Dietrich Fischer-Dieskau, who subsequently recorded the work.

conventional, but they are for men who die like cattle. The Kyrie is choral. The music for solo soprano is calculated with uncanny precision for Vishnevskaya; the eldritch leaps and piercing tone colour of the "Liber scriptus" are typical. "Out there, we've walked quite friendly up to death" is a powerful dramatic stroke, a jaunty scherzo for tenor and baritone, and after the poignant "Ricordare" comes Owen's invocation of a great gun; "May God curse thee, and cut thee from our soul" for baritone solo. The "Dies irae" bursts in.

The "Lacrimosa" is set for the eerie tones of Vishnevskaya, and is followed by Owen's "Move him into the sun". Some of of the music of the "Offertorium" is derived from Britten's canticle "Abraham and Isaac", which tells of God's promise to Abraham, that his seed should be as numerous as the sands, with its ironic ending: "Offer the ram of pride instead of him. But the old man would not so, but slew his son—and half the seed of Europe, one by one." After this the children's choir sing the *Quam olim Abrahae*.

The Sanctus is set for soprano and chorus, to an angular, piercing line over percussion, and the "Pleni sunt coeli" is a great crescendo of muttering. After this affirmation the setting of "After the blast of lightning from the east" is wholly pessimistic. The Agnus Dei is combined with Owen's poem about the mutilated crucifix; after the "Libera me" the tenor solo begins the setting of Owen's greatest poem, "Strange Meeting", which is concerned with a dead soldier who wakes in limbo and finds the enemy he killed yesterday beside him. The immense slowness of harmonic movement, the eloquence of the vocal line for the tenor, who is joined by the baritone, the rising and falling of the last line, "Let us sleep now", create a tension which the final, slow cadence releases into compassion. Britten's War Requiem has a strange kinship with Beethoven's *Missa Solemnis*, and is one of the greatest religious works since that masterpiece.

Michael Tippett's contribution to the opening of the new cathedral was an opera. Like Britten's the work had a background of war; but whereas Britten's great Requiem was a logical continuation of the technique he had always used, Tippett made a radical new departure in the sound and technique of his music. *King Priam*, an account of the seige and fall of Troy, was given in Coventry Theatre by the Covent Garden Opera Company. The story is invested with a depth of symbolism far beyond the actual Homeric narrative. The central idea of this in many ways revolutionary opera is that of the necessity of choice, no matter where that choice may lead us in the end. Tippett invents some extraordinary confrontations and other incidental details to the story, things which only he could have dared or imagined.

Familiar territory for the thoughtful Tippett; the musical technique, however, is entirely new. Up to now it had been based on a complex linearity; in *King Priam* the texture is vertical, the music harmonic rather than polyphonic, consisting largely of perfect concords rendered discordant with added seconds, the scoring empty and bleak in sound, and very percussive. The resulting sound was still Tippett, but shockingly different. The opera disconcerted; some excerpts, like Achilles' war-cry, were singled out as imaginative and powerful, but the change was so sudden that it threw everyone out. Shortly after this Tippett published his Second Piano Sonata, which was based on material of the same kind as that in the opera, and consisted almost entirely of isolated chords, with some hard passage work and brutal, two-fisted octaves. It all added up to a strong sonata, no one could guess how. It was considered an unlovable work by the lovable Tippett, and some of us wondered if it marked a decline or a change of style. It proved, thank heaven, to be merely transitional, for after producing in 1963 the Concerto for Orchestra, a large-scale work in the style of *King Priam*, but rather more lyrical, Tippett passed safely into a resplendent third period, in which, appropriately and gloriously, his mentor was Beethoven.

Among emergent composers who had important first performances in 1962 were Alun Hoddinott (b. 1929), William Mathias (b. 1934) and Gordon Crosse (b. 1937). Alun Hoddinott wishes to be known as a Welsh composer; European possibly, but English, no. His music retains a tenuous hold on tonality, but employs a modified form of serial technique. His Second Symphony appeared in 1962; a colourful, rich work, with unusual orchestration that Hoddinott was going to develop. Glittering yet mysterious, there is a good deal of Welsh magic in the scoring. Cheltenham saw the first performance of a Violin Sonata by William Mathias, Gordon Crosse's *Villanelles*, Benjamin Frankel's Second Symphony, and Elizabeth Lutyens's *Quincunx* for orchestra. Her Music for Orchestra No. 2 also appeared this year; she writes that it is an advance in rhythmic freedom on Music for Orchestra No. 1, and is like a fountain that sweeps upward rather than a linear process. Another important work by a progressive composer belonging to this year was Alexander Goehr's Violin Concerto.

At this time a new work by Walton was an event that aroused delight mingled with trepidation; would this too be a disappointment? As it turned out, the Variations on a Theme of Hindemith marked a stage in his mild recovery. It came as a shock to realise that Walton admired Hindemith. Hindemith has his own virtues, but is rather a plain, glum fellow when compared with that mercurial harlequin, Walton at his best. The morose theme that Walton chose came from the Cello Concerto of 1940, and it seemed to forebode the worst; but Walton becomes more and more himself as the music proceeds, ending in considerable brilliance and something of his old irreverence.

Paul Hindemith himself died in 1963. He had conducted in Edinburgh a few years previously, and was quite well known in England; his Symphony, *Mathis der Maler* had become quite popular, and his vast piano-pedagogic work, *Ludus Tonalis*, had excited attention; he also wrote many volumes of composition lessons. He remains difficult to assess, an academic composer of conservative leanings whose music nevertheless belongs in style to the twentieth century.

Rawsthorne's Third Symphony, written for the Cheltenham Festival of 1964, was his last, and his last large-scale orchestral work; it is dedicated to his wife Isabel, who was earlier married to Constant Lambert. This is Rawsthorne's most impressive symphony, and best orchestral work since the Symphonic Studies. The slow movement is a Sarabande, and one might remember the Sarabande from Busoni's *Doktor Faust*, which it somewhat resembles in atmosphere. Humphrey Searle's Fifth

Symphony was written in memory of his teacher, Anton Webern; in it he achieved the synthesis he had been striving for since his First Symphony of 1953, although, like the Fourth, the Fifth is to an extent fragmented in rhythm. His second opera, *The Photo of the Colonel*, from a story by Ionesco, was produced in Frankfurt in June 1964; this first stage production was preceded by a broadcast by the BBC.

The great Russian cellist Rostropovich inspired many works by Benjamin Britten, and the two were close friends. The Symphony for Cello and Orchestra was written in 1963, and first performed in Moscow in March 1964. It is probably Britten's finest orchestral work, although it must be said that he seldom wrote for instruments without voices. The first movement is also Britten's largest sonata structure. The Scherzo, Presto inquieto, has a ghostly alacrity that is a late Britten fingerprint; it turns up in the three Suites for cello he wrote for Rostropovich in 1964, 1967 and 1974 and may be a development of certain passages from the early *Hymn to St Cecilia*. There is a cadenza link between the slow movement and the finale, which is a Passacaglia. Certain aspects of Bridge's *Phantasm* are evident; *Enter Spring* is also echoed in the fanfare and timpani passages towards the end. As Britten grew older his debt to Frank Bridge became more evident.

The first of Britten's Church Parables was produced in 1964; *Curlew River*, a fascinating piece with fascinating origins. In Tokyo in January 1956 Britten saw a No play for the first time, and was immensely impressed. It was *Sumidagawa*, and on it he based *Curlew River* (which means much the same thing), translated into the terms of an English medieval mystery play. The musical basis of the score is the plainsong "Te lucis ante terminum", and it is designed to be performed in churches, by singers dressed as monks, with a minimum of disguise when they assume the roles of the drama. The story is of an old woman driven mad by the loss of her son, and her seeking of him; he has been killed, but his spirit appears to her, and blesses her, and she returns to her home comforted. It is set by the river, and the significant figure of the Ferryman is an important baritone role. The atmosphere is that of a country church, and the whole work has a great peace and spirituality;

technically, Britten adopts a number of devices of decoration and fioritura which almost undermine the usual sturdy tonality; the score is evanescent, made up of flurries of notes.

There was a small, but profound and elusive, work from Britten in 1965: the *Songs and Proverbs of William Blake*. The songs were written for Dietrich Fischer-Dieskau, and are for baritone rather than the usual high tenor of Peter Pears, so the tone-colour is dark. Six of the *Proverbs of Hell* are set between six of the *Songs of Experience*, and a twelve-note theme, arranged in four three-note segments, is the musical basis of the work; as usual, Britten captures the spirit of his poet. Alan Rawsthorne's Third, and last, String Quartet appeared in this same year. He could always sustain a true sonata Allegro, not a common thing since Wagner, and this quartet is no exception; it is both athletic and intellectual, a fine structure of taut polyphony.

Thea Musgrave's opera, *The Decision*, was completed in this year. Its odd story, of a miner trapped for twenty-three days and brought alive to the surface, only to die three days later, is not a very operatic one. Another first performance was that of Edmund Rubbra's Piano Concerto, by Denis Matthews with the BBC Symphony Orchestra under Sir Malcolm Sargent.

One conservative symphonist who has avoided most of the pitfalls of the genre is John McCabe (b. 1939), whose First Symphony was given at Cheltenham in 1965. He studied at the Royal Manchester College of Music, and also at the Hochschule für Musik in Munich. He is one of the few English composers not to be harmed by the influence of Sibelius. His First Symphony is subtitled "Elegy", and like Sibelius's Fourth is based on the tritone—as is much conservative-radical modern music. The brass writing also recalls Sibelius. The first movement is a Lento moderato which suggests the elegy aspect of the work with tolling bells and desolate tritone-based harmony. The second movement is a mordant Scherzo, with smacking, vicious brass; the finale, Adagio–allegro vivo–tempo primo, is complex, as its tempo changes indicate, and shares the northern colouring of the rest of the symphony. A finely constructed, individual work of considerable power. What separates McCabe from other tonal symphonists, apart from his more imaginative harmony, is the passion of the music, and its acknowledgement of the dark side of things. One has the feeling that Nielsen, for instance, rather saw evil as a loud noise, which could be frightened off with a common chord. In McCabe the drama is interior to the music, not an extraneous intrusion; by acknowledging the dark he triumphs over the dark.

Richard Rodney Bennett (b. 1936) began to be known in the 1960s both as an operatic composer and a symphonist. The year 1965 saw the first performance of two major works which placed him on the map: his Symphony No. 1 and his opera *The Mines of Sulphur*, which share a certain musical atmosphere and language, and even a common compositional impulse. Bennett is a middle-of-the-road composer; in some of his music he accepts serial conventions, but most of it is tonal, and adopts tonal methods of harmonic organisation. He writes: "It's my natural way of composing, although the more I progress the more I think I need tonal references and themes." Debussy is one of his points of departure, and another is jazz, but in spite of this his music bears no resemblance to that of Constant Lambert. His music is technically accomplished, but expressionist in mood, and full of dramatic gestures and extreme dissonance. Yet there is always present a lyricism based on Romanticism. The vocal parts of *The Mines of Sulphur*, the story of a band of thieves who contract the plague from their victims, are thoroughly vocal in the old-fashioned sense. It is significant that Bennett, a fine pianist, sometimes plays the piano music of Boulez, from whom he has had advice.

Edgard Varèse died in 1965. He was born in France in 1883 but it was not until the 1960s that his music began to penetrate England and his significance to be recognised here. It was just beginning to dawn on the western world when he died that he was a great pioneer, and perhaps a great composer. His orchestration was obviously approaching the sound of electronic music when the perfecting of tape-recording produced the inevitable result; Varèse composed the first piece of electronic music. Such things as the famous *Ionisation* of 1931, with its reference to a process in physics, *Density 21·5* (the density of the material of a flute) of 1935, and *Equatorial* (1937) have become monuments of modern music.

Britten's Second Church Parable, *The Burning Fiery Furnace*, was first performed in 1966. Like *Curlew River*, it is based on a plainchant, in this case "Salus aeterna, indeficiens mundi vitae", and the story is that of Shadrach, Meshach and Abednego. More overtly dramatic than *Curlew River*, and concerned with the tyranny of a colourful Oriental monarch, *The Burning Fiery Furnace* has music of considerable glitter and splendour— a few instruments only, but such is the skill with which they are used that the resulting web of sound almost recalls Walton's *Belshazzar's Feast*, at least in colour, except that Britten, once more, has been listening to Boulez, while still remaining tonal and even diatonic.

Walton's second opera appeared in 1967: a one-acter, and a comedy at that, but lacking, in its rather subdued manner, the more obvious faults of *Troilus and Cressida*. The story is from Chekhov, with a libretto by Paul Dehn and Walton; it is a simple character study of a tearful widow swept off her feet by a bear-like land-owner come to collect a debt from her late husband's estate; appropriately called *The Bear*. The music is brilliant and swift-moving, not quite like anything else by Walton; but although this is a more viable opera than *Troilus and Cressida*, the music, I fear, is simply unmemorable.

Rubbra's Eighth and Malcolm Arnold's Sixth Symphonies date from 1967; and if Rubbra seems always to remain the same, Malcolm Arnold does register a subtle change as he grows in experience. The Sixth was performed for the first time by the BBC Northern Symphony Orchestra in Sheffield; it marks a development in Arnold's sense of form, a more deeply thought-out structure than ever before. In the first movement form and material grow out of each other in a way that was new for this composer. The slow movement is less diatonic than usual, and even has the appearance of serial music in places, but the finale is the familiar Arnold, with Stravinsky among his more obvious influences. The Sixth shows an increase in purely musical integration, and a certain gain in restraint. There is less tendency simply to bash about, and even the noisy end to the finale is part of the development of an initial string figure.

Richard Rodney Bennett's Piano Concerto, played at the Birmingham Triennial Festival of 1968, is an extremely brilliant work, and scored a great success; Stephen Bishop Kovacevich has recorded it. Bennett's First Symphony was a fine and serious work which handled a European style convincingly; his Piano Concerto is also serial in structure, and to a certain extent in sound; but it also suggests a latter-day Ravel. Ravel uses the blues in his G major Concerto; Bennett a faster jazz idiom in the finale of this Concerto. Brilliant and sensuous, a marvellous game with the medium, the Concerto is saved from shallowness by its neat structure and obvious seriousness of intent. But after this work it began to seem that Bennett had not fulfilled his early promise. He has written much distinguished music, including three operas; but he needs to concentrate his wide stylistic range, which stretches from serialism to diatonic film music and something like pop.

In 1968 Humphrey Searle's opera *Hamlet* was produced in Hamburg, and Franz Reisenstein, who was born in Nuremberg in 1911, but was resident in England for many years, died. Searle's opera, like Schoenberg's *Moses und Aron*, is based on a single tone-row, derived from a setting of Hamlet's most famous speech, "To be or not to be". Franz Reisenstein was a pupil of Hindemith; he was often heard as a pianist in chamber music, and wrote much chamber music himself, and a Cello Concerto (1948), a Ballet Suite (1940) and a Piano Concerto (1941). His style was eclectic and without much personality.

Lennox Berkeley's Third Symphony was performed for the first time in 1969. It is very short by most standards, a single movement no longer than any single movement from a symphony by Rachmaninov or Shostakovich. Its most successful features are its beautiful textures and graceful, flowing lines; but it fails to integrate the sections of a symphony into its one concentrated movement, in the manner perhaps best achieved in Sibelius's Seventh. The heroic attempts of the Third do not quite ring true. Berkeley is not an heroic composer; even in his operas, *A Dinner Engagement* (1954) is closer to his emotional range than *Nelson*.

Walton's Hindemith Variations had been an improvement on the music that preceded them, though Hindemith's theme and example were somewhat glum. Britten is another matter, as was seen in 1970 when the San Francisco Symphony Orchestra under Josef Krips gave the first performance of Walton's

Improvisations on an Impromptu of Benjamin Britten. This was new: a meeting-place for two great English composers who are so different, yet with a basis in that conservative idiom represented at its most typical by Prokofiev. The theme was taken from the new slow movement which Britten wrote for his Piano Concerto of 1938 when he revised it in 1946. This extremely Brittenish theme, a matter of high strings in poignant and ambiguous harmonies, colours the whole work; but Walton is writing in a new style, a style full of eerie imagination. The whole piece has a third-period feeling, in its almost unearthly quality; and when something of the rhythmic snap of *Scapino* is heard at the end, it has a macabre astringency that is both new and yet recognisably Walton. The harmony is the most advanced he has ever used, and more subtly manipulated than the strident clashes of old. It is not a long piece; a little longer than *Scapino*. But it marks a new phase, and holds out a new hope; Walton has done so much that is splendid and memorable that one would like him to pass out of his fallow period and end in a blaze of glory.

The aftermath of the revolution of 1959 settled down into what was perhaps the best period for English music since the renaissance began. Many prejudices departed, and what was good, both in English and foreign music, was appreciated as never before. If this had not happened it would have been better to have ended this book in 1939, for in the 1950s I could never have predicted the change for the better which has come over the English musical scene. The emergence of Elgar as a world figure, an emergence assisted by the death of so many false legends, and by the advocacy of distinguished foreign conductors like Solti and Barenboim, and also the radical temper of these later times, opened the floodgates as Elgar himself had opened them at the beginning of the century. It was the progressives of the 1970s who recognised the progressive and professional of eighty years before. In Elgar's wake many other English composers received a measure of recognition not accorded them in their lifetimes, Arnold Bax and Frank Bridge especially, while virtually the complete works of John Ireland have now been recorded.

There had been, in the late 1960s, an astonishing revival of interest in Romantic music. The finest musical brains in England from the 1920s until this time had been apt to reject nineteenth-century Romantic music out of hand, perhaps as a reaction against the lazy and prejudiced acceptance of this music by the general public, who, in the main, refused to listen to anything else. But this Romantic revival was not based on the over-played Tchaikovsky, Chopin and Puccini, but on other, unusual, very individual composers. The Berlioz centenary had at last established him as a great composer; there were several complete recordings of Wagner's *Ring*; and the music of Mahler became a positive cult. Many minor figures, like Moscheles, Gade and Raff were revived, and later individualists, Erik Satie being the most prominent, became the object of interest.

Was this Romantic revival the reason for the new interest in the composers of the English renaissance? Not quite; they were aspects of the same broad tendency. The swing from extreme conservatism to fanatical serialism had been too violent; a new mood of tolerance and a broad appreciation of the music of many nations and all periods prevailed. There was great enthusiasm for medieval and Renaissance music, and ancient instruments of all kinds were revived. It had begun with the harpsichord at the hands of Arnold Dolmetsch and Wanda Landowska at the beginning of the century, and now baroque and earlier wind and string instruments reappeared, and with them a proper understanding and appreciation of their music.

A small point, but a significant one, was the group of young conductors, English and foreign, who suddenly through the medium of gramophone records, discovered the art of Wilhelm Furtwängler. During the 1940s and 1950s, and in some cases later, the provincial condescension of some English critics towards the conductor who had led the two greatest orchestras of Europe, the Berlin Philharmonic and the Vienna Philharmonic, for thirty years, passed belief. They wrote of him as though he were some eccentric boy who had taken up conducting as a hobby and made a mess of it, and drew his attention to minor English conductors as a model from whom he should learn. In many points of interpretation and musicianship the English remained isolated from the rest of the world for decades after the ending of the war. For the majority of the younger conductors of the second half of the twentieth century Furtwängler was the most significant conductor of the first half. The rejection of Furtwängler, and many other great interpretive artists of the immediate past, together with much modern music, had been an example of the chronically genteel, inhibited atmosphere which had been the bane of the British.

A great number of composers died in these years; Roberto Gerhard in 1970, Stravinsky and Rawsthorne in 1971, Frank Martin in 1973, and Egon Wellesz and Benjamin Frankel in 1974. Stravinsky was of course a giant, and had been composing gnomic, mysterious works ever since his conversion to serialism. Gerhard and Wellesz were both in their different ways disciples of Schoenberg, and Wellesz was an authority on Byzantine music into the bargain; Martin was a Swiss conservative, and Frankel died writing his Ninth Symphony. Rawsthorne, the English composer in this group, was a reticent composer who had become more conservative after a radical beginning, but one of distinctive personality and inherent originality.

Fine though John McCabe's First Symphony was, his Second, first performed on 25 September 1971 by the City of Birmingham Orchestra under Louis Frémaux, is even finer. It is more subtle; the hard elements of the First have been given an added edge and fire, the harmony is more advanced and sophisticated, and the scoring sounds as though that iron Northerner, McCabe, had been listening to the music of that wild Welshman, Hoddinott. Like the First, the Second resolves into alternate fast and slow. The order of the sections is Vivo–Andante–Allegrissimo–Lento–Vivo; they are more sections than movements. The work is introduced by a short phrase for flute that recurs at the end, cool and almost flavourless. In between is a magnificent orchestral landscape, logical but passionate, wildly coloured like a winter sunset. When the flute theme appears again at the end, the notes are the same, but the meaning is different.

In between McCabe's First and Second Symphonies came a rather unexpected work, *Notturni ed Alba*. Based on medieval

Latin lyrics concerned with night and dawn, this is warm and colourful music, and the influence suggested is that of Szymanowski; in fact, this is an English counterpart to Szymanowski's masterpiece, *The Song of the Night* (the Third Symphony). The vocal line has much the same shape and sensuous inflection as that in *The Song of the Night*, while the vivid and glittering colour of the scoring also suggests the Polish composer.

One effect of *Peter Grimes* and the subsequent Britten operas was to turn England, for the first time, into a country of opera composers. This was helped along by the liberation of the English temperament from its chronic inhibitions, a liberation which may have begun during the 1939–45 war, when English soldiers, stationed in Italy, heard Italian companies presenting Italian opera for the first time. In Britten's wake came a number of English composers of opera, not only Tippett, but Bennett, Searle, and many others, including such progressives as Lutyens, Birtwistle and Peter Maxwell Davies. But Britten was to write only two more.

Britten's penultimate opera, *Owen Wingrave*, was commissioned by BBC Television and was first televised on BBC 2 on 16 May 1971. The libretto is by Myfanwy Piper, based on a short story by Henry James. This was the second time Britten had referred specifically to his pacifism in a major work, and in the War Requiem the reference was only implicit. It is explicit in *Owen Wingrave*, the story of a conscientious objector in an old military family. It is a strange work; the music, like that of the latest works of Michael Tippett, suggests the onset of a third period; it has that elision and unusual quality which marks the final works of a major composer—an atmosphere further confirmed by *Death in Venice*. Page after page of *Owen Wingrave* is eerie, haunted, unique, in spite of its traditional tonal technique. This unusual atmosphere persists until almost the end, when the music begins to tail off.

It is doubtful if the pacifist case can be rendered in a form that is at once operatic and didactic, for opera is emotional and theatrical, an exotic and irrational entertainment, while the arguments for pacifism are realistic and intellectual. The case in the opera *Owen Wingrave* fails on two counts. First, the Wingraves are presented as mere grotesques, and the opposition to

Owen is not formidable, either intellectually or morally. It does make a difference, for he is fighting shadows; and appropriately, but hardly probably, it is a ghost that kills him. It also kills his argument, for the second point is that in accepting the Wingraves' challenge to prove that he is not a coward he is accepting their own appalling values: he dies, according to Henry James, "like a young soldier on the battlefield". The Wingraves have been dying—and killing!—for all manner of bad causes for centuries, but Owen dies for the worst cause of all; to prove that he is brave, to prove, in the end, that killing is valid. Owen's initial case is sound, as is the music that accompanies it. But it is his courage that is tested—or his folly—not his pacifism, or his intelligence; and it is no accident that the music goes to pieces in the last quarter of the work.

Britten's next, and last opera, *Death in Venice*, was performed for the first time in The Maltings, Snape (rebuilt after a disastrous fire), on 16 June 1973. It continues the third-period aspect of his music, and is more subtle dramatically and psychologically. I shall not deal with it here in detail, except to note that it stands up well among his finest works, perhaps his best opera since *Billy Budd*. It is based on Thomas Mann's story of a distinguished novelist, Gustave von Aschenbach, whose gift has failed him. He is brooding on holiday in Venice, when he notices a fourteen-year-old boy of great beauty and grace, who seems to symbolise for him his lost talent. He takes to following the boy around, and watching him, in an effort to find again his creative joy; but gradually realises that he is physically in love with him. In his infatuation he stays on in Venice in spite of a cholera epidemic, and dies of the disease. In addition to the singing protagonist, and the dancing, silent boy, Tadzio, a procession of characters—all played by the same baritone singer—symbolise some beckoning, haunting fate—perhaps the death that von Aschenbach will meet in Venice. Previous hints of a development of Britten's style in the direction of something unusual are fulfilled in this opera; the music is haunting and unearthly, the scoring different. (It has been suggested that it is a development of the orchestration of *Curlew River*, an interesting thought.) Britten was now very ill, and about this time underwent a serious operation, which left him an invalid for the rest of his life.

Three works by Tippett stand out in the English music of the time, and form a climax to these years: *The Vision of St Augustine* (1966), *The Knot Garden* (1971) and the Third Symphony (1972) are a visionary trinity of major works.*

The Vision of St Augustine, for baritone solo, chorus and orchestra, is a setting of Augustine's description, in his *Confessions*, of a vision of time and eternity he shared with his mother, Monica; it is a work of extended ecstasy, an outburst of praise and joy so uninhibited that it was some time before listeners came to grips with it. Passing years, the score, and a very fine recording have given us the measure of this work. It is in three sections, and each section is opened by the baritone soloist with a quiet, almost hesitant phrase. In the first section this phrase, to the words "Impendente autem die" (When the day was approaching), is accompanied by a pedal C on cellos, basses and piano, with bass drum roll, and decorated with a phrase for half the cellos; the wild flicker of the celeste as the chorus enters at bar 5 is typical of the tone-colour of the work. Tippett's characteristic wild-cat writing for instruments in the upper reaches of their compass (usually violins) here reaches a highly developed state, which was later to change subtly in *The Knot Garden*. Part Two begins with the words, "Cumque ad eum finem aermo perduceretur" (And our conversation had brought us to this point) over divided basses, with a variant of the figuration of Part One. The opening of Part Three however is not so mysterious, but ecstatic: "Dicebamus ergo; si cui sileat tumultus carnis sileant . . ." (So we said; if for anyone silent was the tumult of the flesh . . .).

The solo part is high in tessitura, with wide-leaping intervals, and the orchestra fragmented and pulsing with excitement. The ending is awe-inspiring, but also deeply moving: after a final wild swirl of wood-winds, a mysterious line in Greek, murmured by the chorus in major seconds, B flat to C; even

---

* He has since produced another opera, *The Icebreak*, and a Fourth Symphony, both perhaps too new at the time of writing (1978) to warrant comment here, particularly as there is always a time-lag as far as Tippett is concerned.

more mysterious chords from the orchestra; and the final sound is the spoken translation of the line in Greek, "I count not myself to have apprehended".

The sustained ecstasy of the words, in which the vision is analysed in the usual allusive language of the mystics, is expressed by a number of musical devices, one of these the stuttering on one note of the soloist, derived from a similar device in Monteverdi. The music often whirls along, to end in a sudden, short chord, as if words had failed. There are many changes of tempo, the metronome marks for which are meticulously indicated in a table at the head of the score (it must be a nightmare for the conductor); the usual Tippett wild, high writing; sudden brassy climaxes, short and curt; battering timpani figures abruptly interrupting the discourse; austere, cold harmony, developed from *King Priam* but no longer brutal but edged with fire; and orchestral textures which, for all their occasional clamour of noise, are of disembodied luminosity. The work grows in stature with acquaintance; but even so, for one who knows Tippett's idiom, and is temperamentally attuned to it, even the first hearing can be impressive.

The Knot Garden was Tippett's third opera. Once more he wrote the libretto himself, and this time it was accepted that only he could provide the right words for his particular vision. The knot garden of the title is used to enmesh and confront a group of very diverse characters who have come to seek the advice and help of an analyst (Mangus). Act I is called "Confrontation", Act II "Labyrinth", and Act III "Charade", and in this final act not only is the action wound up (rather inconclusively in the case of the musician Dov), but a parody of *The Tempest* is played out by the characters under the direction of Mangus-Prospero. The central problem is the unsatisfactory marital relationship of Faber and Thea, which is resolved. Denise, a freedom fighter badly disfigured by torture, finds a mate in the quasi-homosexual Negro writer Mel; and Mangus also realises that he is not the god of this little world, but has his problems too.

In the music some of Tippett's most persistent mannerisms evolve and soften. The wild-cat writing high above the stave, which had acquired more purpose and a fiery edge in *The*

Vision of St Augustine, here becomes a lucent flickering as of the fire of the spirit; the orchestration achieves a peak of slow-won mastery, a luminous kaleidoscope of melting sound which provides an uncanny equivalent of the changing panorama of psychic events. Another aspect of Tippett's shrill treble writing finds an apt resolution in the part for Denise. The extravagance of this kind of vocal writing is justified by the extremity of Denise's position, and this aspect of Tippett's style here finds unexpected fulfilment. Some see Denise as the central character and catalyst of the opera; she is certainly a catalyst, but Dov, weak, enigmatic Dov, imposes his tortured gentleness on the action.* Denise pairs off with Mel (whose name means sweetness), but for his partner, the abandoned Dov, there is no salvation, only loneliness and his art. In the crisis confrontation of the three characters, Dov, Mel and Denise, the troubled pair, Faber and Thea, are almost thrust out of our consciousness; but it is their uneasy reconciliation that forms the dénouement of *The Knot Garden*, the first opera of Tippett's stylistic maturity.

Beethoven has always presented a twofold challenge to Tippett; the challenge of the music itself, for which he has a particular reverence, and the challenge of Beethoven's optimism, an idealism that believes, not without question, but with faith, in truth, beauty and love. This could be Tippett's creed also, but as a child of our time he is aware of how little that time gives grounds for any such hope. His Third Symphony is concerned with these questions, both the musical challenge of Beethoven to a contemporary symphonist and the metaphysical and moral challenge of our time to Beethoven's optimistic humanism. The symphony is in two sections; but in the first section the first movement and the slow movement are dovetailed together in a remarkable way. Two elements are employed, Arrest and Movement; the Arrest music is the tonally static rhythmic device used by Stravinsky; Movement is Tippett's familiar high scolding strings. They alternate throughout the first part of the first section, extending, modifying,

* Tippett felt that the character of Dov could do with further expansion, and in consequence he wrote a set of *Songs for Dov* outside the body of the opera.

combining, until the snapping brass of Arrest and the rushing strings of Movement are observed to be aspects of the same thing, and merge together in the great sidereal calm of the slow movement, which ends the first section. A kind of scherzo introduces the second section, but it quickly develops into Beethoven's "Terror Fanfare" from the Ninth Symphony. No triumphant baritone challenges this sad music, but a soprano singing the blues. There are four blues songs in the movement, in which humanity is affirmed, compassion proclaimed, but a solution to the terrible questions left uncertain. "What though the dream crack! What shall remake it. Staring with those startled eyes at what we are—blood of my blood,/Bone of my bone/We sense a huge compassionate power/To heal/To love." The last word of the symphony is love.

When Colin Davis was asked by Tippett to comment on the decidedly curious, but painfully moving poems Tippett wrote for his four blues songs, Davis said in effect, not Schiller but Blake. Blake! The prophet of our time, the one English poet with a message for our age, two hundred years after his. If these poems seem strange to us, it is to mad, gloriously sane Blake, with his piercing vision that was the sum of things, that we must turn. Blake died singing; and this is the sort of music he might have written, had he been a composer of our time and not a poet of his. In any case, Blake and Beethoven were contemporaries.

Benjamin Britten died on 4 December 1976. During these last years he was permitted only an hour's composition a day, but he succeeded in writing several short vocal pieces and the Third String Quartet. His last great, cumulative works have been discussed in their place; from the 1950s he shared a pre-eminence with Michael Tippett, and at the time of Britten's death Tippett was still very active on ambitious projects. In spite of some non-basic devices which sound modern, Britten's harmonic idiom was extraordinarily anachronistic. He relied heavily on diatonic harmony, and when, in his last years, his music became a little more radical, the radical elements took the form of decorative flourishes and fiorature which did not affect the basic harmonic structure. From *King Priam* onwards Tippett's technique became much more radical than Britten's, and that in spite of the adaptation by Britten of a form of serial row to his diatonic textures, a device Tippett has shown no interest in. It remains to be seen whether the major works by Tippett that we shall hear during the next few years alter the relative positions of the two composers; Britten so dominated the musical scene in England, and had such a commanding position abroad, that Tippett's closing of the gap between them in the last few years was unexpected. It has been pointed out* that Britten's themes, now that we can see all his music, were obsessional, and his range in some ways narrow. This does not seriously detract from Britten's ultimate stature, but it has to be set against the wide emotional range of Tippett, his electrifying speed of development, and the sense he gives of almost infinite potential. With Tippett still active, the relative stature of the two cannot be said to be finalised.

During the last few decades the number of possible styles in which a composer might write, from extreme conservatism to music more radical than ever before, and the number of composers who have achieved at least performance, has increased to a bewildering degree. In England there is a broad spectrum of techniques, from the extreme conservatism of Robert Simpson and Edmund Rubbra to a fair degree of radicalism. Cornelius Cardew (b. 1936) was for a time associated with the Scratch Orchestra, an *ad hoc* group of instrumentalists playing any instrument they liked, whether they could play it or not, each man a different piece of music, and all at once. Its life was short. Cardew, who became a Marxist, is the author of a book called *Stockhausen Serves Imperialism*; his own music must be a matter of opinion, but personally I find it simple-minded, whereas Stockhausen's is perhaps the most intellectually complex music of today, for all its bewildering variety of idiom and technique the product of a formidably musical mind. David Bedford (b. 1937) has a more secure talent than Cardew, although his music veers disconcertingly between serious and pop, with folky inflections. His orchestral piece, *Music for Albion Moonlight*, is imaginative and powerful, and a recent song cycle

* By Stanley Sadie in his *Musical Times* obituary of Britten.

with chamber orchestra called *The Tentacles of the Dark Nebula* was sympathetically received.

John Tavener (b. 1944) is, like the Jacobean dramatist Webster, "much obsessed by death" and has written a series of requiems. His first considerable work was called *The Whale* (1966), and it begins with a reading of the entry on whales in *Chambers's Encyclopaedia*, and proceeds to elaborate on Jonah. *A Celtic Requiem*, which followed in 1969, draws on a variety of texts, including those of traditional children's games. So far Tavener's music has mixed serious and popular elements in wild confusion, but it retains its emotional coherence, and seems to owe something to the techniques of Penderecki, who avoids both orthodox and modern techniques, and writes music that is a series of noise-like sounds. *Ultimos Ritos* (1975) is a long, impressive work of many layers, taking its main departure from the Crucifixus of Bach's B minor Mass. One small requiem followed it; *Requiem for Father Malachi*, for smaller forces, more traditional in sound, and to the usual liturgical words. It is difficult at this stage to assess Tavener, but he is important in epitomising a tendency of some composers to react against the deadly seriousness and maddening technical complexity of some modern music and to move into a realm of pure expressiveness in which taste is largely irrelevant.

Roger Smalley (b. 1944) is radical in a way that is unique to him. Unlike some other progressive composers in England today, who have developed their techniques out of a burning need to say certain things in a certain manner, his theory appears to be that the idiom matters more than the music, and he is very intolerant of all music being written today that is not of the extreme avant-garde. He is interested in the manipulation of blocks and waves of sound, and he has written mainly for chamber groups with piano.

Two more Welsh composers range from middle ground to distinctly conservative: Denis ApIvor (b. 1916) and Daniel Jones (b. 1912). ApIvor is a very prolific composer, but although he made some stir in the late 1940s, he seems of late to have faded from public notice. Daniel Jones has written six symphonies at the time of writing, in a Romantic style, with traditional tonal technique. Even more conservative are Kenneth

Leighton (b. 1929) and Anthony Milner (b. 1925), both of whom have written liturgical music, or oratorio-type compositions, as well as orchestral works. In Anthony Gilbert (b. 1934) we have another radical, of small but interesting output.

Of the comparatively conservative composers who are still reasonably young, four stand out in my opinion. Apart from Malcolm Arnold, who is a law unto himself, we have Alun Hoddinott, John McCabe, and Richard Rodney Bennett. Hoddinott has written so much music that it is hard to keep up with it all; but his five symphonies (so far), and many concertos and small pieces, including a magnificent short piece with an unwieldy name, *The Sun, the Great Luminary of the Universe*, have such colour, power and magic and are so original that he must be considered to have considerable potential. He has shown some development over the years, tending to become more radical and increasingly original. It is tempting to compare him with Turner, since as time goes on his music seems about to dissolve into light and colour. McCabe writes much more slowly, and his music is less spectacular, but its solid qualities, and the rugged power of his large-scale structures, make a similar outstanding impression. The more radical Bennett seems to be marking time, and a development of his present style would be welcome; he is one of our few radical-conservative composers with a European orientation who manages to make something personal out of it.

One great conservative died in 1975: Sir Arthur Bliss. His last work was the Metamorphic Variations of 1973 in which his considerable talent remained undimmed. Like some others, he began as a radical in the early days of the renaissance, and became steadily more conservative as the years went on; but, unlike some others, Bliss made a success of it.

In 1973 William Alwyn almost ceased to be a conservative; he produced a work of such originality that it sounds far from reactionary. His Fifth Symphony, commissioned by the Arts Council, was first performed at the Norwich Triennial Festival. In one movement, it is "the repayment of a life-long debt" to Sir Thomas Browne, and is based on his strange book of 1685, *Hydriotaphia: Urn Burial*.

The very opening of the symphony, a mysterious and indeed

ghoulish rushing sound, the scoring of which has no parallel in Alwyn's earlier works, alerts one to the fact that something new and exciting is taking place in this composer's musical development. The scoring is indeed adventurous; and although the thematic material as it unfolds has the familiar Alwyn sound, its context is positively unfamiliar. The sheer imagination of this work, and the subtle way in which the tempo passes from the funeral march of one section to weird sounds as of ghostly nocturnal revels, reveals a tremendous extension of Alwyn's range. The score bears quotations from *Urn Burial*, the last of which is "Man is a noble animal, splendid in ashes, and pompous in the grave". The atmosphere of Sir Thomas Browne's magnificently mannered prose has been splendidly caught, and there is an added dimension that is Alwyn's own.

The rebirth of Romanticism, and the increased radicalism of English music, produced some curious hybrids, one of whom may be John Tavener, and another undoubtedly is Robin Holloway (b. 1943) a young composer divided between his reverence for Romanticism in general and the music of Schumann in particular, and his sense of being a twentieth-century composer. He has composed a number of songs, and some large-scale orchestral works, some of them based on the music of Schumann.

I wish to close this book with some account of the latest works of those composers whom I think have the future of English music in their hands. The situation in England in the 1970s is more favourable to our music and our composers than at any time since the renaissance began. A young composer has a better chance of performance, publication and even recording, than ever before; it almost seems as if the national character of the English has changed since the beginning of the century. Part of this improved situation is due to the more liberal, generous social atmosphere which began in the 1960s, and part to the pioneering of Elgar, Beecham and Wood. The operatic success of Britten, and his acceptance abroad, also helped in no small measure.

There are three names, in my view, among the younger composers in England today that are outstanding in world music and bode well for the future of the art in England. These are Brian Ferneyhough (b. 1943), Peter Maxwell Davies and Harrison Birtwistle. Of these, Ferneyhough has lived abroad for some years, and has been better known on the Continent than here; but his very striking music is beginning to be known in the land of his birth. The 1969 recording by the Gaudeamus Foundation of part of his Sonatas for String Quartet brought his name to a wider public, and in the 1970s his music began to be performed in England. But the overwhelming number of performances, and first performances, of his music have taken place in Europe. He is a composer on a grand scale: Sonatas for String Quartet lasts for 45 minutes, and is in 24 linked sections. Sonatas belongs to 1968; in 1969 came *Epicycle for Twenty Strings*, and his next big work was *Sieben Sterne* for organ. The enormous and elaborate *Firecycle Beta* for orchestra was composed during 1969–71, followed by *Transit* for six voices and chamber orchestra. *Transit*, like many of Ferneyhough's mature works, has a metaphysical point of departure; the score has a famous sixteenth-century print on its title page, depicting a missionary who has come to the ends of the earth, sticking his head through the sky to look at Heaven. Various *Time and Motion Studies* followed, and he is at present (1978) working on *La Terre est un homme*, for orchestra.

Ferneyhough's technique takes its departure from Webern, but obviously with such a broad canvas he has to extend Webern's concentrated, minuscule time-scale. Whereas there is a timelessness about Webern's structures, born of their very internal rhythmic and contrapuntal organisation, Ferneyhough admits far more sense of movement, of motor-rhythm almost, although these rhythms are fragmented and subtle. Nevertheless they do move, and have to move to support his vast time-scale. There also seems to be, in his music, a sense of resolution, of increase and decrease of harmonic tension, that is irrelevant in Webern. He is, then, in some ways less radical than Webern, in spite of various elements from the modern avant-garde that occur in his music; this is true, but it comes from what I will call his cosmic romanticism, an element one finds even in such works as *Unity Capsule* for solo flute. Of our three composers Ferneyhough has declared less

of himself than the other two; there is more of him that is as
yet unknown. Both Birtwistle and Maxwell Davies have been
before the public longer, and their styles are less mysterious—
I will not write more mature, for we do not know yet how
Ferneyhough is likely to develop. But there is a very great
talent indeed, already instinct with power and intellectual grip.

Harrison Birtwistle's first published work was *Refrains and
Choruses* for wind quintet (1957), in which his preoccupation
with repetitive forms and tone-colour make an early appearance. *Ring a Dumb Carillon* (1965) for voice, clarinet and percussion, with a text by Christopher Logue, was Birtwistle's first
comparative success. The clarinet part is a tribute to Alan
Hacker, of the Fires of London, who has done so much to
develop and extend the potentialities of the instrument, and
who has been an inspiration to the Manchester group. Birtwistle's first large-scale orchestral work was *Chorales* (1962–3),
which contrasts block orchestral sonorities with solo violin
tone.

Tragœdia of 1965 was an important work; it also indicates
some of the sources of Birtwistle's inspiration. Like many of his
compositions it has a name that is a classical allusion; it means,
literally, a goat-dance, but from this Greek root the original
derivation of the word tragedy evolved. There is a Prologue,
and each subsequent section has a Greek title: "Parados",
"Episodion", "Stasimon", and finally "Exodus". The sound
of the music is savage, aggressive and vivid; the norm of dissonance is very high. These are characteristics of Birtwistle's
music generally. *Tragœdia* was a study for his first full-length
opera *Punch and Judy*, in four Melodramas with Prologue and
Epilogue. Birtwistle has taken the familiar sea-side children's
show, with its roots in the classical *commedia dell'arte*, as a starting point for an opera on the subject of the search for personal
identity. This quest is represented for Punch by a character
called Pretty Polly, and each of the four Melodramas is a ritual
murder. In the Epilogue Punch attains Pretty Polly, that is, he
discovers his true identity. The music aroused some comment
on its first performance because of its violence and brutality.

Down by the Greenwood Side was commissioned for the 1969
Brighton Festival, where it was performed by Alexander Goehr's

Music Theatre Ensemble. It is a curious piece, in which a soprano sings the old ballad about the Cruel Mother, alternating with the mystery play of St George, The Slasher, and Father Christmas. There are works by Birtwistle for all manner of combinations, all stamped with the same individual technique and personality; *The Death of Orpheus, Medusa, Linoi I, Linoi II,* and a large-scale work, *The Visions of Francesco Petrarca,* are among the best of them. His latest compositions have shown a preoccupation with time. *The Triumph of Time* (1972) is a large single movement of considerable power, written for symphony orchestra, and there is a shorter work called *Chronometer* for electronic tape.

Peter Maxwell Davies is fast emerging as one of the greatest composers of his generation in the world. Although his technique is not so radical as that of some of his foreign contemporaries—a certain conservatism continues to be the mark of the English composer—it was sufficiently novel in England in the 1950s to ensure him a rough passage. His struggle has been a tough one, but it is now being acknowledged that he has brought greater recognition to England on the strictly contemporary music scene than any other composer. Medieval and renaissance works are often a source of inspiration for him; once or twice he has begun to transcribe some unfinished polyphonic composition, only to feel the piece taking hold of him, with the result that the end product has been a piece wholly in his own manner. This was the case with *L'Homme Armé* (1968). In the last few years he has transcribed traditional Scottish dances and instrumental pieces in a similar but less radical way.

The Tudor composer John Taverner aroused his interest as an example of a kind of betrayal that has always fascinated him—not the meaningless change of loyalties known as treason, which in our days, when political faiths are more potent than patriotism, has become too complex an issue to analyse, but that inner betrayal of a man's deepest principles which is the soul's death. John Taverner was a Catholic who, when converted to Protestantism, almost certainly under threat of torture or death, and against his inner convictions, betrayed his Catholic friends, and persecuted them; and from this time on he wrote no more music. For a composer of his stature and conviction this suggests a torment of the psyche that appals.

The libretto of Maxwell Davies's opera *Taverner* was compiled from letters and documents of the time, and very skilfully compiled too; the sound of the Elizabethan English has an extraordinarily threatening effect in this sinister work. One of the main characters is a Jester, who is also Death; and the main prop is a "Wheel of Fortune" which dominates the stage, and which indicates who is up, and who down. Does it derive from the Tarot? This would be very characteristic of Maxwell Davies, especially if other Tarot symbolism were present, hidden in the work (we already have The Jester)— what of La Maison Dieu, for instance, that thoroughly sinister card? The opera has three off-shoots, the two Taverner Fantasias and the *Points and Dances* derived from the "musak"—as Maxwell Davies amusingly describes it—which goes on at certain points during the action of the opera; mock Elizabethan music, distorted and sinister.

Maxwell Davies's music shows the example, rather than the influence, of the early free atonal music of Schoenberg. The expressionist vocal line of *From Stone to Thorn* (1971) shows no evidence of *Sprechstimme*, but its wry and piercing vocal line must remind us of Schoenberg, just as its somewhat fragmented but still powerfully lyrical instrumental writing links the work with *Pierrot Lunaire*. Accepting the shadow of Schoenberg, let us acknowledge also that of medieval music. The problem arises how to reconcile them, a problem complicated by another influence: that of the foxtrot and the jazz of the 1920s. This really is a joke in the Maxwell Davies manner; Schoenberg, medieval music, and the foxtrot? Then there is the very genuine merriment which goes on even in his blackest inventions. There is no cruelty or cynicism here; it seems to be a genuine realisation of the interpenetration of laughter and pain in this our human lot.

What does it all add up to technically? The acceptance of atonality, but its modification by innumerable tonal and modal echoes; orchestration and melodic line partially derived from Schoenberg, but perhaps also from Debussy and Ravel. A polyphonic technique which in some works reaches majestic proportions, a polyphony that suggests Busoni, Tallis, even Bach. Rhythms derived both from Elizabethan dances and the foxtrot. The synthesis of these disparate elements is impressive. In his earlier music this synthesis results broadly in two styles: the powerful extended polyphony of the first and last parts of the Second Taverner Fantasia and the *O Magnum Mysterium* organ piece, and the distorted dances of *Points and Dances* and the central section of the Second Taverner Fantasia. As Maxwell Davies developed these elements tended to merge into a texture more rhythmically free and yet more complex. His harmony is perfectly free; there is no obligation to use nothing but discord in every part any more than there is to follow classical consonant harmony.

A further development came when Maxwell Davies went to live in Orkney. Far be it from a contemporary composer to write nature music! But the fact remains that just as the Sussex sea coast inspired Frank Bridge, the Channel Islands and the South Downs John Ireland, and the north-west of Scotland Arnold Bax, so this desolate scene has affected Maxwell Davies.

But a number of important works date from before his Orkadian period: *Revelation and Fall* for soprano and solo instruments, *Eight Songs for a Mad King* for voice and chamber ensemble, *Vesalii Icones* for dancer, solo violoncello and ensemble, and *Worldes Blis* for orchestra, among others. *Revelation and Fall* (1966) dates from Maxwell Davies's most expressionist period, and created a scandal with its extreme violence when it was new, for about this time he was writing the music for Ken Russell's sensational film, *The Devils*. *Eight Songs for a Mad King* (1969) was a refinement on this technique, and has become a modern classic. Fragments of prose associated with the madness of George III are set for a male voice of extreme range; dressed as the king, the singer wanders amid huge birdcages which contain the players, and goes through the motions of teaching the "birds" to sing. Some music for the mechanical instruments the king possessed is incorporated into the score. *Vesalii Icones* (1969) interprets some Renaissance anatomical drawings in terms of the resurrection of Antichrist.

The two great scores of this period are the Second Taverner

Fantasia and *Worldes Blis*; they are of the same kind, long virtuoso compositional exercises for large orchestra. Of the Second
Taverner Fantasia Maxwell Davies writes: "Formally it com-
prises 13 sections. Sections 1 to 6 make roughly a sonata-form
movement, with an introduction and coda; sections 8 to 10
make a scherzo and trio; and section 12 is a closing extended
slow movement." So this splendid work, which sounds like a
meditation by a modern composer on sixteenth-century polyphony, is also a symphony, one of the greatest by an Englishman, and also significant by reason of Maxwell Davies's later
Symphony, which he called by that name. The material of the
Fantasia grew out of Act I of *Taverner*, and refers to the action
at several points. The thematic material is transformed, as in
Liszt and Schoenberg, by a process described by Maxwell
Davies as transformation but not development.

Worldes Blis (1969), described as a motet for orchestra, is like
the Second Taverner Fantasia a vast single movement with
internal sections for large orchestra. It is rather more sectional
than the Taverner Fantasia, resembling in its construction the
later *Ave Maris Stella*. Based on the thirteenth-century monody
beginning "Worldes blis ne last no throwe", which is printed
on the flyleaf, it runs to 151 pages of full score, and is mostly
very slow and concentrated. It begins quietly with the thematic
material forming under high harp sounds, working slowly up to
a climax of shrill scoring; from this climax on, the organ builds
up pedal chords under the orchestral development, which
gradually begins to take on the character of tolling bells. There
is a huge final climax based on bell sounds, with the heavy
brass and timpani joining the organ in massive final chords.

The works after *Worldes Blis* are all affected more or less by
Maxwell Davies's stay in the Orkneys. *From Stone to Thorn,
Stone Litany, Ave Maris Stella, Hymn to St Magnus, Mirror of
Whitening Light*, and his second opera, *The Martyrdom of St
Magnus*, all belong to this place and period. *From Stone to Thorn*
is a setting of verses by the Orkadian poet George Mackay
Brown, whose verses Maxwell Davies was to set on subsequent
occasions, and is a combined Stations of the Cross and a descrip-
tion of the sowing, reaping and threshing of wheat. It is for
soprano and chamber orchestra, a glittering web of sound

encompassing a voice part of wide leaps and enormous compass. *Stone Litany* sets some graffiti, in ancient Norse, that were left by the Vikings in the great prehistoric building on Maeshowe. It is a substantial, restless score in which the soprano soloist intones a florid voice part. *Ave Maris Stella* (Hail, Star of the Sea) is a 40-minute work based on the medieval hymn of the same name. In a form of variations, it is cumulative in effect, and written for the Fires of London—which defines its forces; it is at once an intellectual structure of great thematic manipulation and an uncanny invocation of the presence of the sea. *Hymn to St Magnus* is based on the twelfth-century hymn from St Magnus Cathedral, Kirkwall, Orkney. The actual sung text is fragmentary, and the instrumental parts once more for the Fires of London. The instrumental writing in this work is particularly imaginative; Maxwell Davies writes that the central section is permeated with the violence of the martyrdom and the violence of the sea.

The violence of that martyrdom inspired Maxwell Davies's second opera, which, like so much of his music, is a piece on several levels. St Magnus, the patron saint of Orkney, was martyred on 16 April 1117, on the island of Egilsay, having refused to fight his cousin Earl Hakon over the division of the Earldom of Orkney. He may therefore be considered a pacifist martyr, and this consideration is felt in the opera. Various changes of level and apparent time take place; part of the action implies the twentieth century, as it does in Mackay Brown's novel from which the libretto is taken. The orchestra is a slightly expanded Fires of London. The opera was given its first performance in St Magnus Cathedral, on 18 June 1977, as part of Maxwell Davies's new Orkney Festival. The work is introduced by a symbolic character, Blind Mary, saying the Stations of the Cross; after the martyrdom Blind Mary is seen praying for her sight at St Magnus's tomb. When it is restored she sees the audience as in no wise different from those who expected St Magnus's martyrdom so many years ago: "dark faces, blind mouths crying still for sacrifice". She tells the audience to "carry the peace of Christ into the world".

Peter Maxwell Davies's Symphony was given its first performance on 2 February 1978, by the Philharmonia Orchestra under a brilliant new conductor, the very young Simon Rattle. That a composer so contemporary in spirit should write a work designated "symphony" is remarkable enough, but still more remarkable was Maxwell Davies's confession that the work owed much of its inspiration to his admiration for the Fifth Symphony of Sibelius. The Symphony is in four movements, and lasts fifty minutes; in incorporates a work called *Black Pentecost*, which Davies realised would not stand up on its own, but which becomes, effortlessly, a part of the Symphony, which seems to derive something of its mood from whatever is suggested by the term Black Pentecost. As with so much of Maxwell Davies's music, there is a suggestion of Mahler in the texture and orchestration, especially the Mahler of the last movement of the Sixth Symphony. It is a most pregnant and suggestive conflation of the symphonic essences of both Sibelius and Mahler, a marvellous synthesis of these symphonic opposites, with Maxwell Davies's own personal style and radical technique as the catalyst.

Maxwell Davies's Symphony received an impressive welcome from public and critics alike; Simon Rattle referred to the challenge of conducting the work for the first time as being like conducting a Mahler symphony fifty years ago. It consolidated the already formidable reputation that Maxwell Davies had built up during the years.

The fact that we can produce, at this stage in our musical history, three radical composers of the stature of Ferneyhough, Birtwistle and Maxwell Davies is a signally felicitous portent for the future. It was necessary for English composers to evolve their own contemporary technique because of the peculiar conditions of English musical life; on the one hand we have a rootedly conservative tradition, based on our long eclipse after the death of Henry Purcell, and reinforced in the early days of the renaissance by Stanford's reactionary views and teaching methods; the folk-song movement, adopted by England long after it was abandoned by Europe, was a blind alley, and more conservative in its essence than its followers perhaps realised; and to this we must add our own natural insularity. On the other hand we have the radical music of the century and this means especially the Second Viennese School. Schoenberg, Berg, Webern, were among the greatest composers of the twentieth century, and Schoenberg's revolution was that century's most important musical event. But there is something in the English musical make-up—and I am not writing here of our conservative composers, but of our radicals—which resists undue formalism, and which was crushed by the First Viennese School in the eighteenth century. Those composers who have taken Schoenberg as a model, not as a teacher, imitating his mannerisms, not building on his discoveries, have remained little Schoenbergs, and hence of small importance; the greatest composers of the second half of the twentieth century—and that must include Boulez and Stockhausen—have adapted and extended Schoenberg's actual techniques, to express their own very different musical personalities. In this the music of Webern has been a help, music of dazzling technical brilliance that is actually rather impersonal.

The recurring malaise of English music has been its gentility, a conservatism based on a rejection of passion, commitment, and all extremes. Because of this factor in the English character, which has grown up since the close of the Tudor period, our music has been limited and our composers, with a few exceptions, disappointing, holding out more promise than fulfilment. I have tended to stress in this account the achievements of those composers who have escaped from this pervading conventionality, because I believe that they have the secret heart of England in their keeping, that they speak for that other England of visionaries and even eccentrics, an England that is not inimical to great art.

The greatest of these is Elgar. We can see him now not as the Edwardian figure of the establishment, a wholly inaccurate impression that was maintained far too long, but as the son of a tradesman who won through against impossible odds; and not as the guardian of tradition, but as the rebel who dared to use the language of Strauss and Mahler in Victorian England. Delius still stands aside; a great despiser, an ambivalent and partly foreign figure, who nevertheless was unmistakably English in much of his music. If he had conformed, if he had been respectable, we should have lost all his music.

I have given Arnold Bax and Frank Bridge an unaccustomed degree of prominence, partly because I believe they merit it, partly because their music exhibits characteristics that have passed into the future in a way that the technical idiom of Vaughan Williams could not have done. There is no doubt that Vaughan Williams's *London*, *Pastoral*, F minor and E minor Symphonies and his *Job* are great achievements, but the pastoral idiom was still-born, an assumption of the folk-nationalist idea that Europe had abandoned decades before England discovered it; and after Vaughan Williams had relinquished the technique he had based on folk music, he could assume no more contemporary idiom, although the F minor was a brave try. Bax's music is hampered by his romantic aesthetic, but technically it begins where the last astonishing works of Liszt left off, and there are many passages in his works—the opening of the Third Symphony, and the slow movement of the Third Piano Sonata—that suggest the Berg of *Wozzeck* in their acceptance of a totally chromatic texture. As for Frank Bridge, his last compositions might be thought to have been the bridge between Bax and Peter Maxwell Davies, and the origin of the technique of the young English composers of today, if it were not for the fact that this music was totally unknown except to a few specialists like myself.

Britten was a giant, but Tippett is more likely to have an abiding influence on English music in the future. Britten's idiom was so deeply atavistic—I choose that word rather than conservative, for Britten's music has nothing at all in common with that of the true English conservatives—that nothing can come after it. His style has died with him, and it could not have been otherwise. In many ways he was unique, this pupil of Frank Bridge.

The future belongs to Ferneyhough, Birtwistle and Maxwell Davies. The way in which Ferneyhough has turned the more radical idioms of our time to his personal use, a unique manipulation of a technique derived in the first place from Webern, marks an originality that proclaims an important composer. Birtwistle pursues his own path, which is also a singular one; but Peter Maxwell Davies has achieved the greatest measure of fame. Many threads of our musical life have come together in him; his is the Tudor glory and agony, the mystery of Egdon Heath, the exploratory technique that was pioneered by Frank Bridge in the generation before his, and the irony, humour and nonconformity of all that is best in the art of England. His music is relevant to the twentieth-century experience and predicament, but the old tradition of English nature mysticism is there also, reflected in terms that suit our time by the wild and desolate beauty of the Orkneys.

The English musical renaissance proper ended on 3 September 1939, when politics and war, which have played such a part in the history of England, swept aside our feeble muse. After the war was over England was left isolated in narrow provincialism; but the 1960s saw a great awakening of English music, and I can end at the date on which these words are written, in the contemplation of a living art in England, and a string of magnificent compositions by a group of English composers who are still young.

SELECT BIBLIOGRAPHY
and
INDEX

SELECT BIBLIOGRAPHY

GENERAL

Bacharach, A. L., *British Music of our Time* (1946)
Beecham, Sir Thomas, *A Mingled Chime* (1944)
Bliss, Sir Arthur, *As I Remember* (1970)
Boult, Sir Adrian, *My Own Trumpet* (1973)
Cohen, Harriet, *A Bundle of Time* (1969)
Elkin, Robert, *Queen's Hall* (1944)
Elkin, Robert, *Royal Philharmonic* (1946)
Gray, Cecil, *Musical Chairs* (1948)
Gray, Cecil, *A Survey of Contemporary Music* (1924)
Greene, H. Plunkett, *Charles Villiers Stanford* (1935)
Holbrooke, Joseph, *Contemporary British Composers* (1925)
Howes, Frank, *The English Musical Renaissance* (1966)
Routh, Francis, *Contemporary British Music* (1972)
Wood, Sir Henry, *My Life of Music* (1938)

ELGAR

Burley, Rosa C., and Carruthers, Frank C., *Edward Elgar: the Record of a Friendship* (1972)
Dunhill, Thomas F., *Sir Edward Elgar* (1938)
Kennedy, Michael, *Portrait of Elgar* (1968)
Maine, Basil, *Elgar, his life and work*, 2 vols. (1933)
McVeagh, Diana, *Edward Elgar: His Life and Music* (1955)
Parrott, Ian, *Elgar* (1971)
Powell, Mrs Richard, *Edward Elgar: Memories of a Variation* (1947)
Young, Percy M., *Elgar O.M.* (1955)

DELIUS

Beecham, Sir Thomas, *Delius* (1959)

Delius, Clare, *Frederick Delius* (1935)
Fenby, E., *Delius as I Knew Him* (1936)
Heseltine, P. (Peter Warlock), *Delius* (1923)
Hutchings, A., *Delius* (1948)
Jefferson, A., *Delius* (1972)
Palmer, C., *Delius* (1976)

HOLST, VAUGHAN WILLIAMS

Dickinson, A. E. F., *Vaughan Williams* (1964)
Douglas, Roy, *Working with RVW* (1972)
Foss, Hubert, *Vaughan Williams* (1950)
Holst, Imogen, *Gustav Holst* (1938)
Holst, Imogen, *The Music of Gustav Holst* (1951)
Howes, Frank, *The Music of Ralph Vaughan Williams* (1954)
Kennedy, Michael, *The Works of Ralph Vaughan Williams* (1964)
Vaughan Williams, Ralph, *National Music* (1963)
Vaughan Williams, Ralph, and Holst, Gustav, *Heirs and Rebels* (1959)
Vaughan Williams, Ursula, *RVW* (1964)
Young, Percy M., *Vaughan Williams* (1953)

BAX, BRIDGE, IRELAND

Bax, Arnold, *Farewell My Youth* (1943)
Hull, Robert H., *A Handbook on Arnold Bax's Symphonies* (1932)
Longmire, John, *John Ireland: Portrait of a Friend* (1969)
Parlett, Graham, *Arnold Bax: a catalogue of his music* (1972)
Payne, A., Foreman, L., Bishop, J., *The Music of Frank Bridge* (1976)
Pirie, Peter J., *Frank Bridge* (1972)
Scott-Sutherland, Colin, *Arnold Bax* (1973)

OTHERS

Gray, Cecil, *Peter Warlock* (1934)
Howes, Frank, *The Music of William Walton* (1965)
Lutyens, Elizabeth, *A Goldfish Bowl* (1972)

MacDonald, Malcolm, *The Symphonies of Havergal Brian*, 3 vols.
  (1974–)
Mitchell, D. & Keller, H., *Benjamin Britten* (1952)
Shead, Richard, *Constant Lambert* (1973)
Tippett, M., *Moving into Aquarius* (1959)

INDEX

All works have been indexed under their composer